AUTHEN

CORO

OF

HIS MAJESTY,

King George the Fourth:

WITH A

FULL AND AUTHENTIC DETAIL OF THAT AUGUST SOLEMNITY;

AN ACCOUNT

OF ALL THE INTERESTING PROCEEDINGS;

THE

ADJUDICATION OF THE COURT OF CLAIMS,

WITH AN

HISTORICAL ACCOUNT OF THE ORIGIN OF THE COURT;

A Full and Original Detail of the Regalia,

AND OTHER IMPORTANT PARTICULARS CONNECTED WITH THAT

MAGNIFICENT CEREMONY:

To which is prefixed a concise History of the Coronations of the Kings
of England from the Saxon Heptarchy to the present time.

BY ROBERT HUISH, ESQ.

LONDON:

J. ROBINS AND CO. ALBION PRESS, IVY LANE,
PATERNOSTER ROW.

1821.

In the interest of creating a more extensive selection of rare historical book reprints, we have chosen to reproduce this title even though it may possibly have occasional imperfections such as missing and blurred pages, missing text, poor pictures, markings, dark backgrounds and other reproduction issues beyond our control. Because this work is culturally important, we have made it available as a part of our commitment to protecting, preserving and promoting the world's literature. Thank you for your understanding.

HISTORY OF THE CORONATION

OF

KING GEORGE THE FOURTH.

WESTMINSTER HALL,
as it appeared at the Coronation of George IV.
With the ceremony of the Champion's Challenge.

Published by J. Robins & Co. Albion Press, London, Aug.t 4, 1821.

Br 2070.13.30

INTRODUCTION.

It is only the great and sublime spectacles which possess intrinsically any interest for the human mind; expectation becomes excited in proportion as the magnificence of the spectacle increases, and an anxiety to view it keeps pace with the general importance that is attached to it. If we direct our view to the different nations of the world in their most rude and uncivilized state, at a time when a system of regular government and of polity first dawned amongst them, we shall find particular ceremonies and institutions established, which had a direct reference to the welfare of the State, and without which, a regular and just administration of the laws could not be effected. In the sacred writings we read of the jubilees of the Hebrews; and it is rather singular that our ceremonies of unction and coronation actually existed in Judæa. " And Jehoiada brought forth the king's son, and put the crown upon him, and gave him the testimony; and they made him king, and anointed him, and they clapped their hands, and said, ' God save the king.' " And in the same passage we find the administration of a coronation oath and the ceremony of enthroning : " Jehoiada made a covenant between the Lord, and the king and the people, that they should be the Lord's people; between the king also and the people.—And he took the rulers over hundreds, and the captains, and the guard, and all the people of the land, and they brought down the king from the house of the Lord, and *came by the way of the gate of the guard* to the king's house, and he sate on the throne of the kings."

If we take a rapid flight to another hemisphere, we there behold amongst a superstitious and idolatrous people, the festivals of the Sun in Peru, by which the fealty of the nation to a superior power was confirmed and established, and which placed the ruling potentate only inferior to the sun itself.

Of a similar nature, in point of an imposing ceremony, were the Druidical assemblies of the early Britons, the inauguration of a Cardinal to the Pontificate, and thence we come to the splendid ceremony of a British coronation.

In the contemplation of this splendid pageant, the mind turns away dissatisfied from the contemplation of the scenes which are daily presented to its view, and its attention becomes absorbed in admiration of the institutions established by our forefathers, and which have been transmitted from sire to son in all their primeval dignity and splendour. The antiquarian sees in them the living representation of the scenes pourtrayed by the historians of former times, the doubtful becomes clear to him, and after-ages mention him as their authority. To the historian, however, whether of this or of any subsequent period, an authentic document of one of the most magnificent pageants of a monarch's reign, and by the virtue of which the Sovereign in the face of Heaven enters into a solemn compact with his people to preserve their rights inviolable, and " to cause law and justice in mercy to be exercised in all his judgements," must necessarily possess a value only to be appreciated by the individual who looks upon every event, which affects the interests of his country, as paramount to every other subject, which the common affairs of life submit to his consideration.

The coronation of a King of England may be regarded as an important epoch in the life of every individual, and few there are who can say, they ever witnessed it twice. Even of those great and exalted characters who surrounded the coronation chair of George III.—" who bore the tarbet and the shield, and wore the plumes of dignity"—not one is now living to witness the coronation of his successor. The same venerable walls will indeed hear the sacred anthem, and hundreds and thousands of voices will echo " Long live the King—may the King live for ever—Hallelujah;" but ere a few years be passed, the thousands who composed the gaping crowd, and the hundreds who echoed the solemn anthem, will in their turn have joined their fellows in the grave, and the solitary records of the historian will alone be left, to tell the history of the day.

They, who are now in the heyday of their youth, and to whom Heaven may vouchsafe to grant a lengthened life, will in the perusal of the historian's record of a magnificent spectacle recal to their memory the scenes which once they witnessed; and they who are now standing on the threshold of life will find their enjoyment in tracing the history of one of the most magnificent pageants which their country can present, but which it may never fall to their lot to behold.

In this respect, therefore, it becomes a pleasant task for the historian; he writes for the amusement and instruction, as well of those who did view the splendid ceremony, as of those who did not view it: the former will be able to judge of the correctness of his account, the latter of his assiduity and research.

In regard to originality, the author of the following work can lay little claim, he is barely the narrator of facts; but with those facts are connected some most interesting circumstances extracted from ancient records and documents, which could only be obtained by the most indefatigable research, and which tend to explain many parts of the ceremony, which appear to the general observer to take their origin in causes, which are at total variance with the real one. It is in his laborious research for those records and documents, in the general correctness of his statements, and in a luminous display of every circumstance political or personal, appertaining to or originating from the Coronation, that the author expects the commendation of his readers. He is well aware that there is one subject, into which it may be considered by many as necessary for him to enter, and with which a strong degree of political animosity is connected. It is, however, his most positive intention in the following work to steer clear of all political discussion on one of the most momentous questions which ever agitated the councils of the nation, and which has ended in a firm and determined renunciation of the rights to which the illustrious individual has laid her claim. This is indeed not the place to discuss the right of a Queen Consort to be crowned, scendants of that family who were elevated to the regal dignity.

This regular succession or principle of adherence to the blood of royal line, may be regarded as one of the first rays in the dawn of civil government, and it almost implies a right of regal government in the descendants of the first kings in preference to other men, which right has been incorrectly called *divine*, although it be hallowed by antiquity and long established use.

At an early period, England presented an extraordinary feature in the history of regal governments. It was an *imperium in imperio*, as one of the English princes was often elected to preside amongst the rest as king of the English nation, each state retaining its proper sovereignty, and thus the prophecy was fulfilled, which was pronounced to one of the Anglo-Saxon princes, " *thou shalt be king over kings.*" Indeed, from the above circumstance arose the Anglo-Saxon heptarchy; but in consequence of the failure of some families, the total extinction of others by want of issue or subjugation, the entire dominion of England became vested in the noble house of Wessex, to which the English crown is indebted for its national greatness and its glory.

From the foregoing observations it is evident, that the crown of England has ever been sovereign and independent; it has neither been conferred nor protected by any federal head; but it has gradually descended from the primitive leaders and chiefs of the nation,—the august ceremonies of the Coronation will not only show its magnificence, but it will explain, in a particular manner, by what means it has remained so long in security and respect.

The principal acts connected with the coronation of a king of England, may be divided into two classes, *political* and *feudal*. In the character of sovereign, it is attended with rites and ceremonies, which may be divided into *civil* and *ecclesiastical*.

In the first place, the political act, is that in which

the nation is more immediately concerned; and it is at the same time the most important and the most ancient part of the ceremony of coronation. In the formulary, as it at present consists, the political act consists in demanding the consent of the people, and on the other hand in requiring the protestation of an oath from the king before he receives the crown. This may be called the admission and the introduction of the sovereign to his office; and, as it is no less the interest of the people than it is of the king himself, that his person and character should be adorned with the highest possible honour that worldly pomp, and the solemnities of religion can afford, the church receives him in its sanctuary, and its ministers confirm and strengthen his authority with prayers and benedictions, accompanied at the same time by the most holy and awful rites. He is afterwards invested with the power and prerogatives of royalty, by the formal delivery of the crown, the sceptre, and the sword.

The second act, which is entirely feudal, is grounded on the principle, that, as by the constitution of the kingdom, all territorial dignities and possessions are held of the king as chief lord; the accession of a new sovereign requires a renewal of the reciprocal engagements of service and protection, which these tenures imply. Homage, and the Oath of Fealty, though not forming by necessity a part of the ceremony, have, nevertheless, always followed, and now form an intimate part of it.

These are however not the only feudal circumstances connected with the Coronation; it was the custom of our ancient kings, in the grant of lands to their vassals, to provide for and to consult the maintenance of the nation's power, by a particular reservation of rent or service; and this circumstance tended in a great degree to exalt the dignity and splendour of their court. At the banquet, which always follows the Coronation, and which may perhaps be considered as the most perfect model of ancient courtly magnificence in the world, the various duties of the household are filled by hereditary grand officers of the kingdom, who perform the services enjoined them by the tenure of their estates.

It was for the purpose of establishing the right of these feudal tenures that the Court of Claims was founded, of which further mention will be made in the progress of this history; but the most perfect copy of the ritual used by the Court of Claims, appears on the coronation of Richard II. which is remarkable, as affording us the first record of the proceedings of that court, which was at that time holden on the Thursday before the festival, by John, king of Castile and duke of Lancaster, high-steward of England.

The coronation of the kings of England is considered as a sort of election, and, in fact, it appears to have been a mode generally adopted, not only by regal but imperial governments, even where the succession is absolutely hereditary. Thus the emperors of Germany had their *wahltage* (day of election), and their *krönungs tage* (day of coronation). The election was supposed to be vested in the seven electors of the empire; the city of Frankfort on the Maine, claiming the right of having the emperor elected within its walls, and Aix-la-Chapelle the right of having him crowned.*

The right of election was, however, more observed in England than in foreign countries, and even more so than is generally supposed. A stronger proof of this cannot be adduced than in the speech which the Archbishop delivered at the nomination of King John to succeed to his brother's throne. "It is well known to you all, that no man hath right of succession to this

---

* From this circumstance originates the custom of dispatching from Frankfort a princely deputation to Aix-la-Chapelle, to bring from that city a chest of earth, on which the emperor must stand when he is crowned. I witnessed this chest introduced into the city of Frankfort at the coronation of Leopold, when every cannon on the ramparts was fired, and the whole city was more brilliantly illuminated than upon the entrance of the emperor himself.

crown, except that by unanimous consent of the kingdom, with invocation of the Holy Ghost, he be elected for his own deserts." On this important subject, Sir William Blackstone says: "It is in general hereditary or descendible to the next heir on the death or demise of the last proprietor." The time and place, however, at which the successor is virtually appointed to a throne, must vary with the circumstances which have made it vacant. It is the province of parliament to confer and confirm the crown in a regular course, and the manner of it will be amply detailed in a future part of this work.

The form of election of the sovereign varies considerably in different countries. Amongst the German nations we find that the election form was merely the raising the elected on a shield, or on the arms of the soldiers, and bearing them three times round the camp in triumph. The monarchy of France furnishes us also with several records of the observance of this custom. Pharamond, the first king of the Franks, was placed on a shield when he received his office (A. D. 420); and it is related of the chairing of Tunbal, King of Burgundy, that on the third time of his being carried round the assembled people, the sovereign fell from "his high estate," and was with difficulty kept from descending to the earth. Gregory of Tours speaks of the elevation of Clovis on a shield, and of the popularity of his election. Pepin, at his succession to the throne in 751, was raised upon the target, though he was afterwards anointed and crowned in the church of St. Denis.

Among the Scandinavian nations, the Norwegians, the Swedes, and the Danes, the ceremony consisted in placing the monarch on a stone; and it is a very remarkable circumstance, that a stone is still preserved in the coronation formula of England, though it is considered as having been taken by us from the Celtic ceremonies. This stone (the fatal stone of Tara) is one of the most curious of our inauguration antiquities, of which presently a more minute description will be given, when we come to describe the regalia; but in the mean time we will briefly state, that according to the testimony of the antiquaries of both Scotland and Ireland, the kings of those nations were placed on a stone at the time of their election, and it is not a little remarkable, that the same stone was transferred from the less to the larger island for the same national purpose. This monument is evidently of Celtic origin, and it will afford a curious instance of the wide diffusion of a most ancient practice, which may be said to form a part of the inauguration of our English kings.

The introduction of Christianity, amongst other momentous changes which it effected, in the manners and customs of those nations which were blessed with its light, was a zealous affectation of the laws, customs, and political maxims, derived from the Jewish people, and which formed a part of the Mosaic system of religion. Accordingly, in the election of the English kings, rites of a more sacred nature were adopted, and unction and coronation displaced the target elevation. In regard to the former, the first English king who is recorded to have been anointed, is Egferth of Mercia, in the year 785, who in the language of the Saxon Chronicle was " hallowed to king" by his father Offa, the sovereign of Mercia.

In regard to the crown, Jeffrey of Monmouth says, that King Ethelstan was the first English king that used it. The most ancient mention of a royal crown is in the Old Testament, 2 *Sam.* i. 10. when the Amalekites brought Saul's crown to David. It appears also that David had a crown of gold and precious stones out of the spoils of the Ammonites.

We shall have occasion to enter more fully into the history of the crown when we come to the description of the regalia.

The first English coronation which has been minutely described was that of Richard I. during which, Matthew Paris says, the wine was running through the streets. In this coronation, we trace the existence of many of the feudal services, which have been transmitted to succeeding reigns. The festivity on this occasion was, however, to the great disgrace of the times, interrupted by the massacre of the Jews, who were strictly forbidden to appear in the places appropriated to the ceremony; notwithstanding which they attempted to force their way, but they were driven out with force and blows; their houses were subsequently attacked, and the inhabitants of them killed.

In regard to the festivities, which distinguished the coronation of our early kings, it appears to have been an old and very economical practice to provide for the necessaries of the table, by the king issuing his precepts to the sheriffs of the different counties, calling upon them to provide oxen, swine, sheep, fowls, &c. in quantities proportioned to the extent and means of their respective districts. Thus, at the coronation of King Edward I. orders were issued on the 10th of February, 1724, to different sheriffs, to furnish the following provisions at Windsor on Easter-eve, it being then intended that the coronation should be solemnized at that time and place:—

	Oxen.	Swine.	Sheep.	Fowls.
Sheriff of Gloucester	60	101	60	3000
Bucks and Bedford	40	66	40	2100
Oxford	40	67	40	2100
Kent	40	67	40	2100
Surry and Sussex	40	67	40	2100
Warwick and Leicester	60	98	40	3000
Somerset and Dorset	160	176	40	5000
Essex	60	101	60	3160
	440	743	360	22,560

In the year 1307, King Edward II. issued an order, dated at Clipston, on the 25th of September, to the Seneschal of Gascony, and Constable of Bourdeaux, to provide a *thousand pipes* of good wine, and send them to London, there to be delivered to the king's butler before Christmas, to be used at the approaching coronation. The purchase and freight of the wine was to be paid for out of the revenues of Gascony, by a company of Florentine merchants, who farmed those revenues.

On the 1st of January, 1308, the same king issued an order to the sheriff of Wiltshire, (and probably to all other sheriffs in proportion,) to buy and provide out of the revenues of the sheriffdom 24 live oxen, 24 live porkers, 25 live brawns, and 24 fat bacons, to be delivered at Westminster to those who should be appointed to receive the same, within a fortnight from the festival of the purification.

It is highly amusing to read in some of the chronicles, the account of the solemnities and amusements by which the coronation of our kings was distinguished; and a short transcript of some of them may be considered as not an inappropriate appendage to those of the present day.

Henry III. when only nine years of age, was crowned at Gloucester, and afterwards at Westminster; " to the end," saith Holinshed, " it might be said, that now after the extinguishment of all seditious factions, he was crowned by the general consent of all the estates and subjects of his realm."

One of the most magnificent coronations of the early times appears to have been that of Eleanor, the beautiful young queen of Henry III. which was celebrated on her marriage, on the 20th January, 1236. Matthew Paris, speaking of this solemnity, says, " to this nuptial entertainment, there came such a multitude of the nobility of both sexes—such hosts of religious persons —such crowds of people, and such a variety of jugglers and buffoons, that London could scarcely contain them in her capacious bosom." He further says, " why need I recount the train of those who performed the sacred offices of the church ; why describe the profusion of dishes which furnished the table—the abundance of venison—the variety of fish—the diversity of wine—the gaiety of jugglers—the readiness of the attendants—whatever the world could produce for glory or delight was there conspicuous."

Edward I. and Eleanor his queen were crowned in the new church at Westminster, by Archbishop Kilwarbie, on Sunday, the 19th August, 1274. "At the solemnitie of this coronation," Holinshed says, "there were let go at liberty (catch them that catch might) five hundred great horses, by the king of Scots, the earles of Cornewall, Glocester, Penbroke, Warren, and others, as they were alighted from their backs;" and from the account of a cotemporary writer, we may presume that it was hardly inferior to the last coronation in the number and magnificence of the company assembled, or the richness and splendour of the entertainments.

Richard II. was crowned on the 16th July, 1377, at Westminster, by Simon Archbishop of Canterbury. The proceedings on this occasion, including the progress through the city of London, were full of pomp and magnificence. On St. Swithin's day after dinner, the mayor and citizens assembled near the Tower, when the young king, clad in white garments, came forth, with a great multitude in his suite. They proceeded through the street called *La Chepe*, and on to the palace at Westminster. On the morrow, the king arrayed in the fairest vestments, and with buskins only upon his feet, came down into the hall. He was then conducted to the church, when the usual ceremonial was performed; and returning again to his palace, was carried on the shoulders of knights being opprest with fatigue and long fasting. The banquet, from the character of the age, was most splendid and profuse. The historian Walsingham, forbears giving a description of it, as it might exceed the belief of the reader. He, however, mentions one circumstance worthy of being recorded. In the midst of the palace a hollow marble pillar was set up, surmounted by a large gilt eagle, from under the feet of which, through the four sides of the capital, flowed wine of different kinds during the day, nor was any one forbidden to partake of it. After dinner, the king retired with a number of the nobility to his chamber, and was entertained until the time of supper with dancing and minstrelsy.

The coronation of Henry IV. is remarkable for

the first historical notice of the creation of the Knights of the Bath, although there be little doubt of the observance of this formality in much earlier times. Forty-six gentlemen, including three of the king's sons, watched on the vigil of the coronation at the Tower of London, and received their knighthood there on the day before the festival. The ceremony of this coronation appears to have been peculiarly grand and striking; no less than six thousand horses were employed in the procession from the Tower to Westminster. In addition to the marble pillar mentioned in the last coronation, there were nine similar pillars erected in Cheapside, which continued flowing on the day of the procession, and on the day following. The streets were decorated with hangings of various kinds, and the sword of state was borne by the celebrated Sir Thomas Erpingham.

The coronation, of which the fullest account has come down to us, and which appears to have been one of the most magnificent in the "olden times" of our history, was that of Henry VIII. and Catherine of Arragon. This has been described by Hall with much minuteness; and at this moment, perhaps, some short abstract from his work may not be unacceptable, as showing the prodigal splendour of one of the most gorgeous of our monarchs. This author states, that on the 21st of June, 1509, Henry came from Greenwich to London, and devoted the ensuing day to the ceremonies of the Bath. "The morrow following being Saturday, his Grace, with the Queen, departed from the Tower through the city of London, against whose coming, the streets where his Grace should pass were hanged with tapestry and cloth of Arras, and the great part of the south of Chepe (Cheapside) with cloth of gold, and some part of Cornehill also. The streets were railed and barred on the one side, from over against Gracechurch unto Bread-street, in Cheapside, where every occupation stood in their liveries in order, beginning with base and mean occupations, and so ascending to the worshipful crafts; highest and lastly stood the mayor with the aldermen. The goldsmith's stalls, unto the end of the Old Change, were replenished with virgins in white, with branches of white wax; the priests and clerks in rich copes, with crosses and censers of silver, with censing his Grace and the Queen also as they passed." The apparel of the king must have been, according to this chronicler, most splendid: "His grace wore for his uppermost garment a robe of crimson velvet, furred with ermine: his coat was of raised gold, the placard of which was embroidered with diamonds, rubies, emeralds, great pearls, and other rich stones; the trappings of his horse was damask-gold, with a deep border of ermine. His Queen was borne in a litter by two white palfreys, which were trapped in white cloth of gold: her person was apparelled in white embroidered satin, her hair hanging down her back of a very great length, beautiful and goodly to behold, and on her head a coronal, set with many rich orient stones." The author then goes on to describe the procession to Westminster, which took place on the Sunday following, and the order of the coronation in the Abbey; after rather tediously recapitulating the various forms and ceremonies, he thus ends with his characteristic panegyric: "What should I speak or write of the sumptuous, fine, and delicate meats prepared for this high and honourable coronation, provided for as well in the parts beyond the sea as in many and sundry places within this realm, where God so abundantly hath sent such plenty; or of the honourable order of the services, the clean handling and breaking of meats, the ordering of the dishes, with the plentiful abundance; so that none of any estate being there did lack, nor no honourable or worshipful person went unfeasted. The same author had, in not many years afterwards, to record the coronation of Anne Boleyn, which he does with equal minuteness, and, as it would seem, with equal ardour. After describing the voyage from Greenwich, and the " bathing and shryving" of the knights, he narrates the land-procession, which was enlivened

by many "marvailous conynge pageauntes," amusing
enough to hear of in our day. Mythological allusions
and emblematical pageants were then the courtly
vehicles of flattery; for instance, Apollo and the
Muses saluted her Majesty upon Ludgate-hill, and
the Graces took their station in Fleet-market; Saint
Anne, her Majesty's name Saint, met her in Cheapside, and the "Cardinal Virtues," we fear for the
last time, were seen collectively at Temple Bar. A
fountain, inscribed with the name of Helicon, ran
with hock, sufficient to inspire all the populace of
Parnassus, and the Conduit of Cheap overflowed
with claret. This coronation has been beautifully
described by Shakspeare, who recites the observance of all the ceremonies which have been handed
down religiously to our day:

> "At length her Grace rose, and with modest paces
> Came to the altar; where she kneeled, and, Saint-like,
> Cast her fair eyes to Heaven, and prayed devoutly:
> Then rose again, and bowed her to the people;
> When, by the Archbishop of Canterbury,
> She had all the royal makings of a Queen,
> As holy oil, Edward Confessor's crown,
> The rod and bird of peace, and all such emblems,
> Lay'd nobly on her: which performed, the choir,
> With all the choicest music of the kingdom,
> Together sung 'Te Deum.' So she parted,
> And with the same full state pac'd back again
> To York-place, where the feast is held."

The two queens whom we have mentioned, were
the only consorts of Henry VIII. who were honoured with a coronation. In reference to the pageants and mythological devices played off at these
ancient spectacles, we find the ancient chroniclers are
even eloquent. Thus, at the ensuing coronation of
Edward VI. " Valentine and Orson was exhibited at the Conduit in Cheap." At a goodly distance from this stood " Sapience and the seven Liberal Sciences." " The story of Jason" was also
epitomised, and " an Arragosan descended from the
battlements of St. Paul's upon a rope, which was fas-

tened to an anchor at the Dean's gate, and returned up again, playing certain mysteries all the while." Upon this last exploit Holinshed remarks, that during this coronation " St. Paul's lay at anchor." The coronation of Mary, the elder daughter of Henry VIII. remarkable as having been the first female who swayed the English sceptre, was marked by similar exhibitions; and, as if to outdo the flying phenomenon we have just mentioned, a Dutchman, who seems to have possessed a very anti-national agility, was also induced to make St. Paul's the theatre of his performances: he is represented as having actually stood on one foot on the weathercock of the steeple, waving a streamer five yards long, and occasionally kneeling on his knees, " to the great marvell of all people," and certainly to ours. So says old Holinshed. " We tell the tale as 'twas told to us." On her passing through Cheapside, the chamberlain of London presented her Majesty with a purse of cloth of gold, containing a thousand marks of gold, with which, doubtless, she was almost as well pleased as with the antics of the Dutchman. The coronation of the " Virgin Queen" is the last which we shall notice, because with it the day at least of mythological pageantry may be said to have passed away. Polemics, and the persecutions consequent thereon, now put to flight all pagan pretensions, and in the words of Miss Aikin, " learning lent her lamp to other studies, and, whether in the tongue of ancient Rome or modern England, Elizabeth was hailed in Christian strains, and as the sovereign of a Christian country." In her procession the companies of the city stood along the streets, one by another, enclosed with rails, hung with cloth, themselves well apparelled in many rich furs, and their " liverie hoods upon their shoulders in comelie and seemlie manner," having before them sundry persons clothed in silks and chains of gold; besides a number of rich hangings, as well of tapestry, arras, cloths of gold, velvet, silver, satin, and other silks; " plentifully hanged all the waie as the Queen's highness passed from the Tower through the Citie." That nothing might be wanting, on her arrival at Temple Bar " Gogmagog and Corineus, two giants, furnisht accordingly," held above the gate a tablet, whereon was written in Latin verse " the effect of all the pageants which the city had before erected."

The most minute narrative which exists of an English coronation, is that of James II. and the forms which were then adopted have been followed for the arrangements to be pursued in the Coronation of George IV. It becomes, therefore, unnecessary to notice the different forms used on that occasion, as well as those which were adopted at the intervening coronations, as they will be full and amply detailed in the progress of this history.

On the 29th of January, 1820, it pleased Heaven that George III. should exchange his earthly for a heavenly crown, and he was succeeded by his eldest son, the present George IV. As is usual in similar instances, the Privy Council immediately met to deliberate upon the best measures for proclaiming the new King, and at the same time for issuing those orders which were requisite upon the occasion.

As these orders have no particular reference to the important subject of the present work, being merely official notices of the demise of the late Sovereign, and the accession of the new one; and as they have been amply detailed in the various histories which have appeared of the life of George III. a repetition of them would be in this place superfluous. But as the necessary forms had been gone through relative to the accession of his present Majesty, the public attention began to be drawn towards the splendid spectacle of the Coronation, respecting the celebration of which various rumours began to be circulated towards the close of the month of April, which were in a degree verified by the following proclamation which appeared on the 9th of May, 1821.

BY THE KING.—A PROCLAMATION,

Declaring his Majesty's Pleasure touching his Royal Coronation, and the Solemnity thereof.

GEORGE R.—Whereas we are resolved, by the favour and blessing of Almighty God, to celebrate the solemnity of our Royal Coronation, upon Tuesday, the 1st day of August next, at our Palace, at Westminster; and forasmuch as by ancient customs and usages, as also in regard of divers tenures of sundry manors, lands, and other hereditaments, many of our loving subjects do claim, and are bound to do and perform divers several services on the said day, and at the time of the Coronation, as in times precedent their ancestors, and those from whom they claim, have done and performed at the Coronation of our famous progenitors and predecessors; we therefore, out of our princely care for the preservation of the lawful rights and inheritances of our loving subjects whom it may concern, have thought fit to give notice of and publish our resolutions therein; and we do hereby give notice of and publish the same accordingly: and we do hereby further signify, that by our Commission under our Great Seal of Great Britain we have appointed and authorised our most dear brothers and faithful counsellors Frederick Duke of York, William Henry Duke of Clarence, Augustus Frederick Duke of Sussex; our most dear cousin and faithful Counsellor William Frederick Duke of Gloucester; our most dear cousin and faithful Counsellor Prince Leopold of Saxe Coburg; the most reverend Father in God our right trusty and right entirely-beloved Counsellor Charles Archbishop of Canterbury, Primate of all England and Metropolitan; our right trusty and well-beloved Counsellor John Lord Eldon, our Chancellor of Great Britain; our right trusty and right well-beloved cousins and Counsellors Dudley Earl of Harrowby, President of our Council; John Earl of Westmorland, Keeper of our Privy Seal; our right trusty and right entirely-beloved cousins and Counsellors John Duke of Athol; James Duke of Montrose, Master of our Horse; Arthur Duke of Wellington, Master-General of our Ordnance; our right trusty and entirely-beloved George James Marquis of Cholmondeley, Lord Steward of our Household; Francis Marquis of Hertford, Lord Chamberlain of our Household; Charles Ingoldsby Marquis of Winchester, Groom of our Stole; James Marquis of Salisbury; Richard Marquis Wellesley; John Jeffreys Marquis Camden; our right trusty and right well-beloved cousins and Counsellors George Earl of Winchelsea and Nottingham; Frederick Earl of Carlisle; Cropley Earl

Proclamation of George IV.

of Shaftsbury; James Earl of Lauderdale; George Earl of Macclesfield, Captain of the Yeomen of our Guard; Charles Earl of Harrington; Philip Earl of Hardwicke; John Earl of Chatham; Henry Earl Bathurst, one of our Principal Secretaries of State; Charles Chetwynd Earl Talbot, our Lieutenant-General, and General Governor of that part of our United Kingdom called Ireland; Robert Banks Earl of Liverpool, First Lord Commissioner of our Treasury; Richard Earl of Donoughmore; Thomas Earl of Chichester;. Henry Earl of Mulgrave; William Earl Cathcart; John Earl of Sheffield; our right trusty and well-beloved Counsellors Robert Stewart, esq. commonly called Viscount Castlereagh, one of our Principal Secretaries of State; Charles Cavendish Bentinck, esq. commonly called Lord Charles Cavendish Bentinck, Treasurer of our Household; our right trusty and well-beloved cousins and Counsellors Percy Clinton Sidney Viscount Strangford; Robert Saunders Viscount Melville, First Lord Commissioner of our Admiralty; Henry Viscount Sidmouth, one of our Principal Secretaries of State; our right trusty and well-beloved Counsellor Thomas Hamilton, esq. commonly called Lord Binning; Robert Jocelyn, esq. commonly called Viscount Jocelyn, Vice Chamberlain of our Household; John Thynne, esq. commonly called Lord John Thynne; George Thomas Beresford, esq. commonly called Lord George Thomas Beresford, Comptroller of our Household; the right reverend Father in God our right trusty and well-beloved Counsellor William Bishop of London; our right trusty and well-beloved Counsellors William Pitt Lord Amherst; Charles George Lord Arden; Alleyne Lord St. Helen's; Frederick Morton Lord Henley; John Lord Redesdale; Thomas Lord Erskine; Charles Manners Sutton, esq.; Sir Arthur Paget, knight; William Wellesley Pole, esq.; John Trevor, esq.; Sir William Scott, knight; George Canning, esq.; William Dundas, esq.; Charles Philip Yorke, esq.; Sir William Grant, knight; Thomas Wallace, esq.; Charles Bathurst, esq. Chancellor of our Duchy of Lancaster; Charles Long, esq. Paymaster-General of our Forces; Sir John Borlase Warren, Baronet; Sir Evan Nepean, Baronet; Charles Arbuthnot, esq.; John Hookham Frere, esq.; Nicholas Vansittart, esq. Chancellor and Under Treasurer of our Exchequer; Reginald Pole Carew, esq.; John Sullivan, esq.; Richard Ryder, esq.; Sir John Nicholl, knight; Frederick John Robinson, esq. Treasurer of our Navy; William Vessey Fitzgerald, esq.; Robert Peel, esq.; Sir Thomas Plumer, Knight, Master of the Rolls; William Huskisson, esq.; William Sturges Bourne, esq.; Charles Bagot, esq.;

Sir Henry Russell, Baronet ; Sir Richard Richards, Knight,
Lord Chief Baron of our Exchequer; John Beckett, esq.;
Sir Benjamin Bloomfield, Knight; Sir John Leach, Knight,
Vice Chancellor of England ; Sir Charles Abbott, Knight,
Lord Chief Justice of our Court of King's Bench; Sir
Robert Dallas, Knight, Lord Chief Justice of our Court of
Common Pleas ; Sir Samuel Shepherd, Knight, Lord Chief
Baron of our Exchequer in Scotland ; and David Boyle,
esq. Lord Justice Clerk of Scotland, or any five or more of
them, to receive, hear, and determine the petitions and claims
which shall be to them exhibited by any of our loving subjects in this behalf; and we shall appoint our said Commissioners for that purpose to sit in the painted-chamber of
our Palace, at Westminster, upon Thursday, the 18th day
of this instant May, at twelve of the clock at noon of the
same day, and from time to time to adjourn as to them shall
seem meet, for the execution of our said commission; which
we do thus publish to the intent that all such persons whom it
may any ways concern may know when and where to give
their attendance for the exhibiting of their petitions and
claims concerning the services before-mentioned to be done
and performed unto us at our said Coronation ; and we do
hereby signify unto all and every our subjects whom it may
concern, that our will and pleasure is, and we do hereby
strictly charge all persons, of what rank or quality soever
they may be, who, either upon our letters to them directed,
or by reason of their offices or tenures or otherwise, are to
do any service at the said day or time of our Coronation, that
they do duly give their attendance accordingly, in all respects furnished and appointed as to so great a solemnity
appertaineth, and answerable to the dignities and places
which every one of them respectively holdeth and enjoyeth,
and of this they or any of them are not to fail, as they will
answer the contrary at their perils, unless upon special reasons by Ourself, under our hand to be allowed, We shall
dispense with any of their services or attendances.

Given at our Court at Carlton-house, this sixth day of
May, one thousand eight hundred and twenty, and in the
first year of our reign. GOD save the KING.

In pursuance of the foregoing Order in Council,
the regular official persons connected with the Heralds'-Office, proceeded to make proclamation of the
intended Coronation of his Majesty on the 1st of
August, 1820. The persons appointed to take part
in the ceremony assembled at 11 o'clock, in Old

Palace-yard, and were marshalled by Sir George Naylor in the order in which they were to proceed.

The crowd collected on the occasion was by no means so numerous as might have been expected, and seemed principally to have been formed from persons accidentally drawn to the spot from the military parade which was made, a whole regiment of the Horse Guards Royal being in attendance. At twelve o'clock precisely, the cavalcade prepared to move. The heralds, who were mounted upon horses belonging to the band of one of the regiments of the Horse Guards, came forth from the Court-yard in front of the Speaker's house, and having arrived in front of the great gate of Westminster-hall, were received by a flourishing of trumpets.

Mr. G. M. Leake, the Chester Herald, then took off his hat, and his example being followed by the other official persons in attendance, he read the Proclamation. At the conclusion, the household trumpets, accompanied by the drums, played the popular air of " God save the King."

The whole now moved on in the following order, the band playing the jubilee-march :—

The High Constable of Westminster.
Two Horse Guards.
One Horse Guard.
Four Farriers of the Horse Guards.
The Trumpets of the Horse Guards.
A troop of Horse Guards.

Eight Marshal's men, in full uniform, with their staves, on foot.

Household Band, on foot, and in their state uniforms.

Six Deputy Serjeants at Arms (Messrs. Chas. Brown, Struble, Gardner, Ruddock, Brown, and Nost) on horseback, attired in full-dress Court coats and waistcoats, and cocked hats, wearing also swords, and having over their shoulders silver chains, to which were appended the order of St. George, and the Royal arms. The remainder of their costume consisted of coloured breeches and top boots, which, when contrasted with the full-dress coats, had a most singular appearance, and produced a good deal of risibility among the spectators. Men were employed to walk by the side of these persons to carry their silver gilt maces.

G. M. Leake, Esq. Chester Herald.
Pursuivant.
Joseph Hawkes, Esq. Richmond Herald.
Pursuivant.
James Cuthro, Esq. Somerset Herald.
Pursuivant.

These gentlemen were covered with their official heraldic dresses. The procession was closed by a numerous body of the Life Guards. The whole proceeded slowly to Charing Cross, and up the Strand, till they arrived at a short distance from Temple Bar, the gates of which had been shut. An order was now given to halt, and Blue-Mantle (Mr. Wood), pursuivant, attended by eight Horse Guards, rode up to the Bar, and having rapped, the gates were opened by Mr. Wontner, the City Marshal. Mr. Wontner then asked his business? when he replied that he demanded admission to read his Majesty's proclamation relative to the royal Coronation. Mr. Wontner shut the gate, and immediately joined the Lord Mayor, who was in attendance in his state carriage, and communicated to his lordship the purport of Blue-Mantle's demand. The Lord Mayor directed that Blue-Mantle might be conducted to him. Mr. Wontner, immediately rode back, and again opening the gate, requested Blue-Mantle to advance alone. This he did, and was forthwith introduced to the Lord Mayor, who asked him personally the object of his mission. Blue-Mantle replied, as he had to Mr. Wontner, and handed to his lordship the Order in Council for making the proclamation of the King's Coronation. The Lord Mayor, under the sanction of this order, immediately ordered that the gates should be thrown open. This order was obeyed, and the procession advanced, in the manner already described, to the end of Chancery-lane, where the Richmond Herald read the proclamation, under similar circumstances to those which attended the reading in Palace-yard.

The procession in its further progress to the Royal Exchange was followed by the Lord Mayor, Sheriffs, and several Aldermen, in their carriages. The reading was repeated at the Royal Exchange. The procession then went on to the pump at Aldgate, and returned through Fenchurch-street and Lombard-street to the Mansion-House, where the ceremony was concluded. Every thing was conducted with the greatest order and regularity.

Summonses were directed to be immediately issued to the Peers of the United Kingdom, including Roman Catholics, and Peers of Scotland and Ireland, not Peers of Parliament, to assist at the ensuing Coronation. The following is the form of the summons, adapted to the several ranks:—

G. R.—Right trusty, and right well-beloved cousin, we greet you well.

Whereas we have appointed the first day of August next for the solemnity of our royal Coronation; these are, therefore, to will and command you, all excuses set apart, that you make your personal attendance on us, at the time above mentioned, furnished and appointed as to your rank and quality appertaineth, there to do and perform such services as shall be required and belong unto you: whereof you are not to fail, and so bid you heartily farewell.

Given at our Court of Carlton Palace, the 10th May, 1820.

The only singularity attending this summons, was the omission of the requisition of the Countesses to attend the coronation of the Queen. In the summons which was issued at the coronation of George III. it ran as follows:—

"And whereas we have also resolved, that the Coronation of our royal consort the Queen shall be solemnized on the same day, we do further hereby require the Countess your wife to make her personal attendance on our royal said Consort, at the time and in the manner aforesaid. Whereof," &c.

Circumstances, however, of a very particular nature intruded themselves at this time, to do away with the provisions necessary for the coronation of the Queen, who, at the period of the issuing of the summons, was residing in Italy, and who, if it had not been for particular insults and indignities which she supposed were offered to her by the constituted authorities of Italy, and which she imagined were sanctioned by the government at home, would probably have remained abroad, and consequently saved this country from that turbulence, and that dangerous effusion of party spirit, which have distinguished her arrival and her abode in it.

The omission of the summons to the wives of the Peers to attend upon the royal consort, may on the first view appear as deserving of little notice; but we shall have occasion hereafter to show, that there is constitutionally, and individually speaking, a higher importance attached to it, than is apparent to the casual observer; and indeed it seems to have been determined upon with a degree of foresight, which confers no little credit upon those who advised the measure.

Although the summons to the Peers to attend the coronation of the sovereign be imperative, yet letters of dispensation are always granted to those who by old age, infirmity, urgent business, or services abroad, are rendered incapable of attending the ceremony. On the occasion of the Coronation of George IV. many Peers availed themselves of the letters of dispensation; and in the exercise of the Monarch's prerogative, there is an instance of a Peer not having been summoned at all, on account of his uniform attachment, and decided partiality to the Sovereign's rejected consort.

There is one particular circumstance connected with the coronation of an English king which deserves particular mention, but which has now fallen into desuetude, on account of the English monarchs having changed their place of residence. It is, however, highly interesting, as it concerns principally the creation of the Knights of the Bath, which being a military order, appears in the early times to have been held in the highest estimation at the coronation of the English kings.

It is indeed highly curious and amusing to trace the changes which have taken place in the ceremony of inauguration of an English monarch from the early days of chivalry, when the hardy English warrior bore his coat of mail, to this more effeminate, but civilized age, when the armour, the lance, and the shield, are thrown aside to make way for the frippery and the foppery of a splendid habiliment.

In former times, the Tower of London was the chosen residence of the kings of England, and on the accession of a new sovereign to the throne, it was customary to assemble there the peers of the realm, the great officers of state, and different members of the court, and thence to go in grand procession through the city to the palace of Westminster, which generally occupied the whole of the day preceding the coronation.

Previously, however, to the King's departure, a ceremony was performed which is worthy of the most particular notice, as it furnishes us with a clue to the ceremonies of the creation of the Knights of the Bath, who always hold a distinguished rank in the coronation of the English kings, but who, from reasons not necessary here to develop, are excused at the present day from undergoing those penances which entitled them to be admitted as members of that most noble order. In Mr. Anstis's *Observations introductory to an Historical Essay upon the Knighthood of the Bath*, he says, " this act of royal grace hath been usually displayed upon the coronation and marriage of our Kings; the coronation of both Queens Regent and Queens Consorts; the birth and marriage of the royal issue, and their first advancement to honours; upon the designed expedition of our Kings against their foreign enemies; upon installations into the most noble order of the Garter; and when some grand anniversary festivals were celebrated."

Mr. Taylor, in his excellent work on the Glory of Regality, speaking on this subject, says, " the ancient Knights of the Bath were not an incorporated brotherhood, but like those other kinds or classes of knighthood, the bannerets or bachelors (or knights of the Sword) derived their title from the manner of their creation. This it appears chiefly consisted in the noviciate's being conducted to a chamber where a bath was prepared in which he bathed; he then retired his clothes, with a hermit's weed of russet cloth, and going to the church or chapel of the palace, kept his vigil till almost day-break, when he retired to rest. In the morning, habited in proud and costly robes, he came forth and took horse in the court of the palace, and passing to the hall, received the spurs and sword, and was dubbed knight by the hand of his Sovereign.

"Such were the ceremonies, now, alas! gone with the age of chivalry, 'to that solemne and highe Knighthood apperteynyng' which were used at the coronations of our ancient Kings; but from the reign of Charles II. these, together with the procession through the city of London have been entirely discontinued." Before this time, then, the great festival of which we are now treating may be said to have begun on the evening when the vigils of the Bath were performed. On the following day the creation of the knights was succeeded by a royal feast at the Tower, after which every thing was put in order for the magnificent progress of the King and his court through the midst of the capital. Upon this occasion the streets were cleaned, and the houses decorated with tapestry and arras. Bands of music were stationed at convenient intervals, and four grand triumphal arches were erected, peopled with gods and genii, who saluted the Sovereign with appropriate speeches and songs. The aldermen of the city were placed in Cheapside, and the companies ranged along the streets all in their proper habits. With respect to the procession itself, it will suffice to say, that it consisted of the usual attendants of royalty, and of the judges, peers, great officers of state and princes of the blood. The King rode bare-headed under a canopy borne by four knights, who were to be " chaunged at divers and many places, as well for that the King may be well served of many noble persons to their great honour, as for their ease that beare it." The Queen came after, and like the King, uncovered; she was carried on a sumptuous litter, with cushions of white damask—her ladies following in chariots. All the rest were on horseback or walking, and in this manner they proceeded through the city by Temple Bar to the old palace at Westminster, where the King and his royal Consort were used to lodge that night.

What a singular contrast will the above description form with that into which we shall shortly enter, when the Monarch, instead of being borne upon the shoulders of his subjects, will be enveloped by the swords and sabres of his guards, when thousands of bayonets will bristle in the air, which are superfluous to a monarch like George IV. who lives in the love and the affection of his people.

His Majesty's pleasure respecting his Coronation having now been made public, the Court of Claims was immediately appointed, in the origin and constitution of which, the following account will at this time be found to possess peculiar interest. On the approach of every coronation, a particular function devolves on the Lord High Steward of England, which is to receive the petitions of state officers and of certain of the nobility and gentry, who by the tenures of their respective estates are bound to perform services of different kinds at the coronations of the Kings and Queens of England. At this time the High Stewards of England were used by virtue of their office to sit judicially in the White hall of the king's palace of Westminster, near the chapel, which is the present House of Commons. These petitions or claims the Steward had power to examine, and if supported by documents and precedents, to allow them, or to reject if wanting in the requisite proof; hence this tribunal is called the Court of Claims. For the better understanding of the decisions of this court respecting the services to be described, we quote the following from Mr. Taylor's " Glory of Regality."

" Among the different conditions upon which the lands were formerly granted by the crown was that of performing some defined service by the person of the tenant to the person of the king. This service was sometimes a military one, but more commonly official, and the time of its performance was frequently the day of the sovereign's coronation, when he also received the homage and fealty of those other tenants who held their lands by these forms of submission. Tenure, on the condition above defined, was honourable from its certainty, and from the required service being due to the royal person alone, hence it was called *magnum servitium*, or grand serjeantry. Thus if the crown hath granted a manor or estate to any one on the condition that he shall carry a sword or a sceptre at the coronations of the kings and queens of England, such estate is said to be holden in grand serjeantry by the service of carrying such royal ensign. As another mark of the honour attributed to services of this kind, we find that they cannot be performed by any under the degree of knighthood, nor by a minor or a female tenant; for these a deputy of sufficient rank is appointed, with the sovereign's license."

It may be well to note in the conclusion, that these services are to be considered as the rent or fine due for enjoyment of the lands to which they are attached; and therefore, though the tenants are sometimes said to claim the service, they must be understood in reality as claiming the continuance of the estates by appearing to fulfil the conditions on which they were granted.

We shall now enter without further preamble to enumerate the claims which were brought forward on the memorable occasion, and which in some respects are similar to those brought forward at the coronation of George III.

The Court of Claims on this occasion sat in the

Painted Chamber, and its members consisted generally of Earl Harrowby, President of the Council and of the Court of Claims; the Dukes of York, Clarence and Gloucester; his Grace the Duke of Montrose, Master of the Horse; the Earls of Donoughmore and Mansfield; Lord Henley, Lord Beauchamp, Sir Wm. Scott, Sir J. Nicholl, Mr. Sturges Bourne, Mr. Beckett, and a number of other official characters. A number of ladies of rank usually attended the proceedings, whose elegant appearance conferred additional ornament upon the arrangements observable in the court.

1*st Claim.*—The Bishop of Durham and the Bishop of Bath and Wells claimed jointly of old custom to assist or support the King in the procession, the first walking on his right hand, the latter on his left. These prelates were in the enjoyment of this distinction so early as Richard I. but the manner or time of their obtaining it has not been brought to light. The petition further prayed, that the petitioners might be allowed to perform the service by deputies, on account of their great age.

The court allowed the claim of the petitioners to perform the services stated. But the question of their being allowed to perform the services by deputies, was referred by the court to the King in Council.

2*d.*—The Dean and Chapter of Westminster claim for the Dean, to instruct the King in the rites and ceremonies, and to assist the Archbishop in performing the divine service; also that they should have the keeping of the Regalia and coronation robes. These privileges were enjoyed of old by the Abbott and Monks of this noble monastery, and were continued to their Protestant successors by letters patent of Queen Elizabeth. The fees which are claimed for this service are robes for the Dean and his three chaplains, and sixteen ministers of the church—the royal habits which are put off in the church—the several oblations, the furniture of the church, the staves and bells of the canopies held over the King in the church, and the cloth on which his Majesty walks from the west door to the theatre or platform. This claim was allowed, with the exception of the keeping of the Regalia.

3d.—The Lord Great Chamberlain of England claimed to carry the King his shirt and clothes the morning of his Coronation, and to dress the King; to have forty yards of crimson velvet for a robe, also the King's bed and bedding, and furniture of his chamber where he lay the night before, with his wearing apparel and night-gown. Also to serve the King with water before and after dinner, and to have the basons and towels and cup of assay.*

Allowed, except the cup of assay; but as chief officer of the King, he had awarded to him two gilt chased basins and one gilt chased ewer—the remainder were compounded for in a given sum of money. Counterclaimed by the Earl of Derby, but disallowed.

The most important claim is that of the Lord of the Manor of Scrivelsby, to perform the noble and splendid service of King's Champion, the most perfect, perhaps, and most striking relique of feudalism that has come come down to us from the ages of chivalry.

This office was originally held by the family of Marmion, in right of their possession of the manor of Scrivelsby, no doubt familiar to many of our readers by Sir W. Scott's description, as

"Lord of Fontenaye,
Of Lutterward and Scrivelbaye,
Of Tamworth tower and town."

This manor is holden by the service of "finding, on the day of the Coronation, an armed knight, who shall prove by his body, if need be, that the King is the true and rightful heir to the kingdom." This is

---

* A vessel to contain a portion of the water in which the King is to wash as a specimen or sample of the remainder.

taken from an inquisition held so long ago as the seventh year of Edward III. which shows the high antiquity of the office. It has been for a long series of years in the family of Dymoke, and remains in it to this day. It was disputed twice by the lords of Tamworth, the last time in the reign of Henry IV. since which it has remained as the unquestioned appurtenant to the manor of Scrivelsby. The petition of Dame Margaret Dymoke, asserting her rights, in that reign, is still extant; and another document also remains, claiming the fees which were due, and unjustly withheld from her late husband. His duty is to ride into the hall during dinner, before the second course is brought in, mounted on a spirited charger, and clad in a splendid suit of armour. He is attended by the Lord High Constable and the Earl Marshal, and, by a herald, proclaims a challenge to any one who shall deny the legality of the King's title to the throne. This having been done, his Majesty drinks to him from a gold cup, which, together with its cover, becomes his fee, and the horse and armour: the first was his fee as a matter of right, but the latter was withholdable at the King's pleasure, unless a combat took place. Anciently the Champion used to ride in the procession as well as in the hall, and to proclaim his challenge publicly in both places. Indeed, at the coronation of Henry IV. the challenge was proclaimed in the palace, and at six different places in the city, and in the original form it was used to be proclaimed before the ceremony of crowning. At the coronation of Richard II. Sir John Dymoke, the Champion, came with his attendants to the church door; but the Lord Marshal came to him and told him he must retire until the King's dinner, and then return, which he accordingly did, and so it has continued to the present day. This office is certainly the most characteristic and magnificent remnant of feudalism which has escaped the great innovator.

In the present instance, the claim was advanced by the Rev. T. Dymoke, lord of the manor of Scrivelsby;

but at the same time, in consequence of his being in holy orders, he prayed leave to appoint his substitute, and that leave being granted, he appointed John Reader, jun. esq. At a subsequent meeting of the court, the Rev. Mr. Dymoke presented a petition praying for leave to withdraw a former petition, in which he had prayed for leave to appoint John Reader, jun. esq. his deputy as Champion at the Coronation; the petition also prayed that he might be allowed to appoint his son (a minor) to appear as his deputy in the office of Champion.

The consideration of this petition was deferred until the pleasure of his Majesty should be known, as to whether he would accept a minor as his champion.

At the next meeting of the court, Mr. Gaselee, the king's counsel, was heard in support of the right of the Rev. T. Dymoke, (lord of the manor of Scrivelsby, and the person whose duty it was to perform the office of Champion at his Majesty's Coronation,) to appoint a deputy, he being a clerk in orders, and thereby incapacitated from attending. The learned counsel said, that during the last year the Rev. Mr. Dymoke had petitioned to have Mr. Reader, jun. permitted to officiate for him as champion; but that since that period his son (Mr. Dymoke, jun.), who was abroad for some time, had returned, and he now prayed that he might be permitted to officiate instead of Mr. Reader, jun. A doubt, it was rumoured, had arisen on the right of Mr. Dymoke to appoint a deputy. There was no doubt upon his own right to officiate as champion, he being the lord of the manor of Scrivelsby, and the person possessing the manor being from early times his Majesty's Champion at the Coronation. But he thought the right to nominate his deputy, in cases where the lordship was filled by a person incapable *per se*,—either, for instance, when it was filled by a woman, or by a minor,—was clearly demonstrable by a reference to the ancient records, and the chapter in Coke on Littleton upon Serjeantry and Manorial Rights. The learned counsel called

F

the attention of the court to the words as they stood in the old writs of offices inscribed in the Coronation Rolls in the Record-office. From thence it would be seen, that so early as the time of Henry IV. when the manor of Scrivelsby was vested in a woman, she appointed her husband to be champion; and in another instance, a female nominated her son to act for her. He knew that there were instances from which it was inferred that the Champion must be of the rank of knight; but it would be seen, on looking at these instances (and there appeared many in the Dymoke family), that the appointment of knights champions was accidental, and in no degree a matter of compulsory mandate. Indeed earls had performed the office; and it was remarkable, that they were appointed by persons holding the manor, who were themselves incapable of acting—a circumstance, he thought, fully showing that the right of appointing the deputy was vested in the lord of the manor, and in him alone. In the reigns of Edward III., Edward VII., Henry IV., James I., William and Mary, and other reigns, it would seem, that the Lord of the Manor of Scrivelsby appointed a deputy. There was no qualification of rank or degree required: the words of the writs ran thus: that he should serve the office by a *probus et legalis* person *nomine suo*. The latter words clearly implying his own substitute. In the writ of Henry IV. the words were, to appoint, *aliquis nomine suo;* all through showing that the right of appointment of his deputy was vested in him, and that the only stipulation was, that the person appointed to act as deputy, should be *probus et legalis*. The fact was, that the Lord of the Manor of Scrivelsby was imperatively bound to perform the office of Champion, either by himself or a deputy; for it was on that performance depended his right of tenure to the manor. Mr. Dymoke, the father of the present lord, had performed the office to the late king. It might be said that the constitution of this court, and the very fact of claims being brought here and registered before admission, implied that the appointment of a deputy could not be made without the consent of the King in Council. He humbly submitted that this inference was not conclusive; for that the great object of his summoning this court was, that it should be known who were the parties coming forward to do the services required of them by the King at the ceremony of his Coronation, and to see that those upon whom his Majesty had a right to call, under the penalty of a forfeiture, were in proper attendance. So much then for the right of Mr. Dymoke to appoint a deputy. Then as to the person who was to be his deputy, he had only a few words to offer. Mr. Dymoke, junior, whom he wished to appoint, was only 20 years of age last March, and being consequently a minor, he could not be appointed without the permission of his Majesty; for, of course, if the lord himself, being a minor, could not officiate, it followed that his deputy, in the same predicament, incurred a similar disqualification, unless the King was pleased to dispense with his minority. Mr. Dymoke was most anxious to show his respect for his Sovereign, by having the office of champion filled by his son; but if the court rejected the prayer of his petition, he then hoped they would suffer the name of Mr. Reader to remain as before, his deputy at the approaching ceremony.

When Mr. Gaselee had concluded, the Duke of Clarence asked Mr. Dymoke, jun. what rank he held in the navy, and when he was appointed?

Mr. Dymoke replied, that he was not at present in his Majesty's service.

The court was then cleared; and after a short consultation it was declared, that Mr. Dymoke should be excused from performing the office of Champion in person, and that he should be allowed to appoint a " sufficient deputy."

Considerable interest was accordingly made by the Rev. Mr. Dymoke to obtain the appointment for his son; and his endeavours were ultimately crowned with success.

The reverend gentleman also claimed to have the mantle worn by his Majesty, and the gold cup, out of which he will drink to the Champion, as fees for his services.

The court decided that the petitioner should be allowed to have the gold cup, but not the mantle.

The Lord Mayor and Commonalty of the City of London claimed by prescription, that the said Mayor and twelve citizens to be chosen by them, should assist the Chief Butler of England in the execution of his office; and that they should sit at a table next the cupboard on the left side of the hall. Also that the Lord Mayor should serve the King after dinner with wine in a gold cup, and have the cup and its cover for his fee.

A singular circumstance arose from the presentation of this petition, on account of the Coronation having been postponed from August 1820, to July 1821. In the interim the Lord Mayor mentioned in petition of 1820 had retired from his office, and two of the list of the twelve citizens had died. It became, therefore, an important point to decide on the right of the existing Lord Mayor, to substitute other names in the lieu of those who were dead, and whether the wardens of the former year, or those of the current one, were to attend the ceremony.

Accordingly, at a meeting of the court on the 15th of June, 1821, Sir John Sylvester, the Recorder of the City of London, attended by the City Remembrancer, advanced to the council table, and read an application made on the part of the Right Honourable the Lord Mayor of the City of London, praying that his lordship might be allowed to alter some of the names presented to the court during the last year, by the late Lord Mayor. It appeared, that, according to ancient usage, the Lord Mayor of London, for the time being, has had permission, accompanied by twelve citizens, to attend the coronation of the kings of England, and the festival which follows that ceremonial. When the Court of Claims sat last year, the late Lord Mayor (Mr. Alderman Bridges) presented, by virtue of his office, a petition, praying for leave to attend with the wardens of the twelve liveries of the City of London, as his twelve citizens. The claim was, we believe, then allowed; but since the last year, an alteration by death has occurred in two instances in the list, besides the alteration of the Lord Mayor's name for the time being; and it was the object of the Recorder's present application to the court, to have permission merely that these two or three alterations should be supplied.

When the Recorder had finished reading his petition on the part of the Lord Mayor, and presented it to the Clerk of the Court, twelve gentlemen appeared with another petition; which set forth, that they were the twelve wardens, for the present year, of the liveries mentioned in the Lord Mayor's previous petition; and they, therefore, humbly prayed that their names might be substituted for those of the twelve wardens of the past year, who were no longer in office, and who could not be styled wardens, as the petitioners had, in fact, succeeded to the livery wardenships, at the late election for the current year. They therefore prayed permission to represent the twelve citizens who were to accompany the Lord Mayor, and that their names should be inserted in the list, to the exclusion of the twelve out-wardens.

The Earl of Harrowby, after a short consultation with the other Commissioners, said, that in estimating the claims of persons to officiate at his Majesty's Coronation, that court could not recognise any right on the part of persons calling themselves wardens of the liveries of the City of London, as they were unable to find any precedent for the admission of such a right on similar occasions. That it was true the Lord Mayor of London, *ex officio*, had been allowed the privilege of being present on such occasions, and that it was the ancient custom he should be attended by twelve citizens of London, which twelve citizens were always nominated by the Lord Mayor. That as to wardens, the court knew nothing about such persons: all they had to require was, that the twelve who had the privilege of attending with the Lord Mayor should be citizens.

The wardens begged leave to observe, that the names already in court purported to be those of persons holding livery offices; now they had, in the present year, lost those offices, which were filled by the twelve gentlemen now attending the court, who prayed that their names should be substituted in the room of the preceding names, as in fact they must be, if the existing wardens of the companies are to be those in attendance with the Lord Mayor.

The Earl of Harrowby repeated, that the Court of Claims had nothing to do with the office of wardens. That it was for the Lord Mayor to transmit for approbation the names of twelve citizens,—the civic denomination being alone requested.

The petition presented by the Recorder on the part of the Lord Mayor to alter the names occasioned by demise, was then left for consideration, and that of the twelve wardens, who came in person into court, was rejected.

The mayor, bailiffs, and commonalty of Oxford, claimed, by virtue of their charter, to serve in the office of Botelry with the citizens of London, and to have for their fee three maple cups. In the Cotton MS. the following account of this service appears in a list of the claims of Edward VI.

"The mayor of Oxenford claimeth to ayde the chief butler, in their service of ale at the barr; and for profe shewed olde presidentes, wherin it appeared, that the mayor of Oxenford hade done the service, wheruppon the Erle of Arrondell, chief butler, gave him his livery, and did admit him to do the said service." The claim of the city of Oxford was allowed.

The Earl of Ormond and Ossory appeared in person, to take the opinion of the court upon his claim to attend his Majesty at the Coronation, as Lord Chief Butler for Ireland.

The court admitted the validity of the claim by virtue of the office, but delayed adjudicating upon the right of the present claimant, until the Committee of Privileges now sitting upon the earldom of Ormonde, shall have made their report.

Lord Gwydir also appeared in person, and presented the King's Sign-Manual to his appointment (which he derived by succession) as Deputy Chamberlain of England; in right of which he claimed the performance of his office at the Coronation, to represent the senior chamberlainship, now filled by two ladies the Marchioness of Cholmondeley and Lady Gwydir.

The claim was ordered to be referred to the King in Council.

Sir Andrew Halliday claimed the privilege of attending the Coronation, as one of the officers of state in Scotland; but this claim was referred to the Council Office.

The claim of the Barons of the Cinque Ports to carry the canopy over the King, at the ceremony, was allowed.

The claim of the Baroness Grey de Ruthyn to carry a pair of silver spurs before the King, and to perform other services, was allowed by the court. Her deputy is to be appointed by the King.

The claim of the Duke of Norfolk to present a glove was allowed. The claim of the Duke of Norfolk, as Earl of Arundel, to perform the office of Butler, and to have the great ewer for his fee, was also allowed.

Petitions from the Duke of Bedford and S. Whitbread, Esq. claiming to be Almoners to his Majesty, were allowed.

The claim of the Duke of Montrose, to be allowed to have the care of the silver scullery, was referred to the King in Council.

The claim of Mr. Soames to be allowed to hold the towel and basin, and to have the ewer for his services, was allowed.

The claim of Mr. John Campbell, of Liston, to be the King's Waferer, was allowed.

That the reader may not be ignorant of the composition of these royal wafers, and the quantities of each ingredient allowed to the claimant, the following is a list of them copied from the record of a late coronation.

 Imprimis un pipe de flower.
 Item. xxx loaves de sugre.
 Item. xx li de almonds pur ixille.
 Item. ij li de powdre de ginger.
 Item. ½ li de saffron pur bastrons.
 Item. i pipe d'osey.
 Item. iij gallons d'oyle.
 Item. i dozeine de towailles de Paris.
 Item. i dozeine aulnes de lyn pur covertures.
 Item. ij Paris bulters.
 Item. xl aulnes de streigners.
 Item. xx aulnes de canvas.
 Item. i dozeine basins et bolles pur batre.
 Item. fuel sufficient.
 Item. Vestures pur vostre suppliant et deux homes.

The manor of Liston was holden on the above tenure by the family surnamed De Liston as early as the time of Henry II. or King John, and the conditions have been regularly fulfilled by their successors. The service was performed by W. Campbell, Esq. of Liston, at the coronation of George II.

The claim of Mr. Wiltshire, to present the first cup to the King at dinner, was allowed.

ANOINTING OIL.—The next application was of a very singular character; it was the petition of Messrs. Godfrey and Cooke, of Southampton-street, Covent-garden, chemists, praying to be allowed to prepare and supply the oil for the purpose, after consecration, of anointing his Majesty. These petitioners applied to be allowed to fulfil such service, because their house had supplied the anointing oil used at the coronation of George III. The court, after having made some inquiries, stated, that they had nothing to do with this application. The petitioners did not adduce any warrant or authority for the privilege they claimed; it regarded regulations that were under the exclusive control of his Majesty. The King could appoint such person as he pleased. Petition returned as not coming under the cognizance of the court.

The petition of the city of Dublin, that the Lord Mayor, &c. may have a place at the approaching Coronation, was referred to the King in Council.

The free barons of the port of Dover claimed to hold a canopy over his Majesty, and sit on his right hand at the Coronation-banquet. This privilege was also claimed by the mayor, corporation, and common-councilmen, of the same port. The court did not decide to which of the two parties the right of electing eight free barons of Dover belonged, but said, that it would be expected that eight of them would attend for that purpose. The parties were therefore left to settle among themselves to whom the right belongs.

The Marquis of Cornwallis claimed to act at the Coronation as Butler of Ireland. He founded his claim to this privilege upon his descent from Sir T. Boleyn, who acted in the same capacity at the coronation of Henry VIII. This honour was counter-claimed by the Marquis of Ormond, to whom it was decided to belong, the rights of the Boleyns having merged in the Crown on the marriage of Anne Boleyn with Henry VIII.

One of the most singular claims which was put in was that of Mr. Walker, the King's apothecary. If it had been allowed, it would have been required of him to wear the dress of the Esculapius of Edward II. viz. long shoes turned up at the toe and looped to the knee; a blue stocking on one leg, and a red stocking on the other, with a party-coloured vest and cloak. His office would have been to carry in one hand a bottle of perfumed oil.

The Lord of the Manor of Nether Bilsington claimed to present the King with three maple cups by himself or deputy. This manor seems to have been held by William de Albini, Earl of Arundel, in the reign of Henry I. by a serjeantry of butlership. His descendant Richard Fitz Alan, Earl of Arundel, in the reign of Edward III. alienated it to Edmond Staplegate, who died possessed of it in the forty-sixth year of that reign, holding it by the service of presenting three maple cups. The service however of presenting these maple cups does not appear in some of the intervening records, but is admitted in the reigns of Charles II. James II. and their successors.

The Duke of Athol, as Lord of the Isle of Man, claimed to bring two falcons to the King on the Coronation-day.

The Lord of the Manor of Addington, (called Bardolf's Manor,) in the county of Surrey, to find a man to make a mess of grout in the King's kitchen; and that the King's master-cook might perform that service. It is not easy to give an account of this dish, which is so remarkably perpetuated by this ancient tenure. It can, however, be recorded back as far as the time of the Conqueror.

In the " Environs of London," the author adds the following as a note: " In a collection of ancient cookery receipts of the 14th century, printed at the end of the Royal Household Establishments published by the Society of Antiquaries, is a receipt to make a dish called Bardolf;—although there is no evidence to support it, it would not be an unfair conjecture, as the Bardolfs were lords of Addington at the period above mentioned, to suppose that this might be the dish in question ; it was called a pottage, and consisted of almond mylk, the brawn of capons, sugar and spices, chicken parboyled and chopped."

This manor was sold in 1807 to the present Archbishop of Canterbury, who was the claimant on this occasion.

The Lord of the Manor of Scoulton, alias Bourdelies, in Norfolk, claimed to be Chief Larderer, and to have for his fees the provisions remaining after dinner in the larder. These services were counterclaimed by the Lord of the Manor of Easton and Montem in Essex, but it appearing on reference that other manors were severally holden by the same service, the former was appointed *pro hac vice,** with a *salvo jure* † to the latter.

The Lord of the Manor of Great Wimondley, Hertfordshire, claimed as chief cup bearer to serve the King with the first cup of silver gilt at dinner, and to have the cup for his fee.

The Duke of Norfolk as Earl of Arundel and lord of Kenninghall manor, in Norfolk, claimed to perform the office of Chief Butler of England, and to have for his fees the best cup of gold and cover, with all the vessels and wine remaining under the bar, and all the pots and cups, except those of gold and silver, in the wine cellar after dinner. Allowed, with only the fee of a cup and ewer.

There were several other minor claims put in of trifling importance, which do not deserve particular mention; nor have we noticed those which were presented, but not established.

The following are some further allowances connected with the ceremony of the claims at the coronation of the kings of England.

1. To the Lord Almoner for the day, three hundred and five ounces of gilt plate, in two large gilt chased basons.

2. The gold cup and cover, to the Lord Mayor of London, of twenty ounces of pure gold.

---

* For that duty.

† Saving the right—that is to say, allowing the privileges of the other two claimants, although the service was performed by one of the possessors of the barony only.

3. To the Chief Cup-bearer, a cup and cover, curiously enchased and gilt, of thirty-two ounces.

4. To the Mayor of Oxford, a high gilt bowl and cover, richly chased, of one hundred and ten ounces, as a gift from the King to that city, with his Majesty's arms engraved on it.

5. To the Champion, a high bowl and cover, finely chased and gilt, of thirty-six ounces.

All which cups and bowls are enchased with his Majesty's arms.

6. To the Duke of Norfolk, as chief butler of England, for the day, a cup of pure gold, of thirty-two ounces.

7. To the Lord Great Chamberlain, as chief officer of the Ewry, two gilt chased basons, and one gilt chased ewer.

His Grace the Archbishop of Canterbury as his fee, according to ancient usage, receives the purple velvet chair, cushion, and footstool, whereon he sits at the Coronation.

The officers of the removing wardrobe also usually receive as their fee, the pall of cloth of gold held over his Majesty at the Coronation.

The persons who represent the Dukes of Normandy and Aquitain, receive, in right of the King, a pension of one thousand pounds per annum.

The following are the manors held by coronation services, arranged under their respective counties.

Counties	Towns	Service of
Bedfordshire	Bedford	Almoner.
Dorsetshire	*Wynfied* *	Water-bearer.
Essex	*Easton*	Caterer and lardiner.
———	Fingreth	Queen's Chamberlain.
———	Heydon	Towel.
———	Liston	Waferer.
Hertfordshire	Wimondley	Cup-bearer.
Kent	Bilsington	Maple cups.
Leicestershire	*Kibworth*	Panneter.

---

* The services of the manors printed in Italics are extinct, or not allowed.

Counties	Towns	Service of
Lincolnshire	Scrivelsby	Champion.
Norfolk	Ashill	Napier.
———	Kenninghall	Butler.
	Scoulton	Lardiner.
Nottinghamshire	Worksop	Glove.
Suffolk	Kettilbarston	Sceptre.
Surrey	Addington	Gerout.
———	Sheen	Two cups.
Isle of Man		Falcons.

Having thus minutely described these interesting proceedings precursory of the august ceremony, we shall now enter upon the description of those ensigns of power and dominion, the delivery of which, under forms of the most solemn and imposing nature, invests the possessor with sovereign authority. This is considered necessary, as the Regalia will be frequently mentioned in different parts of this work, and they may be considered as forming one of the most prominent features in the coronation of an English monarch.

The Regalia may be properly said to consist of
The Crown.
The Sceptre.
The Verge, or Rod of Power.
The Orb, or Mound of Sovereignty.
The Sword of Mercy, *Curtana*.
The Ring of Alliance with the kingdom.
The Armillæ, or Bracelets.
The Spurs of Chivalry.

The Ampulla, or the Golden Eagle, and the Coronation Chair, although not coming precisely under the head of the Regalia, merit particular attention, especially the latter, as it is the only one of the above-mentioned royal monuments which can boast of an undoubted antiquity.

It may be considered as not uninteresting in this place to give a brief outline of the history of the Regalia, connected as it is with that of the country itself, and at the same time opening a pleasing view to the manners and customs of our forefathers. On this head, Mr. Taylor, in his Glory of Regality, says, "It appears to have been the practice of several kingdoms to confide the care of these treasures to some distinguished church or convent, as well to honor the shrine of a patron saint as to obtain the security of consecrated walls.

"Before the Reformation the Regalia were constantly kept by the religious of the venerable abbey of Westminster, as appears from the ancient ceremonials, which evidently consider them as under the care of the Abbotts of this house, from whom they were received, and to whom they were always restored at the conclusion of the ceremony. This indeed is still done *pro forma;* the royal ornaments are brought to the palace by the clergy of the church, and several of them are left at the shrine of St. Edward when the sovereign is disrobed."

The right of this monastery as guardian of the national insignia was established by the foundation charter of Edward the Confessor, confirmed by the cotemporary Bull of Pope Nicholas II. and the subsequent ones of Pascal and Innocent II. under every sanction that ecclesiastical or civil authority could afford, and there is every reason to believe it was held sacred till the privileges of the religious houses were subverted by Henry VIII. after which period the more valuable parts of the Regalia were removed in violation of national and local right to the royal treasury of the Tower of London, and kept like the heir-loom of a family by the possessors of the throne.

The destruction of the Regalia by the republican party after the death of Charles II. forms too important a feature in the history of the country, not to be generally known.

At the Restoration, new Regalia were made for Charles II. which, with a few alterations necessary to accomodate them to their successive wearers, are the same which are in use at the present day.

The attempt of Blood to steal the crown and

1. The Crown of State. — 2. St Edward's Crown. — 3.4. Sceptres. — 5. The Orb. — 6.7.8. The Swords. — 9. The Ring. 10. The Staff. — 11. The Coronation Chair.

sceptre on the 9th of May, 1673, in the 13th year of Charles II. is too well known to make a particular account of it necessary. And we shall therefore now proceed to give a description of the Regalia individually, and first of the Crown.

The Crown made expressly for his present Majesty presents an appearance of one unvaried mass of diamonds. The curve of its branches, which meet at the top to support the ball, is not so sharp as the old one, it is more extended and graceful, and the whole is consequently much higher. The velvet with which it is ornamented is unlike the old one, which is purple; it is a beautiful crimson colour. The whole is surmounted by a pearl of immense value.

This, however, may be called the Crown of State; that with which his Majesty is crowned is called St. Edward's Crown, which derives its name from that which is said to have been worn by Edward the Confessor. It is a very rich imperial crown of gold, embellished with pearls and precious stones of divers kinds, viz. diamonds, rubies, emeralds and sapphires, and a mound of gold on the top of it, encircled with a band or fillet of gold, embellished also with precious stones, and upon the mound a cross of gold, embellished likewise with precious stones, and three very large oval pearls, one at the top of the cross, and two others pendant at the ends of the cross. The said crown is composed, as all the imperial crowns of England are, of four crosses, and as many fleur de lys of gold, upon a rim or circlet of gold, all embellished with precious stones, from the tops of which crosses arise four circular bars, or arches, which meet at the top in the form of a cross, at the intersection whereof is a pedestal, whereon is fixed the mound before mentioned. The cap within the said crown is of purple velvet, lined with white taffeta, and turned up with ermine. For a representation of these two Crowns, see No. 1 and 2 of the plate of the Regalia.

THE SCEPTRE.

The Sceptre royal which is borne in the King's right hand is made of gold, 2 feet 9¼ inches in length. At the bottom it is enriched with rubies, emeralds and small diamonds, and above the hilt for 5¼ inches is embossed with precious stones. The shaft is of burnished gold twisted and wreathed. The top rises into a fleur de lys of six leaves, three of which are upright, and the others pendant; out of this flower issues a mound, formed of a large amethyst, valued at 20,000*l.* garnished with table diamonds, and upon the mound is a cross pattée of stones, with a large table diamond in the centre.

THE SCEPTRE, WITH A DOVE OR VIRGE.

This differs materially from the sceptre with a cross, which was described in the last article. It is not wreathed, but of an even surface; it is pure gold, 3 feet 7 inches in height, 3 inches in circumference at the handle, and 2¼ inches at the top; the pommel is adorned by a fillet of diamonds and precious stones of different sorts; the ball or globe at the top is ornamented by a band or fillet of rose diamonds; upon the ball is a small cross, which is surmounted by a dove with extended wings, as the emblem of mercy. His Majesty, in the course of complying with the different forms required, exchanges the sceptre for the ball, or globe of empire. The sceptre with the dove is then held in the left hand, while the right bears the sceptre with the cross.

Sceptres were in very early use by the English kings, and if we consult the earlier periods of history, we find that they preceded the use of the crown.

Homer speaks often of " sceptred," but never of " crowned" kings, and Selden tells us that the Egyptians understood Osiris to be represented by " a sceptre with an eye on it." In the sacred writings, also, the word sceptre is often used metaphorically for the sovereign, as thus, " the sceptre shall not depart from Judah." Its use is very ancient in England, as there is a form for its delivery in the Saxon coronation service. For the Sceptres, see 3 and 4 of the Plate of the Regalia.

THE ORB.

This is ancient, but not so much so as the other ornaments which we have mentioned. It is supposed by some to have been originally part of the sceptre, but this opinion is of doubtful authority. Though it is not enumerated amongst the regalia in any of the ancient rituals, still we find it depicted upon almost all the seals and coins of our kings, from Edward the Confessor downwards. The orb was, however, in use amongst the Roman emperors, and Constantine, or Theodosius, it is uncertain which, first surmounted it with a cross. It is a ball of gold, encompassed with two fillets of precious stones, from the middle of the upper of which a large amethyst rises, which forms the pedestal of a cross, richly adorned with gems, and having three large pearls at its extremities. The whole height of both is eleven inches. The globe is most probably meant as an emblem of dominion, and the cross shows that religion ought to be the crown of empire. (See No. 5 of the Plate.)

THE ROYAL SWORDS.

First,—the Sword of Mercy, called CURTANA: the origin of this name is enveloped in obscurity, and it would defy the most indefatigable examiner of our ancient records to discover it. It appears, however, to have been a name given to the first royal sword of England during the lapse of many ages. In the reign of Edward VI. we read of that monarch having a " sworde called *curtana*." It is also mentioned in the reigns of Henry VII. of Richard III. and Henry IV. Matthew Paris informs us, that a sword *curtana*, or curtein, existed so long ago as the reign of Henry III. at whose coronation (1236) it was carried by the Earl of Chester.

The length of the Sword Curtana is 32 inches, the breadth almost two inches; the handle, which is covered with fine gold wire, is four inches long, besides the pommel, of an inch and three quarters, which with the cross or guard is plain steel gilt; the length of the cross is almost eight inches. This sword, for the purpose of answering allegorically to its name, is made to appear as though its point were broken off; the scabbard is covered with rich brocaded cloth of tissue, with a gilt ferrule, hook, and cape. (See No. 6.)

The second sword in dignity, that of Justice to the Spirituality, is a pointed sword, but considerably more obtuse than the third; the length of its blade is forty inches, its breadth an inch and a half, the handle is covered in a similar manner to the former with fine gold wire; it is also of the same length, and in all other respects coincides with the former. (See No. 7.)

The third Sword, or Sword of Justice to the Temporality, is an extremely sharp-pointed sword; the length of the blade is 40 inches, the breadth an inch and three quarters, the length of the handle four inches, the pommel an inch and three quarters, the length of the cross seven inches and a half, and the scabbard in all respects as the two former. (See No. 8.)

THE RING.

The ring is called metaphorically the "wedding-ring" of England. The ring is of very remote antiquity as an emblem of power. Pharaoh took off his ring from his hand and put it upon the hand of Joseph, as a proof of his delegated authority. The investiture by this emblem can be traced in this country so far back as the days of the Heptarchy. The King's coronation ring is of pure gold, in which a large table ruby, on which the cross of the national saint is engraved. We believe that in the Roman-catholic church, also, when any bishop or dignitary is consecrated, he receives a ring as a mark of his more close and dignified connexion with that body. The following is handed down to us by the "Golden Legende," as the origin of the investiture "per annulum." An old man one day asked alms of King Edward the Confessor, who, finding he had nothing else to give, presented him with his ring. Some years after this, two English pilgrims, travelling in the Holy Land, lost their way towards the evening. There came up to them a fair and ancient personage, whose hairs were white with age, who asked them what they were, and of what region. They told him that they were pilgrims of England, and had lost both their way and their company; upon which he gave them comfort and brought them to a goodly city, and, after giving them a night's rest, and refreshment in the morning, he put them once again in the right path. He seemed glad to hear them talk of the piety and welfare of the English king; and when about to separate, he said to them, " I am John the Evangelist; and say ye unto Edward, your king, that I greet him well by the token that he gave to me this ring with his own hands, which ring ye shall deliver to him again;" and having so said, he departed from them again solemnly. They, of course, took care when they came to England to deliver the ring safely to their sovereign, who immediately recognised it; and in after times it has been preserved, with due care, in the Abbey of Westminster, at the shrine of the Confessor. After this, we apprehend, there can be very little doubt that this is the same identical ring which is in our possession this day, and which had once the honour of being on the finger of John the Evangelist. Indeed, it is quite clear that the saints took especial care of the coronation rings of the kings of this country; as we find in the wardrobe accounts of Edward I. that he was in possession of a gold and sapphire ornament of this description, which Saint Dunstan took the trouble of making with his own hands—a trouble which men bred to this kind of business can alone appreciate, particularly when so kindly undertaken by a person who could not have been accustomed to it. (See No. 9.)

THE ARMILLÆ, OR BRACELETS.

These are of solid gold, which open by means of a hinge, in order that they may be worn on the wrist. They are ornamented with the rose, thistle, fleur de lys, and harp, all chased, and on either edge is a row of pearls. The use of the bracelet among the kings is of very high antiquity. In Samuel we find, " And I took the crown that was upon his head, and the bracelet that was on his arm, and have brought them hither unto my lord." Amongst the northern nations it was a distinguishing mark of the monarch and the warrior; so sacred, that the people of Denmark and of Iceland used to swear by it. King Athelstan was called by way of flattery, " the giver of the bracelets."

THE SPURS.

Which are made of curiously wrought gold, and which have so long been familiar as the almost peculiar symbols and ornaments of knighthood, that it is only necessary here, *pro forma*, to allude to them. Knights are created by the investiture of the spur, and degraded by the ceremony of chopping it from their heels.

THE STAFF.

His Majesty's staff is about four feet seven inches and a half in length, of solid gold, weighing 8lb. 9oz. with a pike or foot of steel about four inches and a quarter in length, and a ball and cross at the top; the ornaments of simple raised gold; three different fillets, or bandages of leaves, are at equal distances; its diameter is three quarters of an inch.— The ball is of pure gold, with a raised bandage of precious stones encircling it, and a half bandage of the same round the top; it is surmounted by a cross, upon an amethyst of immense value, as a pedestal.— (See No. 10.)

THE SALTCELLAR.

The Saltcellar is of pure gold, and a model of the White Tower of London. The four corner towers and the large centre one, separately contain salt. There are also other smaller saltcellars of immense value.

THE AMPULLA, OR THE GOLDEN EAGLE.

This vessel, in which the consecrated oil is contained, has also its miraculous traditions, but certainly neither so credible nor so well attested as those of the preceding. The following is the account connected with it by the ancient writers. They say that while St. Thomas a Becket was in banishment in France, as he was one night praying to the Virgin, she appeared, and presented him with a golden eagle, and a small glass or stone vial, assuring him that the happiest effects would be produced upon such monarchs as might be anointed with the unction it contained. She also specified a monk at Poictiers, to whom it was to be given, and he was to hide it under a particular stone in the church of St. Gregory. Here then it was preserved, together with an account of his vision, written by Becket, till the reign of Henry III. when it was revealed to a man of piety, who brought it to the Duke of Lancaster, by whom it was transferred to the Black Prince, who had it deposited in a strong chest in the Tower. The first coronation in which it was used was that of Henry IV. This tradition, of course, must rest upon the faith of the pious saint with whom it originated. We give it as he gave it; nor would we even add, by way of disparagement, a " Credat Judæus" to the mysterious record. It is, however, curious enough that a similar tradition is attached to the " Sainte Ampoulle," a similar ornament used in the coronation of the kings of France. They say, that during the investiture of Clovis, when the person, who held the chrism, was absent, being held back by the people, the Holy Spirit descended in the form of a dove, which held the sacred oil in its shining bill, and let it fall upon the hands of the minister. This oil, the legend goes on to say, has been carefully preserved ever since, and has, from that day to this, remained undiminished! The vessel, which contains the oil now used in British coronations, is in the form of an eagle, with the wings expanded, and it stands upon a pedestal. There is a spoon, with four pearls on the broadest part of the handle, also used, into which the liquid is poured from the beak of the eagle. We fear this is a modern addition, as the saint is silent with respect to it. Having previously described the crown, we have now only to add that the Confessor's crown is laid aside after the ceremony, and one, less ancient, but more costly, worn during the festival. A much more early ornament, however, even than the crown is the sceptre.

We now proceed to the description of the Coronation Chair and Stone, which is a monument of such undoubted antiquity, that the world perhaps does not produce one so old and so respected. Without at all entering into the marvellous stories of its first employment, namely, its serving as the pillow of the patriarch Jacob, and a thousand other equally credible additions, we may remark, that it is undoubtedly traceable at a very remote age to Ireland, as it is mentioned and minutely described in one of their oldest legends called "The Book of Howth." It was called in that country the "Fatal Stone," or the "Stone of Fortune," and it received this title in consequence of a virtue ascribed to it by the vulgar of discovering the pretensions of the prince who sat on it. Under a pretender it was dumb, but under a genuine legitimate it gave a sound which proved what a modern minister would call, his *fundamental* pretensions to a seat on it. In fact it was that sort of sound, with which the most lawless pretender could prove his legitimacy without much trouble or difficulty.

It was in all probability used by the Irish Druids

in their sacrifices, and was afterwards transferred to the Hall of Tara, where the Milesian sovereigns were crowned. The author of the " Antiquities of Cornwall," in alluding to the history of this stone, coneeives it to be not improbably of Druidical origin, the Druids being strongly attached to divination. The Scots had a remarkable prophecy attached to it, that wherever this Stone was fouud their posterity would reign. It ran as follows :

" Ni fallat fatum, Scoti quocunque locatum
Inveniunt lapidem ; regnare tenentur ibidem."

which implies that the Scottish race, although of legitimate descent, should fail to preserve regal power unless in possession of the Fatal Stone. Sir James Ware gives the prediction another form. He says an Irish prophecy concerning this Stone gained credit, which foretold, that in whatever country it should be preserved, a prince of the Scythian race should govern. The prediction of the Scots continues to be fulfilled in that branch of the family of James I. which now fills the British throne, and this prophecy is said to have reconciled many Scotsmen to the Union.

The fullest account given of this Stone by any single writer, is that by Farden, who has devoted nearly an entire chapter of his " Seate Chronicon" to its early history ; the substance of his statement is as follows: " there was a certain king of Spain of the Scottish race, called Millo, having many sons; one, however, named Simon Breck, he loved above all the others, although he was neither the eldest nor the heir. His father therefore sent him to Ireland with an army, and gave him a marble chair, carved with very ancient art by a skilful workman, and which the kings of Spain of the Scottish nation were wont to sit on when inaugurated, from which cause it was carefully brought into his region, as if it were an anchor. This Simon having reached the above island with a great army, reduced it under his dominions, and reigned in it many years. He placed the aforesaid Stone or Chair at Themor the royal residence, a noted palace at which his successors were accustomed to reside, distinguished with kingly honours. Others relate that Simon Breck having anchored on the Irish coast, was forced by contrary winds to withdraw his anchors from the billowy surge, and whilst strenuously labouring to that end, a stone in the form of a chair cut out of marble, was hauled up with the anchors into the ship. Receiving this both as a precious boon from Heaven, and as a certain presage of future dominion, he, trembling with excessive joy, adored his Gods with the gift, as if they had absolutely appointed him to the kingdom and the crown. It was then prophecied likewise that he and his posterity should reign wherever that stone should be found.

Others affirm that Gathelus brought the chair with other regal ornaments with him from Egypt to Spain. In Holinshed's " Historie of Scotland" there is a long account of this Gathelus. He is there said to have been a Greek, the sonne of Cecrops, " who builded the citie of Athens." After leaving Greece, Gathelus resided some time in Egypt, where he married Scota, the daughter of King Pharaoh; but being alarmed at the judgements pronounced by Moses, who was then in Egypt, he quitted that country with many followers, and landed in Spain. Here he " builded a citie, which he named Brigantia," yet not without great opposition from the native Spaniards. Having at length succeeded in making peace with his neighbours, he sat upon his marble stone in Brigantia, " where he gave lawes and administered justice unto his people, thereby to meinteine them in wealth and quietnesse." This Stone was in fashion like a seat or chair, having such a fatal destiny (as Scots say) following it, that wherever it should be placed, there should the Scottish men reign, and have the supreme governance. Hereof it came to pass, that first in Spaine, after in Ireland, and then in Scotland, the Kings which ruled over the Scottish men, received the crown upon that Stone, until the time of Robert I. King of Scotland.

Buchanan, speaking of the same monarch in the Scottish history, mentions the Stone in the following manner. "Kenneth having enlarged his kingdom, and settled wholesome laws for the good administration of the government, he further endeavoured to confirm the regal authority by mean and trivial things almost bordering on superstition itself. There was a marble stone," he continues, "which Simon Breccus is reported to have brought out of Spain into Ireland, and which Fergus, the son of Firchard, is also said to have brought over into Scotland and placed in Argyle. This Stone Kenneth removed out of Argyle into Scone, by the river Tay, and placed it there, enclosed in a chair of wood. The kings of Scotland were wont to receive both the regal title and insignia sitting in that Chair till the days of Edward I. King of England."

Chalmers asserts that the last of the Scottish kings who had the felicity to be crowned in this essential seat was Alexander III. and it is said that the Earl of Fife, as it was his privilege to do, placed the king in *cathedrum marmoreum*.

The era had now nearly arrived when the regal power of Scotland was doomed to succumb before the blood-stained prowess of Edward I. That monarch having formed a league with Bruce against John Baliol, defeated the latter in a desperate battle near Dunbar, in April, 1296, and quickly subduing all Scotland, resolved to deprive the nation of every vestige of its independence. With this intent he caused the crown, sceptre, and inauguration stone, with all the public jewels, archives, charters, &c. to be conveyed to London, there to remain as lasting memorials of his conquests, and of the entire subjugation of the Scots.

Rapin, after alluding to the intention of King Edward to unite the two kingdoms, and his removal into England of the Scottish Regalia, together with the famous Stone on which the inauguration of their kings was performed, proceeds thus, " the people of Scotland had all along placed in that Stone a kind of fatality; they fancied that whilst it remained in their country, the state would be unshaken, but the moment it should be elsewhere removed, great revolutions would ensue; for this reason Edward carried it away, to create in the Scots a belief that the time of the dissolution of their monarchy was come, and to lessen their hopes of the recovery of their liberty.

Nothing, indeed, can show the vast importance attached to this stone in a more forcible point of view, than the circumstance of it having been made not only the subject of an express article in a treaty of peace, but also of a political conference between Edward III. and David II. of Scotland. By the treaty of Northampton, 1328, which was actually confirmed by parliament, it was agreed, that the stone should be returned to Scotland; and for this end writs were issued by Edward III. which however were never executed. When Edward 1. had this stone placed in a new chair, which now forms the coronation-chair of the kings of England, the sum which was laid out upon it was 1*l*. 19*s*. 7*d*. no inconsiderable sum in those days. This chair is in height 6 foot 7 inches; in breadth, at the bottom, 38 inches; and in depth 24 inches; from the seat to the bottom is 25 inches; the breadth of the seat within the sides is 28 inches, and the depth 18 inches. At nine inches from the ground there is a bottom-board, supported at the four corners by four lions; and between the seat and the said bottom-board is enclosed the *Fatal Marble Stone*, being an oblong square, about 22 inches long, 13 inches broad, and 11 inches deep, of a blueish steel-like colour, mixed with some veins of red.

This antique Regal Chair, having, together with the Golden Sceptre and Crown of Scotland, been solemnly offered by the forementioned King Edward I. to St. Edward the Confessor, anno 1297, (from whence it hath the name of St. Edward's Chair,) has ever since been kept in St. Edward the Confessor's Chapel, with a tablet formerly hanging thereto, whereon were written, in the old English letter, these verses:

> Si quid habent veri, vel Chronica, cana fidesve,
> Clauditur hac Cathedra nobilis ecce Lapis.
> Ad Caput eximius Jacob quondam Patriarcha
> Quem posuit cernens numina mira Poli,
> Quem tulit ex Scotis spolians quasi Victor Honoris
> Edwardus Primus, Mars velut Armipotens,
> Scotorum Domitor, Noster Validissimus Hector,
> Anglorum Decus, & Gloria Militiæ.

This Tablet has, however, shared the fate of many other memorials with which the Abbey once abounded.

This celebrated Chair, at the Coronation of George IV. was situated about the centre of the Sacrarium, in front of the altar. The dilapidated state to which the ancient ornaments were reduced, induced Mr. Mash, of the Lord Chamberlain's Office, to have them removed, and to substitute others precisely of the same character. These ornaments, which consisted of crockets and fretwork, were richly gilt, and the remainder of the chair was covered with gold frosted tissue; a cushion was added, covered of the same material. The " prophetic stone," of which our northern neighbours were so jealous, maintained its usual place under the seat of the chair, but was hid from observation by a deep fringe, which was looped up to show the lions and the gilt moulding upon which the chair stood, and which had been repaired and beautified.

The garments with which the King is invested at his Coronation next claims our attention; and the first in importance is the *Dalmatica*, or open Pall,* other-

---

* A Pall was a habit anciently worn by persons of the highest rank only, but the word also signifies a part of the dress of an archbishop, shaped like a Y, and decorated with small crosses. This robe is likewise termed Dalmatica, having been first used in the city of Dalmatia.

wise called the Imperial Pall. It is a three-cornered mantle, in fashion of a cope, with one straight side of about 3¼ yards in length, to cover the shoulders and hang down in front, the other sides sloping into a train reaching about a foot upon the ground. At one period, it was a piece of rich embroidery with golden eagles, but being in the time of the civil wars carried away with all the rest of the regalia except the ampulla and spoon, a very rich gold and purple brocaded tissue is made use of instead. The ground, or outside, is shot with gold thread brocaded with gold and silver, with large and small flowers of the same frosted; all the ornaments and flowers are edged about with purple or deep mazarine blue. The lining is a rich crimson taffeta, and the fastening a broad gold clasp.

It is a peculiar feature in the inauguration of our kings, that they are admitted into a sacred as well as a civil character, and the investiture of the clerical garments particularly proves the two relations in which his Majesty stands with his people.

The *Supertunica, Surcoat*, or close Pall, is a coat with plain sleeves, of a very thick and rich cloth of gold tissue, shot with gold, and ornamented with flowers of the same, brocaded and frosted, without either silk or velvet. The length behind is about four feet, and in front a yard and a quarter, having only one division, which forms it into two skirts, each skirt being a yard and a half; so that the whole width at the lower part is three yards. To this belongs a belt or girdle made of the same cloth of tissue, lined with a white-watered tabby, with a gold buckle, &c. to which clasps of the same are affixed for the sword with which the King is girded.

The Armilla, or the Stole, as it ought more properly to be called, is made of the same cloth of tissue as the supertunica, and is lined with crimson Florence sarcenet. The length of it is about an ell, and the breadth of it three inches, with two double ribbons at each end of crimson taffeta, *viz.* two at the corners of the ends to tie it below the elbows, and two a little higher, for tying it above them.

The Armilla, or Stole, is an ecclesiastical ornament used at the celebration of the mass; it has also been employed for a long time in the investiture of kings. Walsingham, in his account of the coronation of Richard II. mentions, that the king was invested first with the tunic of St. Edward, and then with the dalmatic. Henry IV. is said to have been arrayed at the time of his coronation as a bishop, that should sing mass, with a dalmatic like a tunic, and a stole about his neck.

The *Colobium Sindonis*, or Surplice,* is without sleeves, and is the last garment put upon the king after the anointing; it is made of very fine white cambric, and is in length somewhat deeper than the supertunica. It is laced about the neck, round the armholes or opening of the shoulders, down the breast, up the slip of the sides and round the lowest part with fine white Flanders lace surfled on very full. The Colobium is one of the sacred habits; it is an ancient dress of bishops and priests.

The *Surcoat* of rich crimson satin, is made like the supertunica, or close pall, and consists of about the same dimensions; the lining is crimson Florence sarcenet.

The ornaments appropriated to the legs are the caligæ or buskins, and the sandals; the former are made of the same cloth of tissue as the supertunica, and lined with crimson Florence sarcenet; the height of them is eighteen inches, the compass at the top fifteen inches, and the length from the heel to the toe is eleven inches.

The Sandals are made with a dark-coloured lea-

---

* These names are originally derived from two Greek words, signifying a short linen dress;—although the noun Ενδουος sometimes means a sepulchral covering for the dead. In the seventh chapter of the spurious gospel of Nicodemus, the cloth in which Joseph of Arimathea wrapped the body of Christ, is called *Syndonia*, from the name of the knight's daughter who worked it.

ther sole, and a wooden heel covered with red leather; the bands (of which two go over the foot, and the third behind the heel) are of cloth tissue lined with crimson taffeta, as is also the inside of the sole; the length of the sandal is ten inches.

The purple Boot, or Sandal, is a well known distinction of imperial rank, and was long used by the eastern emperors. The right of wearing it was asserted by the kings of Bulgaria, together with the superior title of Basileus. The Pope, when he presents his foot for the kiss of homage, has a shoe of crimson velvet adorned with a golden cross.

The habits just described are those which are used during the investiture, but there are some vestments which are not used at that ceremony, but which still make a figure in the procession. The whole of the dress in which the King comes to the Coronation is indeed prepared for the occasion, and adapted as well to the splendour of the ceremony as to the convenience of performing that part of it which requires exposure of the person. In the elaborate history of the coronation of James II. the following robes are mentioned, which are conspicuous in the processional solemnities, and which are retained to the present day.

1st. The Parliament Robes, which are put on by the King in the Palace, at Westminster, before he comes down into the Great Hall, consist of a surcoat of crimson velvet, a large mantle of crimson velvet, with a hood suitable, furred with ermine and bordered with rich gold lace; also a cap of state of crimson velvet turned up with ermine.

2nd. The Robes of Estate are of purple velvet, of the same fashion as the former; these he takes with the imperial crown at St. Edward's altar when the coronation is finished.

It may perhaps not be uninteresting to our readers to draw a comparison between the Regalia of England and those of foreign countries; and, accordingly, we present them with a description, in the first instance, of the Regalia of Germany, as they are given in Dillon's Political Survey of the Sacred Roman Empire.

"The Imperial Ornaments of Germany consist of, 1. Charlemagne's crown; 2. His dalmatic robe or mantle, embroidered with large pearls; 3. The golden apple, or globe; 4. His sword; 5. His golden sceptre; 6. The imperial cloak, embroidered with eagles, and bordered with large emeralds, diamonds, sapphires, and chrysolites; 7. The buskins, covered with plates of gold; 8. The gloves, embroidered with curious stones; and 9. The hereditary crown of the Emperor Rodolph II.

The Regalia of France are, 1. The great imperial crown, said to have been received by Charlemagne from Pope Leo III. when he was crowned Emperor of the West; 2. The sword of Charlemagne, called *Joyeuse*; 3. The sceptre of Charlemagne, six feet high, with the figure of an emperor at the top sitting in a chair, garnished with two lions and two eagles; 4. The Hand of Justice, which is a virge of gold a cubit long; at the end is the figure of a hand, in ivory, with a ring on the fourth finger enriched with a sapphire; 5. The spurs of Charlemagne. The vestments are the dalmatic, tunic buskins, or sandals, and the royal robe; these are sometimes of sky-blue satin, and sometimes of purple velvet, but always seeded with fleur-de-lis embroidered with gold. Buonaparte changed these fleurs-de-lis to bees."

The function of consecrating the sovereigns of England has almost uniformly been discharged by the Archbishop of Canterbury, and is a privilege which has been assumed and exercised by the prelates attached to that see from the early ages of the monarchy. In the reign of Henry II. Pope Alexander III. interdicted the Archbishop of York and his coadjutor bishop, because they crowned that monarch's son, Prince Henry, in the absence and without the license of Thomas a Becket, who then filled the chair of Canterbury. In the time of Queen

Elizabeth this privilege of this see was violated. The see was vacated, and the Archbishop of York refused to officiate on account of the change of religion; a duty which was afterwards imposed upon Oglethorpe. The Metropolitan has however ever since, without interruption, performed the office, and receives as his fee the purple velvet chair, the cushion, and the footstool assigned to him during the ceremony.

[margin note: Bishop of Carlisle]

The usual place of the coronation of the kings of England, was, in the time of the heptarchy, the capital of the prevailing state, Winchester, in the kingdom of Wessex. It was, however, not the exclusive privilege of that city. Westminster, London, and various other places, had occasionally the honour of being its scene; and Kingston-upon-Thames derived its name from the circumstance of Athelstan, Edwin, and Ethelred being crowned there during the Danish wars. When the new monastery of Westminster was built by Edward the Confessor, who was crowned at Winchester, he transferred the right thither, and with few exceptions this has continued to be the case ever since.

Our attention must now be drawn to the hereditary great officers of state, and to the history of the remarkable services which they have been used to perform in the august ceremony which is the chief subject of the present work.

The first officer in rank is the LORD HIGH STEWARD. It was formerly his duty to control the kingdom during both peace and war, immediately under the monarch; and upon the demise of the Crown, and the subsequent coronation, a great share of intermediate power devolved on him. He now walks next before the King in the procession to the church, where the ceremony is to be performed, and bears, *pro tempore*, the crown of St. Edward. He is also considered as chief of the Court of Claims. In late years, however, this presidency has usually been vested in commissioners appointed by the Crown. Accordingly we find in the present Coronation that the Earl of Harrowby was appointed President of the Court of Claims, occasionally assisted by the members of the Royal Family, the noblemen, privy counsellors and commoners mentioned in the proclamation of his Majesty.*

The next in rank is the LORD GREAT CHAMBERLAIN. He is the governor of the palace, and is a principal assistant during the whole of the ceremony. His duty is to carry the clothes on the morning of the coronation; and, with the assistance of the Lord Chamberlain, to dress him. Upon the coronation of a Queen, this part of the office is performed by a female, and accordingly, Sarah, Duchess of Marlborough, is said to have filled this station for Queen Anne. He is allowed various perquisites, all of which are now commuted for a sum of money, with the exception of a robe of crimson velvet, forty yards long, which he receives. Amongst his other duties, the investiture of the sword and spurs appertains to him, and the oblations for the altar are delivered by him to the King.

The next is the LORD HIGH CONSTABLE. He attends the royal person during the processions, in which he walks with the Earl Marshal, next to the High Steward, bearing in his hand the staff of office, He also assists at the delivery of the Regalia, and

---

* In the foreign courts, particularly in the German, we find some curious claims advanced at the coronation of the Emperor. The claim of the Arch Marshal was as follows:

"Before the palace gate there used to stand a heap of oats to the breast of a horse—then comes the Arch Marshal, the Duke of Saxony, mounted, having in his hand a silver wand, and a silver measure stood by, which was to weigh two hundred marks; he fills the measure, sticking his wand afterwards in the remainder, and so goes to attend the Emperor. The three Archbishops say grace; the Marquis of Brandenburg comes also on horseback, with a silver basin of water, of the value of twelve marks, and a clean towel, which being alighted, he holds to the Emperor; then comes the Count Palatine of the Rhine, on horseback also, and being alighted, he carries four-dishes of meat, every dish of the value of three marks, then the King of Bohemia comes with a napkin on his arm, with a covered cup of twelve marks, which he presents."

conducts the Champion into the hall for the purpose of the challenge. This office, has, we believe, since the attainder of the Duke of Buckingham, in the reign of Henry VIII. been granted only *pro tempore*. Before that reign it was filled by the Earls of Hereford, as a matter of hereditary right. On the Coronation of George IV. it was filled by the Duke of Wellington.

Following in rank is the EARL MARSHAL, &c. This officer's functions are much more limited than they formerly were. He is now merely a master of the arrangements: in ancient times, however, he was very differently estimated. Gilbert, Earl of Pembroke, by a document still extant, claimed, in the time of Henry II. " to stand next the king on the day of his coronation; to bear in his hand the royal crown; to assist in setting it on the king's head; and when placed there, to hold it by the *fleur de lis*, on its front, so as to sustain its weight, during the solemnity, during which time no other person was to presume to touch it." Amongst his other perquisites, during these times, we find him entitled to " the chines of all the swans and cranes served up at the feast, and to fourpence a-head for every person committed to his custody, by the Lord High Steward, during the coronation." The officers whom we have hitherto named, require no recognition by the Court of Claims: not so, however, those which follow, whose names will sufficiently describe their duties. These are the Grand Almoner, the Chief Butler, the Dapifier or Sewer, who brings up and arranges the dishes at the feast; the Grand Carver, the Chief Cupbearer, the Chief Lardiner, all of which are held by persons of noble blood, in whose families they have been hereditary; but they all require both to be claimed and to be recognised.

We cannot close this part of our history without making mention of a splendid petition, written in letters of gold, and in the legible black English letters of the 14th century, which was presented to the

King by the Laird of Glenalva, on a very interesting subject. The petition states, what is recorded in history, that it was the custom of the Scotch monarchs to have at their coronations a Highland gentleman, dressed in the warlike and graceful national garb (philibeg, plaid and bonnet, target, claymore, &c.) who in the name of the Clans, and of all the other Scotch, made a most dutiful loyal speech and allegiance to the sovereign; and the famous speech made by such an officer before Alexander III. at Scone, Aug. 15, 1249, is too well known to admit of any doubt as to the existence of such an ancient feudal service. The Laird, therefore, humbly beseeches his Majesty to revive this service of antiquity, and offers himself, at considerable expense and on substantial grounds, to appear in the true garb of Scotia at the present magnificent coronation. He finishes his petition in the following dutiful, loyal, and national words:—" May it therefore please your Most Excellent Majesty to take the petitioner's request into Royal consideration, and to grant him permission to surrender the above domain at your Majesty's feet, to be held *de jure* only, and in all time coming, on the ancient feudal service, of appearing before your Majesty and your Majesty's successors in the ancient garb of Caledonia, and respectfully repeating, in broad Scotch, a short speech of loyalty and allegiance, as to your Majesty shall seem meet; and your petitioner, as in duty bound, shall ever fight for your Majesty's cause either on land or sea, without reward or fee."

It is scarcely necessary to state that the petition of the Laird of Glenalva was not granted.*

It may, however, be considered necessary to make

---

* We can recollect the circumstance of the Laird of Colbecks appearing at the court of George III. in " the true garb of Scotia," when the Highland chieftain, on making his obeisance, bent so low, that the kilt was not long enough to conceal a certain part of the chieftain's form, which occasioned his Majesty to exclaim, " Keep the ladies in front—keep the ladies in front."

mention of one particular department which belongs to the office of the Earl Marshal, which is the regulation of the coronets and robes to be worn at the coronation by the various degrees of nobility, expressive of their rank in the kingdom. The order which was issued by the Earl Marshal on the occasion of the Coronation of George IV. is similar to those issued on former coronations, with the exception that no pearls were to be used in the coronets, but balls, silver gilt.

The Barons of England, who constitute the lowest part of the peerage, had formerly neither coronets nor velvet robes, but only a cap of scarlet edged with fur, and a habit of cloth of the same colour. In the thirteenth year of the reign of King Charles II. he issued a grant, permitting them to use the coronet which they now wear; and which consists of a plain circle of gold, having six pearls* set upon the upper rim, the lower part of the circle edged with ermine, and the whole surmounted by a cap of crimson velvet, with a tuft and tassel of gold. At the coronation of King James II. in 1684, the Barons petitioned for robes conformable to their coronets, and accordingly a grant was issued, stating, that for the future their robes should be of crimson velvet, with capes and edgings of white minever, and two rows of ermine, as a distinction.

A Viscount, which is the next degree upwards, has for his coronet a circle of gold, richly chased, edged with ermine, and sixteen pearls, placed on the rim, with a cap and tassel similar to a Baron's. His robes are also of crimson velvet, lined with white sarcenet, with white fur capes, and two doublings and a half of spotted ermine.

The Coronet of an Earl is a circle as before, richly chased, having eight pearls raised upon high points of gold, which spring out of the upper rim, with an equal number of strawberry leaves, formed of the same metal, standing upon lower points between them. It

---

* These ornaments are both denominated and painted as pearls, but in the Coronets themselves they are made of silver.

has also a doubling of ermine, cap, and tassel, as already described. An Earl's mantle is similar to the former, except that it has three guards of ermine.

A Marquis's Coronet differs from an Earl's in the number of pearls and strawberry leaves, and in the manner of placing them. It consists of four of each ornament placed alternately, on short equal points, with the same doubling, cap, and tassel. The robes have three guards and a half of ermine.

A Duke's Coronet is formed of eight golden strawberry leaves only, raised on short points of the same height above the rim ; the fur, cap, and tassel, are the same as before. The robes belonging to this degree have four rows of ermine.

It has been mentioned that some of the golden circles are richly chased or embossed, and this probably gave rise to the idea that they were to be set round with various kinds of precious stones. In consequence of this error, it is not uncommon for the Earl Marshal to issue his order at a coronation, peremptorily forbidding all artists to make use of such decorations. The following is a specimen of such an order, published at the coronation of King George I.

THE LORD MARSHAL'S ORDER.

In Pursuance of an Order of the *Lords Justice's* in Council, dated the eighth of *September* last past. These are to give notice to all the Peers of *Great Britain*, who are to attend his *Majesty* in the Royal Proceeding to his Coronation, upon *Wednesday*, the twentieth day of this instant *October*, that they, and every of them, forbear to set or use any *Jewels*, or *Precious stones*, in their Coronets.

And least coachmakers, carvers, *embroiderers, painters*, or other artificers, do presume (both upon coaches, and in making the coronets for this present Coronation) to raise the *Pearls* of the Baron's Coronets upon *pins* or *spikes*, (whereas they ought to lie flat upon the *Rim* or *Ring* of the Coronet;) This is to warn all such workmen from the like error ; and to enjoin and order them, to take care to make all such Coronets exactly as they are allowed to be worn by the grant of his late Majesty King Charles the Second, as they will answer the contrary at their perils.

And it is also ordered, that no person whatsoever that shall be present at the said Coronation, either attending the Proceeding, or as Spectators, do appear in a mourning habit for that day.

I do hereby appoint John Nutt, Printer in the Savoy, to print this Order; and that no other person do presume to print the same.

6, October, 1714.   SUFFOLK, M.

But robes, as well as coronets, are regulated by the Earl Marshal's orders at every coronation; those issued previous to the crowning of King George II. after having detailed the differences of the various mantles already described, thus proceed concerning the other parts of the Peeresses dresses:—

" The Surcoats, or Kirtles, to be all of crimson velvet, close-bodied, and clasped before, edged or bordered with Minever pure, two inches broad, and scolloped down the sides from below the girdle, and sloped away into a train proportionable to the length of the Robe or Mantle for each degree,* *viz.* about a third part thereof; the sleeve of the Surcoats also to be of crimson velvet, about five inches deep, scolloped at the bottom, edged with Minever pure, and fringed with gold or silver.

" The caps of their Coronets to be all of crimson velvet, turned up with Ermine, with a button and tassel of gold or silver on the top, suitable to the fringe of their sleeves.

" The Petticoats to be of cloth of silver, or any other white stuff, either laced or embroidered, according to each person's fancy.

" The Mantles to hang back, being fastened on each shoulder with cordons of silver or gold, suitable to their fringe, with tassels of the same hanging down on each side of the waist.

" The Surcoats, or Kirtles, to open before, that the Petticoats may appear."

---

* The length of a train was regulated by the rank of the wearer; thus, that of a Baroness might lie three feet on the ground, a Viscountess might have one of a yard and a quarter, a Countess's was a yard and a half, a Marchioness's a yard and three quarters, and a Duchess's two yards.

No other order was issued from the Earl Marshal's office relative to the dress of the Peeresses at the Coronation of George IV. than that it was expected they should appear in " full dress."

Whilst these preliminary matters were adjusting, the preparations for the Coronation proceeded in Westminster Hall and Abbey, with the greatest activity. The Courts of King's Bench and Chancery were removed, and the place where for nearly a century the jargon of the gowned tribe was heard, labouring zealously in their profession to prove that wrong is right, and right is wrong, now resounded with the sturdy blow of the mechanic, or the hoarse bawl of the architect giving directions to his workmen. The Court of King's Bench, however, continued to sit for some time after the workmen had commenced their operations in the Hall, when the noise disturbing the solemn proceedings of the Court, it was judged expedient to remove it to the Guildhall of Westminster; and accordingly one morning, without due notice having been given of the change, the judges took their seats in the Guildhall, whilst in all the pomp of wig and gown, of worsted and of silk, sat the briefed and the briefless barristers, wondering at the non-appearance of the judges, and the judges in return wondering at the non-appearance of the counsel. At last came the intelligence to Westminster Hall, that the judges were sitting in the Insolvent Debtor's Court in the Guildhall, and now arose a confusion worse than at Babel, or in Pandemonium. The lawyer run against the attorney, the attorney against his client, remnants of tattered gowns strewed the flag-stones, and a wig lay here and there, degraded from its lofty state, to be trampled on by the plebeian feet of the workmen. In the scramble the gouty barrister was laid prostrate, and over him rolled his more youthful competitor, till one by one they formed a huge mass of black rolling matter; in the midst of which rose here and there something like a cauliflower, amidst some hillocks of soot. It was " confusion worse confounded," and a more ludicrous scene could not present itself to the eye of the passenger, than to behold the numerous tribe hurrying across the street from Westminster Hall to St. Margaret's church; and certain suspicions arose in the beholder's mind, that his satanic majesty had suddenly made his appearance among his elect, to claim their company in his abode, they being already duly qualified for it. But in the words of that most humorous song, called the "Maid of the Sky-Light," who once routed all the lawyers from Westminster Hall with her mop—

> One appearing however less scar'd than the rest,
> Their absurd apprehensions soon turn'd to a jest,
> Crying, Courage, Old Nick will not take you this bout,
> He'll be punctual no doubt—but your time is not out.

Leaving, however, the lawyers to those who have a keener relish for them than ourselves, we shall return to notice the "din of preparation" which sounded within the venerable walls of Westminster Hall and the Abbey. Every day in the week presented a repetition of the same scene of bustle and anxious curiosity in the immediate neighbourhood of the arrangements for the joyous and imposing solemnity. Crowds of persons of every rank and description flocked to Westminster, to witness the progress of the works, and by inquiry to satisfy the doubts which for some reason, which was in a short time too well explained, had been excited, of the precise day on which the ceremonial was to take place. Rumours of a particular nature, respecting an illustrious individual at that time abroad, began to be circulated; and at last it was decidedly stated, that her Majesty had resolved to return to England, to participate in the ceremonies of the Coronation as Queen Consort. This intelligence was at first discredited, but by degrees the truth of it became apparent, and negociations were consequently set on foot; the result of which it was anticipated would lead to her Majesty's constant residence abroad. It would be superfluous to enter in this place further into the nature and character of these negociations, as they have been already sufficiently detailed to the public; it will be merely necessary to state, that they were not attended with the desired effect, and that on Monday, the 5th of June, her Majesty actually landed at Dover.

Fresh negociations were now commenced, but with as little success as before, and ultimately, the Bill of Pains and Penalties against her Majesty was introduced into the House of Lords. The progress and fate of that Bill are too fresh in the recollection of the public, to require any observation here. It is only necessary to state, that the ceremony of the Coronation of his Majesty was postponed, and it was generally believed that the postponement arose from the proceedings which were at that time carrying on against her Majesty; but that opinion was in a degree negatived, by the avowal of Lord Castlereagh in the House of Commons, who, on Colonel Beaumont giving notice on the 25th of June, of an address to his Majesty, praying that the Coronation might be suspended, until the termination of the proceedings against her Majesty, said, that the motion was unnecessary, because his Majesty had already signified his intention that the ceremony of the royal Coronation should not take place on the day originally named, nor was any other day fixed for that purpose. The postponement, however, was not in consequence of any proceedings respecting her Majesty.

It must, however, be admitted that, in the opinion of the English people, the most penetrating and reflecting in the world, the postponement of the Coronation was to be attributed solely to the proceedings against her Majesty; for as no other ostensible reason presented itself, and as no idea of any postponement existed previous to the Bill of Pains and Penalties, on the contrary, that every exertion had been used in the different departments to have the works ready by the time appointed, it was a very natural conclusion, notwithstanding the declaration of Lord Castlereagh, that her Majesty was the sole and only cause of the postponement.

It must be allowed, that the sense of the country was decidedly in favour of the postponement. The friends of his Majesty very wisely and properly considering that the celebration of a ceremony, which is justly considered as a national fête, would be highly indecorous at a period when the Queen of the country was actually upon her trial; and on the other hand, the friends of her Majesty were most vociferous in calling for the postponement, on the grounds that her innocence would be manifest, and then it was their belief that her Coronation must take place also, the thoughts of which were highly gratifying to them, from the supposition that it would be a source of annoyance and vexation to her illustrious husband. The sequel will, however, show that the postponement of the Coronation arose more from a sense of decorum existing in the mind of his Majesty, than to any intention on his part, that even in the event of the establishment of the innocence of her Majesty, she should be allowed to partake in the ceremony of the Coronation.

The public mind was, however, kept in a high degree of suspense respecting the postponement of the Coronation; for, from the appearance of activity which prevailed in the immediate vicinity of the place where the superb pageant was to be performed, no idea could be drawn of an intended abandonment of the ceremony.

The question was, however, at length put to rest by the appearance of an official notice in the Gazette of July 15, in which it was announced that the Coronation was postponed, and that all persons summoned, whether abroad or in England, were discharged from their attendance.

The Court of Claims did not again assemble, and the works which were carrying on in Westminster Hall, Westminster Abbey, and Cotton Garden were suspended.

In this state, matters rested until the beginning of May, 1821, when the renewed labours of a limited number of men in Westminster Hall, led to a belief that the immediate Coronation of his Majesty had been determined on; and the Queen joining in this belief, although no official announcement had been made to that effect, wrote a letter to the Earl of Liverpool on the 5th, demanding to be present at the ceremony. To this she received a reply, apprizing her "that his Majesty having determined that the Queen should form no part of the ceremonial of his Coronation, it was his royal pleasure that the Queen should not attend the said ceremony."

This answer, on the part of his Majesty, had not been long made public, before it became a matter of parliamentary inquiry; and on the 21st of May, Mr. Monk in the House of Commons, the House being at that time in a Committee of Supply, said, that it would be in the recollection of the House, that in the last session of parliament the sum of 100,000*l.* had been voted for the purpose of defraying the expenses of the Coronation, that vote had been passed under circumstances very different from those which existed at present. At that time it was not known whether her Majesty would return to this country, and he, therefore, conceived that the expenses of the Coronation had been calculated under the idea that she would not be present at it. He, therefore, wished the Chancellor of the Exchequer to give him an answer to two questions, on which every person felt a deep interest who was at all solicitous for the honour of the royal family. The first question was, whether any provision had been made for the part which her Majesty was to have in the ensuing Coronation; and the second was, whether any and what additional expense would be incurred in consequence of her presence in that ceremonial?

The Chancellor of the Exchequer replied, that with respect to the expense of the Coronation, and whether it would exceed the sum voted last year, all he could say was, that he did not intend during the present session to propose any additional vote.

Some of the members were by no means satisfied with this half-answer of the Chancellor of the Exchequer, and considered that he was blinking the question respecting the part which the Queen was to take in the ceremonial of the Coronation; on which, the Marquis of Londonderry stated, that it appeared clear to him that it required an act of the Crown to authorize the coronation of her Majesty; for though it was equally clear that her Majesty was in the eye of the law the Consort of the King, yet there was no prerogative of the Crown more clear at common law, more sound, or more indisputable, than that it rested with his Majesty to decide whether his Consort was to participate in the honours of the Coronation. He might, however, as well now say, that neither he nor any of the other servants of his Majesty were prepared to recommend an act of the Crown to include her Majesty in the ensuing ceremonial.

Mr. Brougham said, as to the strict legal right of the Crown to select those whom it thought proper to participate in the honours of the Coronation, he merely rose to protest against being considered as concurring in the opinion just laid down by the noble lord.

The conversation here dropped; but a sufficiency had been extracted from the ministers, to enable the public to form a decided opinion as to the line of conduct which they meant to pursue in regard to her Majesty.

As late as the 4th of June, no official notice had been issued of the precise day on which the Coronation was to take place. The officers of the Heralds' Office were thus placed in particular embarrassment, as much of the details of their business required considerable time for preparation. It appeared to be the intention of giving only three weeks notice in the *Gazette,* instead of six as is customary, and it was the apprehension of every thing being to be done at once, which created the greatest difficulty in the minds of those, on whom the chief labour of the splendid pageant would devolve. Considerable inconvenience was likewise felt by those families, who were desirous of being present at the ceremony, and who from the incertitude in which they were placed, could scarcely resolve whether to remain in town, or to depart and take the pleasures of the country at a season, when those pleasures are the most desirable. There was, however, a very good and sufficient ground existing for this apparent delay in appointing the precise day for the Coronation, as both houses of parliament were then sitting, and were the Coronation to have taken place previous to the prorogation of parliament, there were some ancient usages which must have been complied with, and which would have required the members of the House of Commons to be invited, which would have added considerably to the expense.

It was, however, certain that the day of the Coronation was not far distant, as in the *Gazette* of Tuesday, June 5, notice was given that the Right Honourable the Commissioners appointed by his Majesty's Commission to hear and determine all claims of services and offices to be performed at the Coronation of his Majesty, and of fees to be received for the same, would resume their sittings in the Painted Chamber at Westminster, on Thursday, the 7th day of June next, at one o'clock in the afternoon, when and where all persons having claims of services were required to give their attendance.

Accordingly, on Thursday, the Lords Commissioners appointed by proclamation to receive and adjudge claims to perform the services at the approaching royal Coronation, resumed their sittings in the Painted Chamber of the House of Lords. There were then present the Duke of Clarence, Lords Amherst and Henley, Sir H. Russel, Sir J. Nichol, R. P. Carew, Esq. &c. Mr. B. Bathurst, at the request of the other Commissioners, took the President's seat. The court, below the bar, was much crowded. There were many ladies present.

Mr. Butt, the Deputy Serjeant at Arms, having opened the Court in the customary form, several claimants appeared.

Lord High Steward of Ireland.—A petition was presented from Charles Talbot, Earl of Shrewsbury, as Earl of Waterford and Wexford, in Ireland, claiming to be the Hereditary Lord High Steward of Ireland, and to be allowed to perform that office in the same manner as was claimed by the Lord High Steward of England. The claim purported to be founded on a grant of Henry VI. The Lord High Steward of England, at the Coronation of the King, proceeds immediately before the King, above all other officers of the Crown, and bears in his hand St. Edward's crown, which is the first and principal diadem. This petitioner was understood to claim to walk in the procession, and to assist in the performance of such office.

Napery.—A petition from an individual, named Green, claimed, as proprietor of the Manor of Ashill, or Ashele, in Norfolk, by serjeantry, in respect of the tenure of this Manor—to perform the office of Napier, to take charge of the napery, table-cloths, and other linen; to cover the tables; and to have for fee all the table-cloths in the Hall, &c. when they were removed.

Ewry.—Thomas Weld, as Lord of the Manor of Winfred, in the county of Dorset, held under the tenure by grand serjeantry, counter-claimed to serve water for the hands of our Lord the King, on the day of his Royal Coronation; and to have the basin and ewer for his fee. This service was previously claimed by J. E. Buchel, as Lord of the Manor of Heydon, in Essex.

King at Arms, Scotland.—The Earl of Kinnoul claimed to be allowed to perform, by himself or his deputy, the office of Lord Lyon, King at Arms of Scotland, such office being his lordship's hereditary right; to appear in his tabard, carrying his crown in his hand.

Great Chamberlain.—Mr. Dillon, a barrister, appeared with a petition and a parchment roll, consisting of a pedigree, and counter-claimed (against Lord Gwydir and the Duke of Northumberland) to perform the office of Lord Great Chamberlain of England, on behalf of his nephew, who was a Baron of the Holy Roman Empire, absent in the service of the Emperor of Austria, and claiming by virtue of descent. The claim was urged from anxiety to sustain the honour of the family.

Armour Bearer.—Sir G. Nayler handed in a claim on behalf of Mrs. Jane Seton, who appeared by her attornies, Sir J. C. Hippesley and Co. petitioning as the heritable Armour Bearer and Squire Royal Body to the King of Scotland, in pursuance of a grant, to be allowed to perform such service at the Coronation, by deputy.

Standard Bearer.—Felix O'Hanlon, Esq. put in a claim to perform the office of Standard Bearer for Ireland, and he appeared with divers parchments and documents to establish his right to put in the claim. The court considered it of a novel character; and without going into his proofs, or troubling him to go into any detail of them, he was desired to attend at the next sitting, and then to be fully prepared with such proofs as he had to urge.

Usher of the White Rod.—Sir Patrick Walker, Knight, as heritable Usher of the Black Rod for Scotland, claimed to appear in the procession of the Coronation, to carry the White Rod of Scotland, bearing the Unicorn, in conjunction with the Black Rod of England surmounted by the Lion. The arms were now united. He claimed also to appear girt with a sword; and added, that from (or in) 1651, his ancestry performed such service.

Grand Almoner.—John Russel, Duke of Bedford, claimed as seized of part of the barony of Bedford, to execute the office of Almoner; and, as the fees of that office, to have the silver alms' basin, and the distribution of all the silver therein, &c. The court observed, that Lord Exeter, Sir S. Blundell, and Mr. S. C. Whitbread, M. P. had already claimed to perform this office.

On former coronations, the court granted three hundred and five ounces of gilt plate in two large chased basins.

A petitioner for a portion of the alms appeared. He was a very aged man, in humble attire, and of much lowliness of demeanour. He held a petition, praying to be remembered by the King's Almoner; but his mistake was pointed out to him. He was told that his Majesty would have the selecting of the individual from amongst the claimants to perform the office of Almoner, and that the present application would then be made properly, on being presented to such Almoner. Mr. Butt, the Deputy Serjeant at Arms, kindly explained the several matters to him.

Standard Bearer, Scotland.—Henry S. Wedderburn, Esq. as hereditary Standard Bearer of Scotland, claimed to appear in the procession to perform such service, and to be allowed to present proofs in support of such claim.

Great Chamberlain.—Dorset Fellowes, Esq. secretary to Lord Gwydir, the Lord Great Chamberlain of England, appeared, and presented to the Commissioners the grant of his late Majesty George III. to Lord Gwydir, to hold such office. It was admitted.

Golden Rod and Dove.—Edmund Devereux, Esq. of Wexford, by his ancestor, W. Devereux, Esq. claimed to be allowed to walk in the procession of the Coronation, and to carry before his Majesty St. Edward's Staff, or the Gold Rod, and the Sceptre with the Dove—the one by himself, and the other by his deputy. St. Edward's Staff is four feet eleven inches and a half in length. It is a staff or sceptre of gold, having a foot of steel about four inches and a quarter in length, a mound, and a cross at the top. The ornaments are also of gold, and its diameter is upwards of three quarters of an inch. The King's Sceptre with the Dove is a sceptre of gold, three feet seven inches in length, three inches in circumference at the handle, and two inches and a quarter round the top. The pomel is decorated with a circle, or fillet, of table diamonds, and in several places with precious stones of all sorts, and the mound at the top is embellished with a band or fillet of rose diamonds. Upon this mound is a small Jerusalem cross, whereon is fixed a dove, with wings expanded, as the emblem of Mercy.

Crown of Scotland.—The Duke of Hamilton and Brandon, counter-claimed (against Lord Douglas), founding the petition of claim on hereditary right, to carry the Crown of Scotland before the King, in the procession of his royal coronation.

Several of these petitions were presented by Sir G. Nayler. There appearing no other persons to present petitions,

The court stated that on the present occasion the examination of proofs would not be gone into. Several of the Lords Commissioners were absent, whose co-operation it was desirable to have: the court, therefore, ordered that those who appeared on the present occasion with proofs in support of claims previously urged, should attend on the following Friday, when the evidence would be received.

The court then adjourned, with the customary forms, proclamation being made by the Deputy Serjeant at Arms, till the Friday following.

It was now determined that the Coronation should take place about the middle of July. His Majesty, in order to put an end to all doubts on the subject, sent for the heads of the several offices to which preparations for different parts of the ceremony belong, and demanded to know whether they would be ready by the 16th of July, and he gave them one day to make the necessary inquiries. They generally answered that they could be completely prepared by that day, by which every obstacle on the part of the ministers was removed.

Accordingly, on the 9th of June, the following Proclamation was issued:

BY THE KING.

A Proclamation appointing a day for the solemnity of the Coronation of his Majesty.

GEORGE R.

Whereas, by our Royal Proclamation, bearing date the 6th day of May, 1820, we did, amongst other things, publish and declare our Royal intention to celebrate the solemnity of our Royal Coronation upon Tuesday, the 1st of August then next ensuing, at our Palace at Westminster; and whereas, by our Royal Proclamation, bearing date 12th of July, we thought fit to adjourn the said solemnity until our Royal will and pleasure should be further signified thereon; and whereas, we have resolved, by the favour and blessing of Almighty God, to celebrate the said solemnity upon Thursday, the 19th of July, at our said Palace at Westminster, we do, by this our Royal Proclamation, give notice of and publish our resolution thereon: and we do hereby give strict charge and command to all our loving subjects whom it may concern, that all persons, of whatever rank or quality soever they be, who, either upon our letters to them directed, or by reason of their offices and tenures, or otherwise, are to do any service at the time of our Coronation, do duly give their attendance at the said solemnity, on the said 19th day of July, in all respects furnished and appointed as to so great a solemnity appertaineth, and answerable to the dignities and places which every one then respectively holdeth and enjoyeth; and of this they or any of them are not to fail, as they will answer the contrary at their peril, unless by special reasons, by ourself under our sign manual to be allowed, we shall dispense with any of their services or attendance.

Given at our Court the 9th day of June, 1821, second year of our reign.

On the 12th, the following circular was sent to the Lord Mayor:

"*College of Arms, June* 12, 1821.

"MY LORD,—In pursuance of an order of council, bearing date the 9th day of this instant, June 1821, directing me to cause the Proclamation for appointing a day for his Majesty's Coronation to be proclaimed at the usual time and

places, and with the usual solemnity, I have to request your lordship will cause a sufficient number of constables to attend the Proclamation, on Thursday next, the 14th instant, at 11 o'clock in the forenoon, from Temple Bar (where the constables of Westminster are to leave the procession) to the Royal Exchange.
"I have the honour to be
your Lordship's most obedient humble Servant,
(Signed) "H. H. MOLYNEUX HOWARD, D. E. M."
"To the Right Hon. the Lord Mayor, &c."

PROCLAMATION OF THE CORONATION.

Thursday, June 14th, having been appointed for the public Proclamation of the Coronation of his Majesty, the curiosity of many thousands in the metropolis was gratified by witnessing that curious ceremony.

A short time before 11 o'clock, the Heralds, Serjeants at Arms, and other official personages connected with the business of the day, assembled at the northern gate of Westminster Hall. The first regiment of Life Guards arrived soon after in New Palace-yard, where some slight inconvenience in arranging the procession occurred, in consequence of the space occupied by the frame-work on which the platform for the coronation procession was about to be raised. At about half-past eleven o'clock, the Heralds, Serjeants at Arms, &c. mounted their horses, and their trumpets having sounded thrice, Windsor Herald (Francis Martin, Esq.) read the proclamation in a loud and distinct voice. At the concluding prayer of "Long live King George the Fourth," there were loud cheers.

The procession then moved on towards Charing-cross in the following order:

Constables to clear the way.
Two of the Life Guards.
Mr. Lee, High Constable of Westminster.
Farriers of the Life Guards, with their axes erect.
Troops of Life Guards.
Eight Knights' Marshals-men marching two and two.
Drums two and two.

Trumpets two and two.
Serjeant Trumpeter, in his Collar, bearing his
Mace (J. Nost, Esq.)
Blue Mantle, (Wm. Woods, Esq.) and Rouge Dragon
(F. Townsend, Esq.)
Pursuivants, in their Tabards of his Majesty's arms.
Rouge Croix Pursuivant (William Radclyffe, gent.) in his
Tabard of his Majesty's arms.
Two Serjeants at Arms, in full court dresses, wearing silver
chains, and their maces newly gilt, borne on each side
of them (Mr. Strubel and Mr. Gardner.)
Lancaster Herald (Edmond Lodge, Esq.) in his Tabard
and Collar.
Windsor Herald (Francis Martin, Esq.) in his Tabard
and Collar.
Two Serjeants at Arms (Messrs. Ruddock and Nost, jun.)
attended and dressed as before.
A Troop of Life Guards closed the Procession.

The progress of the splendid cavalcade was varied by alternate performances on the drums and trumpets.

The cavalcade then proceeded up the Strand, and arrived at Temple Bar a few minutes after twelve. The gates of Temple Bar had, as usual on such occasions, been closed a short time before the procession arrived. Here a delay of nearly half an hour took place before the parties were admitted, in consequence of the Lord Mayor not having arrived at the usual place within the bar. As soon as his lordship arrived, his state-coach was drawn up at the end of Chancery-lane. From thence the City Marshal was sent to know who demanded admittance. He was answered by one of the heralds from without in the usual manner. The Marshal returned to the Lord Mayor, and having obtained his lordship's permission, he proceeded to open one side of the gate so as to admit one herald only. This officer was escorted up to the Lord Mayor's coach by the Marshals, and having formally delivered his authority for proclaiming the Coronation, leave was given for the admission of the procession. The herald then retired without the gates, which were immediately thrown open, and the whole party entered in the order before described.

The cavalcade now moved on towards St. Paul's. The Lord Mayor and sheriffs, in their state coaches and robes of office, having joined and taken their places, immediately following the heralds. The proclamation was again read at the Royal Exchange. As soon as the proclamation was read opposite the Exchange, the procession went on to the end of Gracechurch-street, and returned by Lombard-street in nearly the same order back to Temple-bar. The Lord Mayor quitted the procession at the Mansion-house on its return, but his state-coach accompanied it through the city.

The proclamation was not read at Charing-cross, nor at the end of Wood-street.

CORONATION COUNCIL.

The Commissioners appointed by his Majesty's Proclamation to arrange the ceremonies of the Royal Coronation assembled on Wednesday, the 13th, at one o'clock, at the Council-office, in Downing-street. The Dukes of York, Clarence, and Sussex; Lord Harrowby (President); the Right Hon. Sir William Grant, the Right Hon. George Canning, &c. were particularly summoned. The Council met to receive reports of the progress made in the works for the Coronation; and to sign the warrants for the services of those whose cases have already been adjudged by the Court of Claims. The adjudication of the claim is not complete till the party possesses the warrant of this council.

We shall now enter into a minute description of all the arrangements made in Westminster Hall, previous to the commencement of the ceremony of the Coronation.

The antiquity of Westminster Hall, as well as the fact of its having been repeatedly the scene of coronation and other festivities, is familiar to us all. According to the account of many authors, it was built by William Rufus, about the year of Christ 1097, and since that period has undergone a variety of repairs, particularly in the reign of Richard II. after a great fire, by which much of the ancient palace was destroyed. On that occasion, the two towers at the north end of the Hall were erected. In more modern times the floor of this celebrated edifice was raised two feet, in consequence of its being subject to repeated inundations from the Thames, which rendered it necessary on some occasions to approach the courts of law by boats.

In 1819, it became requisite to survey the whole building, with a view to a thorough repair; a circumstance which was expedited by the dilapidated state of the north window, from which pieces of stone were constantly falling. The usual estimates having been submitted to the Lords of the Treasury, warrants were issued to the Board of Works to commence the repairs forthwith. The works accordingly proceeded with despatch, and every part of the building underwent a close inspection. The roof of such general curiosity and admiration was found in an excellent state of preservation; but wherever any unsoundness was discovered, the decayed wood was removed, and sound oak substituted. It may not be uninteresting here to state, that of the pieces of wood thus taken from the roof, and which were coeval with the building itself, a great number of snuff-boxes were made, on many of which was the following inscription:— " This box is formed of oak which composed part of the roof of Westminster Hall, and which was removed during the repairs previous to the Coronation of his Majesty George IV." One of these boxes has been presented to his Majesty, and many others have been distributed among persons of distinction.

Originally the upper part of the roof was involved in obscurity from the absence of all light, save what was obtained from a few flat sky-lights, and thus the gothic beauty of the structure could not be duly appreciated. To obviate this defect, new dormer-windows were introduced between each compartment of the succession of arches by which the roof is supported, and thus the day-light scenes of the Coronation were relieved from the gloom in which they would otherwise have been involved. Independently of this improvement, the great south window was thoroughly repaired, and the north window was completely renewed. The facing of the north towers were taken down, and that on the east was completely restored to the exact resemblance of the original. The other tower could not be finished in time, and was enclosed in a case of boards, in order to preserve uniformity.

During the progress of these works in 1820, orders were issued to the Board of Works to prepare estimates of the expense for making the requisite preparation for his Majesty's Coronation, the nature of which were particularly specified. In complying with these instructions, the Surveyor-General Colonel Stephenson, Mr. Brown, and Mr. Hiort, the principal architects of the office, had occasion to consult a great number of ancient authorities; but that upon which they most relied was, Sandford's Description of the Coronation of James II. The crowning of that monarch was performed on so expanded and magnificent a scale, that a writer on this subject, in 1761, observes, " it was unquestionably designed for the model of all future coronations; and accordingly by the king's express commands, was recorded in the most pompous manner, which has been followed with little variation in the several coronations since."

In the course, however, of those valuable researches that have recently taken place into the contents of the state papers, a minute and an interesting account of the coronation of James II. was discovered. It gave what was much wanted, some details on the subject of costume.* The manuscript was laid before Lord

---

* In regard to royal and other costumes used at the coronation and other festivals, it is said by some heraldic authorities, that the ancient custom was to take the livery coat from the field, and the appendages from the bearings. There was some propriety in the custom, since it

Sidmouth, who forwarded it to the Coronation Commissioners.

Colonel Stephenson, however, and his able coadjutors did not feel themselves bound to adhere strictly to any of the precedents which they had discovered; but resolved to adopt such improvements as their own experience, and it may be added their own ability, justified the public in expecting, and to the combination of their joint efforts may be ascribed the preparations which met with such universal commendation, and which stood the test of so much public criticism.

The whole length of Westminster Hall, from north to south is 240 feet, and the width from east to west is 68 feet. On the south side it will be recollected

---

denoted particular families. It was customary so to clothe retainers. As the number of heraldic colours is very limited—*or, argent, gules, vert, azure, purpure, sable*—these should each comprise all those tints that come nearest to them. In Scottish heraldry, there are two other hues, *sanguine* (orange red), and *murrey* (dark red.) But many of our most ancient families do not take the coats from the field, but from the bearings. Scarlet is not uncommonly used for hunting parties, for outriders, postillions, &c. Our modern gentry pay no regard to old rules, but choose liveries after their own or their ladies' fancies. Several foreign Courts, too, disregard them. The German Emperors did not, for their field is *or* charged with a black eagle, now the Austrian.

On the whole, it appears that purple is oftener used figuratively than scarlet; and it is safer to say purple of modern costumes and bearings in the modern sense of purple. Shakspeare makes a bold figurative use of scarlet, when he calls ambition "a scarlet sin." By the way, there is a distinct name for scarlet in Latin (*coccus*.) Our translators of the Pentateuch have made a distinction of colours, when they say "purple, scarlet, and fine linen."

In describing the costumes used at the coronation of George II. an error crept in, in saying that the yeomen's dresses were like some of the French kings, "in colour." They were only so in form; the French were probably *azure*, powdered with the *fleurs-de-lis*, the shield of France; those of Navarre (Bourbon), which afterwards accompanied it, is *gules*, with links or disposed in a triangle; and the dalmatics of the supporters (angels) are sometimes dexter *azure*, sinister *gules* in correspondence.

With respect to robes, the King never officially wears any but at his coronation, when he goes to the Abbey in crimson, and is invested there with the purple; or to Parliament, when he wears red. Judges, Mayors, and Prelates, wear constantly officially a greater variety of robes than belong to Majesty.

were situated the Court of Chancery, and the Court of King's Bench. These courts it was discovered had been removed on former occasions, and it was, therefore, determined to remove them on the present. Before, however, the intention could be carried into effect with regard to the Court of King's Bench, it was necessary to obtain an Act of Parliament, which was accordingly passed through both Houses, and these buildings were forthwith taken down. The flood of light admitted into this magnificent chamber, the largest in Europe, exhibited it in a point of view which had not been witnessed by many living persons, and excited the warmest admiration of every individual who entered it, accompanied by a fervent hope that its beauties might not again be obstructed, by again introducing the courts to this spot.

These preliminary steps having been taken, the construction of the buildings for the Coronation commenced immediately. In the first instance a flooring of wood was laid down upon an elevation of fourteen inches above the flags. This extended over the whole area of the Hall, to the foot of the steps formerly leading to the courts of law.

The galleries on each side of the Hall were next erected; of these there were two tiers. The first or under tier was raised on an elevation of about nine feet from the floor, or twelve feet to the top of the rest on which the spectators leaned; they extended about fourteen feet from the wall, and each contained about seven rows of seats. These galleries reached from the royal box, which we shall shortly proceed to describe, to the bottom of the Hall adjoining the triumphal arch, and were entered by five separate staircases, which were perceptible from the bulk-head that rose above the benches; they were each supported by two iron pillars with Gothic caps, which were painted of a bronze colour. These pillars were cast by Mr. Moorman.

The second tier of galleries were erected on a level with the bottoms of the principal window-places of

N

the Hall, and gradually rose to the bases of the oak arches by which the roof is supported. Each window formed as it were a separate box. There were three seats, extending from one end of the galleries to the other without interruption; and in each window-place there were two rows of seats, making together five rows. These galleries were approached by doors made in a section of the casements. Measuring from the windows, the projection into the Hall was ten feet; and the elevation from the floor about twenty feet. They were supported like the gallery below with iron bronzed pillars. The fronts of the galleries were covered with canvass and paper, and afterwards painted in Gothic pannels, to correspond with the general ancient character of the building. Blocks were particularly raised for this purpose. The tops of the fronts on which the spectators leaned were covered with scarlet cloth, cushions, and gold lace fringe. And as a farther security to prevent the possibility of accident, an iron-rail was added to the fronts of about twelve inches in height, which was covered with scarlet cloth in harmony with the rest of the decorations.

The appropriation of the seats in these galleries, devolved by virtue of his office upon the Lord Great Chamberlain. The box for the female branches of the royal family was on the right of the throne, or on the east side of the Hall, level with the royal platform. Opposite to this box, was that appropriated to the foreign ministers. The gallery above this box was also devoted to foreign ministers; and the large box over that of the royal family, was divided between the Earl Marshal, the Lord High Steward, and the Lord High Constable.

The lower gallery (on the east side) was devoted to persons having the Lord Great Chamberlain's and Peers' tickets.

The upper gallery being divided by windows into sections, was thus appropriated:—

First and second windows (back benches) Heralds; front seats, the Lord High Steward of Scotland.

Distribution of the Seats. 91

Third window, Lord Steward.
Fourth window, the Speaker of the House of Commons.
Fifth window, the Surveyor General.
Sixth window, the Auditor of the Exchequer.
Seventh window, the Board of Green Cloth.
Eighth, ninth, tenth, eleventh, and twelfth, the Lord Great Chamberlain.
The seats next the music gallery, the Board of Works.
Lower gallery (west side) Peeresses' places, and Peers' tickets.
Upper gallery, the second and third windows, the Lord Chamberlain.
Windows fourth, fifth, sixth, seventh, eighth, ninth, tenth, eleventh, and twelfth, the Lord Great Chamberlain.

It is due here to state, that at former coronations almost all the places which were the privilege of the Lord Great Chamberlain, were sold at enormous prices. Lord Gwydir, with a nobleness of mind which became his high station, declined pursuing a similar course, and voluntarily presented tickets to all those whom he considered entitled to the privilege.

The royal platform was situated at the south end of the Hall, on the site of the old courts of law, and immediately under the south window. It extended from the wall twenty-six feet forward, and there terminated with three steps; then came a landing place of about five feet in depth, leading to five other steps; and then another landing place, which led directly to the floor which we have already described; the width of the platform was forty-two feet. At the coronation of George III. there was a railing in the front of the platform; but at the coronation of George IV. it reached from one side of the Hall to the other, and presented an uninterupted view of the King's table, and of all the forms observed in paying him the customary attentions. The different landing places were made for the purpose of performing the different ceremonies on approaching the person of his Majesty.

The box for the reception of the royal family was situated on the right of the south window. It was eleven feet in height, and extended from the wall to the first three steps descending from the platform. It contained two rows of benches and one row of splendid gilt chairs. It was approached by a door and a passage leading from the Hall on the first landing place from the platform, as well as by a sort of half-door on the platform itself; the whole of it was lined with scarlet cloth.

The foreign ministers' box was immediately opposite that of the royal family, and was of the same dimensions. It contained four rows of benches, stuffed with horse hair. The box immediately over it was also devoted to foreign ministers; it contained seven rows of seats, and was nearly upon a level with the second tier of galleries, from which it was separated by a rail.

The box immediately opposite that of the foreign ministers erected over the royal box, was divided between the Lord High Constable, the Lord Steward, and the Earl Marshal, each having twenty-four places.

The Lord Great Chamberlain's box was taken off the first tier of galleries next the royal family's box, and was only distinguished from the remaining part of the gallery by having the seats stuffed with horse hair, and covered with crimson cloth.

The flooring of the galleries were all lined with sheet lead, and afterwards covered with matting, with the exceptions already made. The backs of the galleries to a height of four feet were lined with crimson cloth, and each had an iron rail in front, covered with the same material. The seats were stuffed with horse hair and covered with crimson cloth, a crimson silk fringe hanging down in front, four inches in depth.

Immediately under the south window, and about

five feet in advance of the door, which was completely hidden from view, stood his Majesty's throne. This magnificent structure was about nineteen feet in height and seven in width. The canopy was of a square form, and was surrounded by a beautiful carved and gilt cornice, prepared by Mr. Evans. Beneath the cornice hung a succession of crimson velvet helmet drapery, each helmet having embroidered upon it a rose, a thistle, a crown, or a harp. Surmounting the cornice in front was a gilt crown upon a velvet cushion, over the letters George IV. supported on each side by an antique gilt ornament. The entire back of the throne, as well as the interior of the canopy, was covered with crimson Genoa velvet, which was relieved by a treble row of broad and narrow gold lace surrounding the whole. In the centre of the back was the royal arms, the lion and the unicorn rampant, embroidered in the most costly style. Under the canopy stood his Majesty's chair, which was richly gilt, with elbows terminated by lions' heads. The frame of the back was surmounted by the royal arms, carved in the most exquisite style, also richly gilt, and the back and seat were covered with crimson velvet, pannelled with gold lace, as were also the elbow rests. On the floor stood an elegant footstool, the frame-work and legs of which were gilt, and the top covered with the same material as the chair. Six gilt Gothic elbow chairs with cane bottoms and scarlet cushions were prepared for the members of the royal family who dined at his Majesty's table.

The sideboards to receive the plate consisted of a series of shelves, which were so constructed as to be fitted at pleasure against the drapery on the wall behind the throne. The sideboards were placed on the right and left of the throne, and being covered as they were before the banquet with massive gold plate, brought both from Carlton House and Windsor, the effect produced was extremely brilliant.

It would indeed be a difficult task to convey an

adequate idea of the splendour of the decorations which distinguished the royal platform, they were at once tasteful and magnificent, and reflect the highest credit on Mr. Frederick Westmacott, the brother of the Academician, to whom the merit of the greater part of the designs, both in the Hall and the Abbey is due.

We have already stated, that on the right and left of this platform were situated the boxes of the royal family and foreign ministers; these, as well as those above them, were lined completely with superfine scarlet cloth. The galleries above were supported each by four Gothic pillars, richly gilt with burnished gold. The front of these galleries presented a splendid succession of luxuriant drapery, looped up with scarlet ropes. The corners of the festoons being surmounted with large gilt rosettes and wreaths of laurel; to the whole of this drapery was affixed a deep gold coloured silken fringe. The front of the boxes beneath was also decorated with festoons of scarlet cloth reaching to the floor, and looped up to the base of the gilt pillars by lions' heads, also gilt. The effect of this was extremely elegant. The same luxuriance of drapery extended round the corners of the boxes to the commencement of the adjoining galleries.

The whole back of the platform, from the termination of the south window to the floor, was covered with a rich and profuse antique scarlet drapery, falling from cornices formed of a double row of gold twisted rope, and ornamented with a succession of magnificent gold helmets and rosettes. The front of the door which entered from the passage without was covered with a curtain of scarlet cloth, trimmed with deep gold fringe, and looped up on each side with silken ropes.

The floor, and to the extremity of the first three steps was covered with a splendid Persian pattern Wilton carpet, with a raised nap, which almost surpassed the softness of the Turkey carpets, and the remainder of the steps were covered with scarlet baize.

But one of the most interesting objects which presented itself to the notice of the spectator, was the triumphal arch erected at the north end of the Hall and immediately facing the throne. This beautiful structure was purely in the Gothic taste, and was composed of the various orders of architecture existing in the Hall itself and in Westminster Abbey. The merit of the arrangement and composition are due to Mr. Hiort, one of the architects of the Board of Works, by whom it was submitted to Colonel Stephenson, the Surveyor General, and Mr. Brown, of the same office, and by them approved. The execution of the colouring was performed with great skill and effect by Messrs. Greenwood, Latilla, and Phipps. Mr. Latilla was the gentleman who designed the Temple of Concord in the Green Park, during the celebrated Jubilee fête. The height of the arch destined for the entrance of the Champion was nineteen feet, and the width fourteen. The height of the two towers was thirty feet, and of the gallery over the arch twenty-six feet, the whole width of the composition was thirty-six feet. The ceiling of the arch was painted in Gothic fret-work, and on each side were three doors also of Gothic form, the first on the right and left led to the music gallery, the second on the right to the Court of Exchequer, in which part of the procession dined, and the second on the left to a place of retirement; the third on both sides which were covered with crimson curtains, richly trimmed with silken fringe divided in the centre, led to the kitchen passages, and it was through these doors the King's dinner was served. The two figures in the front of the arch represented Richard II. by whom the Hall was repaired, and Edward the Confessor. The entrance to the arch from the platform was by a pair of massive folding doors, painted in imitation of Gothic pannels of oak. These gates were constructed in the manner of flood-gates, and were calculated to resist any ordinary pressure. The whole had the appearance of one of the castles built by the powerful barons of the middle ages, but at the same time it would be difficult to find words adequately to describe the impressive grandeur of the whole. It was a sight worthy of a great nation priding itself in the antiquity of its institutions, of which the venerable roof that covered the whole was an appropriate emblem.

The Champion's stable was situated about fifty yards from the north gate of Westminster Hall, east of the platform. It was a substantial boarded edifice, consisting of four stalls, which were provided with mangers, racks, and other conveniences. There was also a dressing-room for the Champion, furnished with some chairs, a table, and looking-glass, together with a closet, in which to deposit his armour, and the trappings and housings of his horse. There were two horses in the stable, which had been obtained from Astley's Amphitheatre, the one a piebald black and white horse, known by the name of Cato, on which the Champion rode; and the other a small white horse, called Billy, one of the principal performers on the boards of Covent Garden Theatre. This horse was ridden by Lord Howard of Effingham, who acted as Deputy Earl Marshal.

The Duke of Wellington as Lord High Constable of England, rode one of his own chargers, and the Marquis of Anglesea as Lord High Steward, rode his favourite dun coloured horse.* Mr. Blythe, the riding master of Astley's school, superintended the care of the Champion's horse, and also assisted the Champion in preparing for his duties. Over the stable were 150 seats for spectators, and a covered way reached from the door to the platform. The Champion issued tickets for fifty to the seats over the stable, and the rest were given to the artificers of the Board of Works.

---

* A bon mot is related of his Majesty on this occasion, who being informed that the Marquis of Anglesea was to ride his *favorite dun*, replied, " It is the first time I ever heard of a *dun* being a favorite."

Preparations for the Banquet.

In the body of the Hall there were six dining tables, each of which was fifty-six feet long and seven feet wide; they were placed lengthways, within three feet of the pillars supporting the galleries, thereby leaving a large space in the centre of the Hall, the whole of which was covered with matting. The chairs placed on each side of these tables consisted of a sort of antique settée, with a Gothic back, and two distinct seats; they were stuffed with horse hair, and covered with crimson cloth, and were 166 in number; they were composed entirely of Norway deal. In the centre of the Hall was a space nineteen feet wide, which was separated from the dining tables by an iron railing three feet high; a blue cloth twelve feet wide, extended along this, from the steps of the royal platform to the north door.

In addition to the preparations for the banquet in the Hall, other arrangements took place for dining nearly two thousand members of the profession in the different parts of this ancient palace. Tables for this purpose were laid in the Court of Exchequer, the Exchequer Chamber, the Barons' room, the Court of Common Pleas, the Judges' room and the Serjeants' room, the King's Bench Treasury Chamber, and the retiring room of the Judges of the Court of King's Bench. Another suit of apartments was fitted up for the same purpose in the House of Lords, which included the old House of Lords, the Painted Chamber, the old robing room, and No. 4. committee room, and a third suit of rooms in the House of Commons, comprising the Long Gallery, which leads off from the lobby committee rooms, No. 10, 11, and 12, and the Members' waiting room, commonly known as the coffee room of the House of Commons. Mr. Bellamy's (the housekeeper) kitchen was converted into a waiting room. The House of Commons itself became a rendezvous for the lords' attendants, who were not admitted into the Hall until the dinner was served.

The house of Mr. Ley (the Clerk of the Works) was given up to the Lord Steward; it consisted of

O

four rooms, all of which were converted into dining rooms.

All these rooms were covered with matting, and preparations were made for lighting them with argand and other lamps. The Court of Exchequer was lighted with lustres.

The kitchen, and other apartments in which the banquet was to be prepared, consisted of twenty-three rooms on the ground, built of wood and brick, and covered with tiles. They were provided with every possible convenience which the art of cookery might require.

In the roasting kitchen were four immense ranges, in a line with each other, each capable of receiving four rows of spits, which were turned by one man in an adjoining scullery. The dripping pans and furniture connected with these fires were upon the same scale of magnitude. Besides this, there were other kitchens, with every requisite of hot hearths, stoves and boilers for cooking soups, made dishes, fowls, hams, tongues, fish, puddings, &c. There were likewise pastry and confectionary rooms, vegetable dépôts, larders, fruit rooms, dishing rooms, and a bakehouse; in fact, nothing was wanting which could afford facilities to dressing a banquet of such magnitude. These offices were taken possession of on the 12th of July, and the preparations for the day of Coronation immediately commenced. Every thing was conducted with a degree of regularity and precision that excited the admiration of all who had the opportunity of witnessing the operation; and the manner in which the dinner was subsequently served, showed that the system laid down had been strictly adhered to, and was of the most complete and excellent description. The communication with the kitchens consisted of long passages, extending the whole length of the Hall, and terminating with the triumphal arch; they were four feet wide and seven feet in height, their sides were papered and the floors matted. Above these passages were those leading to the first tier of galleries, which were canvassed, papered, and matted. Commodious avenues were opened from Cotton Garden to these passages.

The sideboards from which the dinner and wines were served, extended in a line immediately under the first tier of galleries, and consisted of small closets or cellarets, in which there were commodious shelves. At the back of these cellarets there were sliding partitions communicating with passages behind. Their fronts were in the form of a Gothic arch, and were painted of a deep stone colour; there were nineteen on each side. There were originally twenty, but two of them at the bottom of the royal platform were fitted up for Mr. Watier, the clerk comptroller of the kitchen.

The original intention was to have finished the ceremonies of the Coronation, as well as the banquet, while it was yet day-light; upon giving this matter, however, every due consideration, it was found impossible to effect so desirable an object, and orders were in consequence given to Mr. Perry, of Bond-street, to make the necessary arrangements. Although the notice was short, the work was accomplished with a rapidity which excited general surprise. The great difficulty lay in that the orders were obliged to be sent to Birmingham to be executed; but in spite of every obstacle, and in defiance of every difficulty, Mr. Perry completed his task to the satisfaction of the Lord Chamberlain, as well as to the admiration of the spectators.

The preparations consisted of twenty-eight magnificent lustres in the form of a Worcester vase, each containing sixty wax lights, in brass sockets and glass saucers. At the bottom of the brilliants which formed the vase, were crimson silk tassels in unison with the several decorations of the Hall. They were suspended from the angels in the roof by gold chains, ten feet in length, and were surmounted by coronet caps, composed of or molu and brilliants. The hooks to which they were attached were hidden by two gilt rosettes.

Immediately over the sideboards for the plate were hung two buhl chandeliers. The six tables in the body of the Hall were lighted with twelve or moin candelabras, each containing sixteen wax candles in glass saucers. The royal table was lighted with silver candlesticks only. The cellarets received sufficient lights from the Hall, but the passages behind were lighted with small oil lamps. All the other dining rooms were lighted with argand lamps suspended against the walls.

The illumination of the Hall became a matter of necessity, and indeed the coronation of George III. took place by candle-light, but the latter was at a season of the year when the heat was not oppressive; on the contrary the Coronation of George IV. took place in the dog-days, when although the weather was not extremely hot, and every precaution had been taken to give a proper ventilation to the Hall, yet towards the close of the banquet, the heat became so oppressive, that several of the ladies fainted, and the superb dresses of the peers and peeresses were spoiled by the profuse globules of melted wax which were continually falling upon them; and to increase their embarrassment, an escape was impossible from the place where their unlucky destiny had placed them. If a lovely female dared to raise her look to discover from what quarter the unwelcome visitation came, she was certain of receiving an additional patch upon her cheeks, which, in order to disencumber herself of, obliged her to wipe away also the roseate hue which had been imparted to her countenance at her toilet, thereby obliging her to wear a double face, of nature on the one side, and of art on the other. Many a sly attempt was made to obtain a change of situation, which in a general sense may not be considered as extraordinary in a lovely woman; but the wretched tenants of a slave ship were never more closely packed together, and the powers of locomotion appeared to be confined solely to the head. As to the ministers, and some others who attended the ceremony, a desire to change their places, could not be expected from them, although there are many in the country who think they have retained them long enough.

His Majesty's retiring room was situated immediately behind the throne, in the passage leading to the House of Lords. It was covered with a rich carpet, and furnished with a large reposing-chair, some smaller chairs, table, and other necessary articles.

The regalia room was a small room situate immediately opposite to his Majesty's retiring-room, and it was here the regalia were deposited, both before and after the ceremonies. It was plainly furnished, and covered with a Brussels carpet.

The avenues leading to the Hall were numerous, but extremely well arranged; there were several doors of ingress. The royal family, foreign ministers, and peeresses, were appointed to come through the passages of the House of Lords, and so in by the south door of the Hall; the other spectators were admitted by the north door of the Hall, and by side doors, communicating with the Speaker's Court, and with Parliament Square. Behind every gallery were retiring rooms of the most commodious description, and in every way suited to the convenience of those who had so many hours to remain.

Outside the north gate and communicating with the external platform was a Gothic vestibule or hall, somewhat of a circular form; the ceiling and sides were painted by Mr. Latilla, to represent stone fret work, and looked completely in unison with the antiquity of the building. The porch was painted in the same manner, and by this contrivance the unpleasant effect of an abrupt egress from the Hall to the platform was avoided.

The coffee house of the House of Lords was reserved for the especial use of his Majesty, if he should wish to retire thither for refreshment, and coffee was ordered to be kept constantly ready.

The passage from the House of Lords to the Abbey

was formed of close boarding, and was lined with crimson cloth and matting. This was the course by which the members of the royal family, the foreign ministers, and the peeresses, proceeded from the Hall, to their seats in the Abbey, after the procession had moved.

We have now simply to describe the platform over which the procession moved to Westminster Abbey. The extent of this structure, from the north door of Westminster Hall to the west door of the Abbey, was 1500 feet. The centre, on which the procession moved, and which was enclosed by a railing of about three feet in height, was 25 feet in width; outside the railing, upon a descent of about twelve inches, there was a smaller platform, three feet wide, upon which the soldiers afterwards stood. The whole of this platform was covered with a canvass awning, upon an elevation of fourteen feet, which was so contrived as to be removable at pleasure, by means of cords and pullies, affixed to the pillars by which the canopy was supported. The whole of the platform was covered with matting, and twelve feet of the centre with blue cloth. The side railings were also covered with blue cloth; and the pillars and frame work were painted of a stone colour. The elevation was upon an average three feet from the ground floor.

Before we proceed to the description of the preparations in Westminster Abbey, our duty impels us not to pass unnoticed the scurrilous and malignant attacks which were at this particular period made upon the Coronation, on account of the expense attending it. The severity with which it was treated, was as illiberal, as it was unjust. It would be an idle departure from the point to which our attention is now directed, were we to discuss the question, whether a monarchy like ours is or is not the form of government best calculated to ensure tranquillity and happiness to the people of England; because the experience of ages and of centuries, has long since set that question at rest. But although all classes of the people agree in the wisdom, and utility of placing the executive power in the hands of an individual of one particular family, it is a matter of great importance to know, what degree of rank and consequence that individual and the members of his family ought to hold in the state, and whether any advantage, even in a financial point of view, could be gained, should the spirit of republican parsimony ever be aple to pull them down to a level with common subjects.

It became now the fashion of a particular party, to rail against the Coronation, as a gaudy, useless, pageant, and as entailing a great expense upon the public. These very sentiments were promulgated by several members of the House of Commons; they may, however, apply whatever epithets they please to the Coronation, but men of enlarged views and of sound principles, can see nothing in that pomp and splendour inconsistent with the feelings of moral propriety, by which even a cold calculating philosopher would regulate the conduct of others, while the practice is sanctioned by the usages that have been observed among us from the earlier times, and during the best periods of our history. It belongs not to every one to discover the importance of forms, ceremonies, and splendid decorations, and the aid which the cause of virtue derives from them; but it does belong to many to decry those forms and ceremonies, as being attended with an expense producing ruin to the country—an expense which, if compared to the income of the kingdom, is no more than a glass of water taken from a reservoir. Magnificent ceremonies serve to affix a stamp of obligation on the most important engagements; they are the cheap means of conferring a value upon that which otherwise might be passed over with indifference; they give " body to opinion, and permanence to public esteem;" they enable the imagination to expand, and preserve the finest feelings of the human heart.

The sum, however, which the Coronation costs, is not lost to the country; it comes from the pockets of those who can afford to give, and goes to those who want it. Employment was afforded for several months to many hundred persons, who otherwise might have remained in a state of comparative beggary. Great impulse and activity were given to trade. The metropolis was considerably benefitted by the multitudes which flocked to it, as well as by the extraordinary number of foreigners who came to witness the grand ceremonial. Even in a financial point of view, the country cannot be said to have sustained any loss by the Coronation; because the extraordinary demand for taxable commodities, which it occasioned on the part of private individuals, must have added to the revenue even a greater sum than was expended by government in preparing it. We never hear any of those economists and calculators, who would deprive royalty of the splendour which belongs to it, say a word about the splendid banquets, the fêtes and routs given by noblemen, merchants and tradesmen. They will say that these persons defray all the expenses attending such magnificent entertainments, but that the money expended in royal magnificence comes out of the pockets of the King's subjects. We tell those economists that whatever money is expended for the use of the King, whether for his private purposes or for supporting his state and grandeur, is the property of the King, to which, according to law and to the principles of political justice, his Majesty has as much right as the Duke of Devonshire has to his estate, or Mr. Baring to the money which he lately lent to the sovereigns of Europe.

Did our limits or the patience of our readers admit of any extent of argument on this point, we should prove that the liberties of Englishmen depend more upon, and are more firmly secured to them by their Monarch, than by any other branch of the Constitution, aye, even than by their House of Commons, were the members of that House elected by all the people of the kingdom. A monarch, situated as ours is, can have no temptation to encroach on the rights and freedom of his subjects. He is placed beyond the possibility of being actuated by any such feeling, and that he should continue in that high *protecting* situation, it is essentially necessary that he should enjoy a degree of wealth and splendour superior to that of any other person in the realm. If ever he should, with regard to his means, be brought down to a level with those placed under him, the liberty of the people is immediately put in a state of danger. Now we would ask those persons who so often complain of the expenses of our monarchy, and of extravagance on the part of the royal family, whether there are not many noblemen and even private gentlemen who live in a state of much greater magnificence than many Princes of the Blood in England? Have there not been men among us, who after having made fortunes by traffic had their palaces, their domains, and retinues, almost rivalling those of the monarch? And what must be the consequence, if the distinctions which ought to exist between these orders were to be done away, by impoverishing the sovereign, and curtailing the splendour and magnificence, with which he should ever be surrounded, merely upon a principle of narrow and mischievous economy! It is for these reasons we must repel the attacks which were at this time made against the sovereign, on account of the expenses necessarily incurred in preparing for the Coronation, and which were greedily seized upon by the carpers and cavillers to increase the disloyalty and disaffection of the people.

We shall not protract this description to any greater length, but proceed immediately to the description of the preparations made at Westminster Abbey, which, like those in Westminster Hall, took place under a warrant from the Treasury; and the first step taken was to insure completely all the valuable monuments with which it is stored, with boards, so as to prevent mutilation or injury. It is also worthy of being recorded, that all the galleries and every other building were elevated without a single hook or nail being driven into the ancient fabric.*

The view of the interior of this magnificent pile, on entering the great western door, was such as to excite surprise and admiration in the breast of every beholder. The space from the door to the entrance of the choir, embracing the two side aisles, was from ancient usage considered the privilege of the Dean and Chapter; and as pecuniary speculation does not properly belong to the clerical character, the whole of the space claimed by the Dean and Chapter was let for a large sum to a person of the name of Glanville, by whom the whole was fitted up with commodious boxes and benches, for the accommodation of spectators, to view the procession as it entered the Abbey. The same observation applies in regard to the galleries or nunneries, as they are called, over those aisles which were also fitted up as places for the spectators. These boxes and benches were all covered with matting, and their fronts and backs decorated with crimson cloth. From the entrance to the choir, all the rest of the space occupied by galleries and erections of every sort, was under the dominion of the Earl Marshal, by whom tickets were issued according to certain privileges, which were founded and recognised upon precedents of ancient date. The distance from the west gate to the choir is exactly one hundred and ten feet, and along this was raised a platform, four and twenty feet wide, upon which the procession was to move, and on each side of which there was a smaller platform, for those persons by whom the grand pageant was to be flanked. The whole of this was covered with matting, and along the centre was spread a line of blue cloth of the same width as on the exterior platform.

From the choir all the stalls, reading desks, and

---

* This was not the case at the coronation of George III. on the contrary, it was the boast of the workmen, that they had broken the noses, and cut off the ears of a whole legion of angels.

pews, were carefully removed, and this part of the building being thus cleared, a more elevated platform was raised, which was approached from under the organ loft by six steps. On each side, on the site of the stalls, five benches were placed; they were separated by a low partition from the passage in the centre, which was twelve feet wide, and were approached by openings to the right and left as the steps were ascended; they were set apart for the reception of the Knights of the Bath, Knight Commanders, Privy Counsellors, Judges, and others who formed part of the procession. Above these seats were two galleries, and above them the nunneries, all of which were devoted to spectators.

At the further end of the choir six other steps led to the theatre or pulpitium, which was situated exactly in the middle of the Abbey, between the two transepts. In the centre of this theatre, the diameter of which was forty feet, was raised a small stage of about four feet square, which was ascended by five steps. On this theatre, facing the altar, stood his Majesty's throne or chair of state, on which, after his Coronation, he was to receive the homage of his subjects.

The throne itself presented a most splendid and beautiful appearance. The back was of a square form, richly carved and gilt, bearing on its top the royal arms, also carved and gilt, immediately under which were the letters G. IV. This device was precisely the same on both sides, so that whatever way the object was examined it looked equally rich. The elbows and legs were likewise carved and gilt. The inside of the back, against which his Majesty was to lean, was in the form of a square pannel, stuffed and covered with gold and silver coloured brocade. The seat and resting place for the elbows were also stuffed and covered with the same material. From the bottom of the seat on the four sides, being a deep fringe of gold lace. There was also a footstool corresponding in every particular with the throne itself.

To the stage, and to the bottom of the first step descending from it, was covered with gold-plated tabby, bordered with a gold fringe seven inches in depth. The remaining four steps were covered with a beautiful Turkey carpet, and the rest of the theatre was lined with crimson baize, which was placed over the matting.

At each corner of the theatre were semicircular rails, designed as places in which the Heralds were to stand.

The north and south transepts were filled up with benches, which ascended amphitheatrically towards the window; of these there were thirty-seven; the front seats were reserved for peers, and all those at the back for peeresses and peers' tickets.

The most splendid object, however, in point of decoration, and the most magnificent part of the preparations was the sacrarium. It is impossible, in fact, to withhold the most unqualified praise from those who were engaged in forming and completing the designs which were here presented to the spectator.

The first object which naturally attracted the eye was the altar. The table, which measured six feet nine inches in length, stood upon a platform a little above the elevation of the floor, and had a small shelf behind; the whole was covered with blue and gold brocade. The top of this covering was pannelled with broad gold lace. It was likewise edged with gold-looped fringe. The bottom and sides were bordered with gold lace, and the whole was finished with a deep gold fringe seven inches deep. On this was subsequently placed the chalice, the patina, the ampulla, which contained the holy oil, the anointing spoon, and the other articles necessary in the ceremony of the Coronation.

The back of the altar was likewise covered with blue and gold brocade, clipped on each side with golden palm branches, which rose from the floor to a height of twelve feet, and then gradually spread till they became intermingled with the drapery above.

This drapery, which consisted of blue and gold coloured silk damask, extended along the front of the gallery, and was coiled up with ropes of gold. It was surmounted by a cornice, composed of two inch and a half gold and silk rope, with large gilt rosettes to each pipe. The fringe was of gold and silk, four inches deep. From under the upper drapery on each side of the altar, was suspended some bold antique banner drapery, which swept the floor, but which was capable of being drawn up on both sides so as to give entrance through two doors to the King's Traverse behind.

On the left hand, or north side of the altar, stood the chair of the Archbishop of Canterbury, which was composed of oak. The back, seat, and elbows, were stuffed and covered with that description of velvet which is called bishop's purple, and these were pannelled with gold lace. There was a corresponding footstool, which was covered with purple velvet and ornamented gymp. Added to which there was a kneeling cushion for the Archbishop, covered with purple velvet, with four gold tassels, and a similar cushion for the Dean on the other side.

The step leading to the altar and the floor of the sacrarium were covered with a rich garter blue and gold Wilton carpet, with what is called a cutpile, which gives it all the softness of a Turkey carpet. The pattern was the Norman rose with the ermine.

On the right of the altar stood the offering table, which was covered with garter blue Genoa velvet, bordered with lace and fringed with gold. Upon this, preparatory to the ceremony, was placed a cushion, upon which his Majesty's offering was to be made, covered with garter blue velvet, pannelled with gold lace, and with gold tassels at the corners, together with the offering itself, which was a pall or altar covering of gold brocade, five feet square, bound with gold lace and fringe, and an ingot of pure metal of one pound in Troy weight.

Among other things provided for the occasion, also,

was a kneeling cushion for his Majesty, which was to
be placed in front of the altar when he made his
offering. This was covered with crimson and gold
brocade, fringed with gold lace, and each corner decorated with a gold tassel.

The anointing pall was made of gold and silver
brocade, lined with silver tabby, with a deep gold
fringe, loops and tassels at the four corners, and four
silver staves by which it was to be supported. There
was also a carpet of gold and silver brocade provided,
which was to be spread for the reception of his Majesty before he received the sacrament.

On the south side of the sacrarium was situated
the royal box, on the top of which was a carved and
gold helmet cornice, composed of the rose, the thistle,
and the shamrock alternately with the cross pattée
between them. The drapery which hung from the
cornice was of crimson velvet, decorated with loops
of gold rope, and bordered and fringed with gold lace.
It was lined with crimson sarsnet. The interior of
the box was lined with fluted crimson sarsnet, furnished at the top with crimson silk rope. The front
was hung with crimson velvet in drapery, bordered
with gold lace, and gilt chairs were provided for
those who were present.

On the side opposite the royal box the drapery was
similar to that in the front of the altar, and along this
was placed a bench for the Bishops who were to assist
in the ceremonies, the Lord Mayor of London, and
other persons who were to walk in the procession.
This bench was covered with garter blue and gold
damask, with drapery along the front, edged with
gold lace.

On the south side of the sacrarium, near to the
royal box, was placed his Majesty's litany chair and
faldstool. The frame work of the chair was fluted
and gilt, and enriched with gilt ornaments. The
back and seat were stuffed, and covered with garter
blue velvet, pannelled with gold lace. The faldstool,
which was about three feet in height, and was to be

used after the manner of a reading desk, was placed in front. It was covered with garter blue velvet, pannelled with gold lace, and richly trimmed with gold fringe. There was a pillow on the top, also covered with blue velvet, with gold tassels at the corners.

This chair, on which his Majesty was to sit when the recognition was made, and when he first entered the Abbey, was situated at the foot of the royal stage, which we have already described, on the south side. In form it was somewhat similar to the litany chair, but the decorations were different; the lining too was of crimson velvet, pannelled with gold; and the faldstool was likewise covered with crimson velvet and gold lace. Beyond the recognition chair, but in the same line, was placed a faldstool for the two bishops, by whom the litany was to be read. This was covered with crimson lutestring; bordered with crimson silk twine. At the bottom of the faldstool were two pillows, covered with crimson velvet, for the bishops to kneel on. The tops were pannelled with crimson silk lace. When the litany was over, this faldstool would be removed away, as being no longer necessary.

The pulpit was of a hexagon form, and was situated close to the pillar on the north-west corner of the sacrarium, opposite to the royal box. The desk was covered with a crimson velvet cushion, and the sides with plain crimson velvet, with the exception of the centre pannel, on which was embroidered a glory, with the letters I. H. S. in the centre. The ballustrade was in the Gothic style, and the steps were covered with a garter blue gold Wilton carpet. There was no canopy.

We shall now describe the traverse into which his Majesty was to retire to robe and repose himself during the ceremonies, and which was immediately behind the altar. The floor of this chamber was covered with a rich carpet, and the table or altar, which stood at the back, was covered with crimson lutestring, bound and bordered with crimson silk. There was a chair of state and footstool prepared for his Majesty, which were gilt and covered with crimson lutestring. The walls were distempered of a peach colour. There was likewise a large dressing-glass in the room, and a small mirror. This room was close to St. Edward the Confessor's shrine, and, in fact, in his chapel.

Above the altar, and over the traverse, was situated the music gallery, the two front rows of which were devoted to spectators;—behind these were the seats for the choristers, and behind them again the seats for the instrumental performers. The organ was in the centre; above it was the royal crown, with a figure of Fame on each side; and beneath the crown a medallion of his Majesty. This was painted by Mr. Drummond.

The foreign ministers' box was opposite to that of the royal family, and the Lord Great Chamberlain's box was over that of the royal family. The remaining boxes and galleries were divided among different officers of state, to whom a certain number of tickets were issued. The places prepared were considered equal to the accommodation of four thousand persons.

The avenues of ingress to the Abbey were various, but every thing was so arranged as to produce as little confusion as possible.

Proper places of retirement were provided, and female attendants were appointed to attend upon the ladies; in fact, every thing which could contribute to the comfort of the visitors was studiously consulted.

A new front was added to the organ, the design was of Gothic character, and prepared and executed by Mr. Latilla, the artist, and Mr. Phipps, of the Office of Works. The pipes of the organ all stand separately, and furnish their own shade; the decorative part was painted and gilt in exact representation of rose-wood inlaid with brass. The effect, when viewed from the bottom of the choir, was extremely grand. Seats were prepared in front of the choristers for one hundred and fifty persons, the vocal and instrumental performers being arranged close to the organ.

Withdrawing our attention for a short time from the interior to the exterior of the Abbey, a most singular spectacle presented itself to the eye of the spectator. Some powerful magician appeared to have been at work, and by his potent influence so to have completely changed the vicinity of the Abbey, that few of the objects which we have been accustomed to see on that site could be recognised. The whole area was so completely altered by the carpenters in their busy speculations, that nothing was to be seen but structures raised in amphitheatrical, and indeed every other form, to accommodate those who wished to be spectators of the approaching solemnity. In these structures collective uniformity was entirely out of the question; every shape, and size, and plan, were adopted, according to the taste and means of the architect; and when the passenger became involved in the confusion of the bustling scene, he could survey nothing around him on that spot hitherto consecrated to the repose of the dead, and the transactions of the ordinary business of the living, but

" Towers and ports
Three times a thousand, lift thereon their brows
At equal spaces and in prospect round."

the " dreadful din of preparation" was heard afar and near, and on every countenance sat the look of anxious toil and labour.

That these expensive undertakings were not made in vain, was obvious from the unusual concourse of persons which daily flocked to the spot; we do not mean that description of crowd, which any spectacle ordinarily collects in a capital city, but one of a very different description—persons evidently from the proximate and distant parts of the country, who arrived in town with full purses to participate in the enjoyments of the Coronation, many of whom, whilst gazing with wondering eyes upon the busy scene before them, were very dexterously relieved of their stock of ways and means by the light-fingered gentry. But besides our own countrymen, the place

"Close swarm'd with busy crowds of many a realm."

The Italian, the German, and the Frenchman, the haughty Spaniard and the savage Russ,

"Men of all climes, of fashion, and of form,"

were seen intermingled, and Babel with its confusion of tongues seemed to be restored in England's metropolis.

The whole area in front of the Hall, the Abbey, and the adjoining streets which could possibly command even a transient glimpse of the procession, presented nothing but piles of scaffolding, covered in and fitted up with seats, and the spectator had the means of judging and selecting for himself according to the intensity of his curiosity and the depth of his pocket, for here happily there was a graduated scale of prices well adapted to the various classes of society, from one guinea to twenty. Indeed the anxiety to accommodate was so great, that many persons kindly provided seats at still more moderate prices, where the spectator, if he could not have a bird's-eye view of the procession, would be at least far exalted above the noble and the ignoble crowd, and tower over the multitude congregated together upon the occasion. The owner of the second horse at a race feels some pride that it was not the last, and to have the next number to a capital prize in the lottery is always considered a great consolation for a blank. So in some of the seats we suppose the spectators were consoled for the total absence of a prospect of the procession by the reflection that they saw the roof of the royal platform, and were behind those who actually saw the King, during which time they were comfortably annoyed by some dense volumes of smoke issuing from the chimneys, which served them as a resting place to their backs, and which gave such an African tinge to the fair countenances of the females, that they could scarcely recognise each other—but then, they could hear the cannons fired—the drums beat—the trumpets sound—the bells ring—they could hear the uproarious din of the assembled thousands, and they could afterwards declare that the Coronation was a glorious sight.

These buildings, however, rose with the talismanic rapidity of the transformations of a play, many of them were upon a construction at once solid, spacious, and commodious, fitted up with every accommodation of retiring chambers, particularly for the reception of those parties who repaired to their seats on the previous night.

We shall proceed in the description of these edifices in the order in which they appeared from the grand entrance to Westminster Abbey.

Over the great gate, and beneath the towers, some small galleries were erected; that on the left was called the Select Gallery, which was splendidly fitted up in boxes like the theatre, with scarlet and white hangings and gilt ornaments, and the price of the seats in this gallery was for the first and second seats six guineas each person. The gallery at the right was called the Royal Gallery, and was fitted up like the other; the seats were five guineas each. The whole area in the church-yard was fitted up as the Bishop's Cathedral Gallery, and was contracted for by the beadles of St. Martin's Church. This great gallery was subdivided into different compartments, which were underlet, and called by the respective owners by particular names. The prices varied from two to five guineas each seat, according to the view of the scene of the procession. The front of the Westminster Sessions House was fitted up into seats, many of which were engaged by the police magistrates and their friends. The garden within the railing at the opening of Great George Street, was subdivided into a variety of structures, and fitted up as substantial galleries; the first was called the Royal Platform, enclosed within the garden, extending from the end of George Street, and the tickets were two guineas each. The second division was called the Royal Amphitheatre, and was a continuation of the same garden, and the price of the tickets was three guineas. The third was the Royal Garden Pavillion, extending westward of the Sessions House, and the price of the tickets was the same as the preceding one. The space facing Palace Yard, and within the railing near St. Margaret's Church, was called the Grand Central Pavillion, which commanded a front view of the procession, as it proceeded to and returned from Westminster Hall. The seats were commodiously arranged and well fitted up, and the price was three guineas. The seats on the one side commanded the Palace Yard view, and on the other the Westminster Abbey side of the procession; the Grand Central Pavillion extended nearly 1500 feet, and was capable of containing 7000 persons, with suitable arrangements for provisions and refreshments of every description. It was a most complete and elegant structure. In front of the Court of Exchequer in Palace Yard were some neat galleries, with accommodation at from three to four and five guineas each; at the river side of the Hall, galleries were also fitted up. The fronts of the houses in Palace Yard were all fitted up for the reception of company, in galleries calculated to afford every accommodation, at various prices, and in some places amounting to from fifteen to twenty-five guineas each person. From some of the houses the front and side walls were taken down, and the roofs supported by substantial props, the whole of the rooms being appropriated for the reception of company. These places bore a variety of names, and some as whimsical as caprice could make them.

The curious reader will be amused in reading the following statement of the prices given for a good place at successive coronations, as it will show that the price of *seeing* has increased in the same ratio as the price of every thing else.

In 1761, the first symptoms were advertisements in the newspapers for the hire of windows, and seats on scaffolds, in view of the procession. There is generally a clause in the lease of the houses in view, entitling the landlord to their use at the coronation. In 1761, some of these houses cleared from 700*l.* to 1000*l.* Ground for the scaffolds was let, in some situations, at three and four guineas a foot.

At Edward I.'s coronation, the demand for a seat was *half-a-farthing*. At Edward II.'s the people had doubled either their wealth or their passion for royal shows; for the price had risen to an entire *farthing*. At Edward III.'s it was a *halfpenny*. At Richard II.'s it was a *penny;* and the Chronicler seems to think that the show was not worth the money. At Henry IV.'s it was still a *penny*. Henry V. was popular, and the people paid down to the extent of *twopence*, in testimony of their admiration. Henry VI. of whom Shakspeare says, " that he could neither fight nor fly," was no favourite, yet old English liberality prevailed, and gave *twopence* to see him crowned. But coronations became more frequent in his time than was good for the setters of windows; the market was choked, and the prices dropped from their original loyal elevation of twopence to a *penny*, thence to a halfpenny, and, in some disastrous instances, " the glory of regality" might be seen for *nothing*. Better times then came round, and Edward IV. saw the price of a seat *twopence* once more. Here it seemed to have gravitated, and twopence was the price at the coronations of Richard III. and Henry VII. But those were days of trouble, and the wisdom of Englishmen was better occupied in preserving the few pence left to them by the York and Lancaster plunderings. The country grew opulent and curious again, and allowed *fourpence* for a view of Henry VIII.'s coronation. The same amount was upheld in the days of Edward VI. and even in those of bloody Queen Mary, who had, however, been popular, and had ascended her throne with an *oath* to preserve Protestantism. The nation exulted in Elizabeth's appearance, and, in their joy, disbursed a *sixpence*. The progress of liberality and loyalty were thenceforth rapid; for James I. and Charles I. each brought a *shilling*. Charles II. found the nation in a paroxysm of absurd joy, and was beheld at the expense of *half-a-crown*, the most rapid advance on record, and to be altogether attributed to the rapture of getting rid of the Roundheads. James II. obtained the same price: for it is observable, that, but in the single instance of Henry VI.'s tumultuous and overwhelmed time, the prices once raised on popular folly have never fallen. William and Queen Anne saw the advance *half-a-crown* more, and they were worth it. The House of Brunswick came among us when we were a divided nation, and it was thought too formidable an experiment by the scaffold-makers to raise their prices, while the Jacobites were so fully determined not to *see;* the seats thus continued at a *crown*. Jacobitism was gradually giving way during the reign of George I. under a process of exile, starving among the Highlands, or chains in the English castles; and at George II.'s coronation, loyalty spoke out, and bid up to *half-a-guinea*. The coronation of the late king found England without a disturber at home, and with nothing but triumphs abroad; the prices accordingly sprung up to an extravagance unparalleled. The front seats in the galleries in Westminster Abbey were let at ten guineas and upwards each. Seats in the street were from one guinea to ten; and every tile, from which a glimpse of the procession could be had, was a place of eager canvassing and exorbitant demand.

It must be allowed that the appearance of many of the erections was calculated to produce a shudder for the safety of the occupants, but every one of them were repeatedly visited by Mr. Hiort and the Committee of Safety, and were pronounced to be perfectly secure. It was, however, almost ridiculous to behold a number of persons expending large sums of money in erecting galleries from which not a single part of the procession was to be seen; the price indeed was moderate, but it was paid to behold a crowd, and nothing more.

But while so many caterers were at work for the visual appetite, others were not less active in preparing more solid sources of gratification, and waggons laden with provisions of all kinds, together with potables in equal variety and abundance were seen pouring into the neighbourhood for several days previous to the Coronation. A vast number of persons residing on the spot, desirous of profiting by the general attraction, opened their doors to visiters, whom they regaled with viands of every description at comparatively moderate charges. For the last three or four days previous to the important 19th, the influx of strangers to Westminster from all quarters to view the preparations was immense, and the throng was frequently so dense, that there was no possibility of moving.

But in order to preserve as much as possible a system of regularity, without which it would have been impossible to proceed, it became necessary to erect barriers in the different avenues leading towards the Hall and Westminster Abbey, and to issue clear and positive orders as to the course which each class of visiters was to pursue. This task, which came under the direction of the police department, was superintended by Lord Sidmouth, Sir Robert Baker, and other magistrates, and the whole was most admirably arranged. A lithographic map of the whole city of Westminster was prepared, and upon this the routes which the carriages took coming from different parts of the town were distinctly defined by coloured lines, and the places to which the tickets were to be admitted intelligibly pointed out.

Instructions for the Routes.

The following were the instructions issued by Lord Sidmouth:—

Whitehall, July 13, 1821.—In pursuance of an order of his Majesty's most Hon. Privy Council, the following instructions have been framed for securing the commodious access and return of carriages conveying persons to and from Westminster Hall and Abbey on the occasion of his Majesty's Coronation on the 19th instant. In conformity with these instructions the necessary directions have been given to all his Majesty's officers and servants concerned in carrying them into execution. The doors of the Hall and Abbey will be opened at three o'clock in the morning. At the same hour all the gates of Hyde-park, except the Kensington-gate, will be opened for carriages, and the Stable-Yard-gate will be opened for the passage of such carriages as will be permitted to use the second route laid down in the instructions. The doors of the Hall and Abbey will be shut at seven o'clock in the morning against all visiters, except those who are entitled to be set down at the House of Lords, and the doors of that House will be shut at eight o'clock. All carriages are then to depart, and the gates of the Park will be open at three o'clock in the afternoon to those which are to wait there for the return of their owners, as stated in the second and third routes. SIDMOUTH.

No. 1.—Route for the Foreign Ministers, for all those who are to form part of the procession, and for those who have tickets from Peers, Judges, Privy Councillors, and Grand Crosses of the Bath.

N.B. The holders of such tickets may also use the route No. 4.

Pass down Grosvenor-place, Eaton-street, and the Vauxhall-road, along Millbank-road, Millbank-street, and the east side of Abingdon-street; set down at the House of Lords; and go home by the west side of Abingdon-street, along College-street, Little College-street, Wood-street, North-street, St. John's Church Yard, Little Tufton-street, Tufton-street, the Horse-ferry-road, Carey-street, the North and West sides of Vincent-square, and Bentinck-street.

Persons of the above descriptions from the eastern parts of the town, will fall into this line most easily by crossing Vauxhall-bridge.

All the foregoing persons will be excluded unless they arrive at eight o'clock in the morning.

In the evening the carriages to take away the above-mentioned persons, will wait in Vincent's-square, with the hind wheels against the rails of the square, will come from thence (when required) by the reverse of the morning route, up the west side of Abingdon-street, and go home by the east side of that street, the Millbank-road, and Vauxhall-road.

No. 2.—Route for all persons who have tickets for the south side of the aisle of Westminster Abbey.

Enter St. James's Park, at the Stable Yard, passing along the Mall, cross the Parade, and leave the Park by Storey's Gate, pass down Prince's-street, set down in Dean's-yard; and go home by Bowling-street, Little Smith-street, Smith-street, Dean-street, Tothill-street, the Broadway, York-street, James-street, into the Park at Buckingham Gate, up Constitution-hill, and out at the Hyde Park Corner Gate.

All the foregoing persons will be excluded, unless they take their seats by seven o'clock in the morning.

In the afternoon the carriages to take away the foregoing persons will enter St. James's Park from Piccadilly, and wait in the Bird-cage Walk with the hind wheels against the houses, and the horses heads fronting the canal, and (when called for) will take up and go home by the same route as in the morning.

This route will be used by those who have seats in the booths which open into Prince's-street.

No. 3.—Route for all persons who have tickets for the north side of the aisle of Westminster Abbey.

Fall into the line in Cockspur-street, pass on the west side of the statue at Charing-Cross, down Parliament-street and the Broad Sanctuary, set down at the stairs which will be provided to cross the platform, and go home through Little George-street, into George-street, and through Delahay-street, Duke-street, Charles-street, and King-street, into Whitehall.

All the foregoing persons will be excluded, unless they take their seats by seven o'clock in the morning.

In the afternoon the carriages to take away the foregoing persons will enter St. James's Park from the Stable Yard, turn to the left and wait on the parade in the Park, with the hind wheels against the railing, and the horses heads fronting the Horse-Guards, and (when called for) will pass through the Horse-Guards, down King-street, take up where they set down in the morning, and return home by the west side of Parliament-street.

This route will be used by those who have seats in the Guildhall, and in the booths in the Abbey Church-Yard, and St. Margaret's Church-Yard, and in the Gardens of Parliament-square.

No. 4.—Route for all persons having tickets for Westminster Hall, and the Exchequer, and Duchy of Lancaster Offices.

Fall into the line in the Strand, pass on the east side of the Statue at Charing-cross, down Parliament-street, set down at the platform near the corner of New-Palace-yard, from whence the parties will walk along the platform into the Hall, and the carriages will go home along Bridge-street, and over Westminster-Bridge.

All the foregoing persons will be excluded, unless they take their seats by seven o'clock in the morning.

In the evening the carriages to take away the foregoing persons will wait round the Asylum with the hind wheels against the walls, and (when called for) will take up where they set down in the morning, and will go home along the east of Parliament-street.

This route will be used by those who have seats in New Palace-yard.

The aid of barriers was in these routes resorted to, and the lines so preserved as to preclude the possibility of confusion, unless produced by wantonness. Independently of the barriers thus disposed, other barriers were erected, to preclude the multitude, who might be attracted towards the platform, from approaching beyond a certain distance. These barriers were placed in the following stations:—South end of King-street; south end of Parliament-street; south end of Cannon-row; east and west ends of Bridge-street; east end of Great George-street; east end of Tothill-street: north and south ends of Abingdon-street; Mews, between Dean-street and the gateway to Dean's-yard; the open thoroughfares west of Prince's-street. To prevent the crowd from encroaching beyond the barriers, the military and police were judiciously stationed.

The tickets, both for the Hall and Abbey, were of the same character, only printed in different coloured ink. They were designed and printed under the direction of Sir William Congreve. In the centre was a medallion, on which was represented his Majesty in his full Coronation dress, seated on his throne, and an angel descending from heaven to place the crown on his head. In his hands he held the sceptre and orb; on his right stood the allegorical figures of Britannia, Hibernia, and Scotia; and on the left the figures of justice—one holding the scale and the other the sword. The figures were white, on a blue ground. The whole was surrounded with a garter, containing the inscription—" Georgius IIII. Dei Gratia Brittaniarum Rex, Fid. Dei." upon a red ground, shaded with black. This again was encircled with a luxuriant wreath of rose, thistles, and shamrock—the roses and thistles red, the rest black. At the bottom were two vigorous boughs of laurel bound together with a ribbon—leaves alternately red and black: from that wreath surrounding the medallion sprung a radiant circle, at the extremity of which, on one side was the figure of Fame, with her trumpet—and on the other the figure of Peace, with a wreath of laurel in one hand and an olive branch in the other. Surmounting the whole were the King's Arms, with the letters " G. R." on one side, and " IV." on the other. At each corner was an oval space for the name of the place for which the ticket was intended, " Abbey," or " Hall," and the number. On the outer edge was a beautiful embossed border of oak leaves and acorns, terminated at each corner by the crown placed on the insignia of England, Ireland, and Scotland. The name of the party to whom the ticket was granted, " not transferable" was at the bottom on the left, and the signature of the Lord Great Chamberlain, or the Earl Marshal, on the right. The official seal was in the centre. The place or box to which the ticket would admit, was likewise distinctly specified.

The procession-ticket presented in the centre a medallion representation of his Majesty in a triumphal car, drawn by four fiery steeds, in most animated style, enclosed by engine work in blue and red. This was encompassed by a beautiful specimen of the richest embossed work. At the top, in the centre, was the royal crown, emitting its rays of regal glory; on each side appears the Union badge; and thence, in scroll ornament, are introduced the head of the British lion, and branches of oak; on each side of the Congreve print, the rose, shamrock, and thistle, hang luxuriant pendent in relief; and, in the same style, at bottom, were vigorous branches of oak and laurel.

The Abbey pass-ticket was a print of the north elevation of the Abbey, in a blue ground, supported like the former, with engine work, and stars of the Orders, and inscribed " Abbey pass-ticket." This again was enclosed with embossed work of the Crown Royal, Union Badge, and Scroll, with oak and laurel on each side, while, at the bottom, the peaceful palm branches were appropriately introduced.

The Hall pass-ticket presented an appearance of rays emitting from their centre in subdued red, surrounded entirely by the circular Union Badge in blue, as used in the large Hall and Abbey tickets. Above appeared in relief the double cypher of G. R. IV. in beads, the Badge of Union being thrown boldly into Scroll on each side, the words " pass-ticket" in the centre, and the signature and seal of Lord Gwydir at the bottom.

The Hall and Abbey tickets were issued according to a scale of privilege recognised by the Lords of Council—namely, to a Peer five tickets; to Privy Councillors, four tickets; to Knights of the Grand Order of the Bath, three tickets; Clerks in Council, two; Peeresses, in their own right, one.

The pass-tickets were delivered to persons engaged in the ceremonies, and entitled them to free egress and ingress, where their duties might call them.

Independent of the tickets issued to Peers and other certain officers of state, the official departments were entitled to a given number each. The Lord High Steward, the Lord High Constable, the Earl Marshal, the Lord Chamberlain, the Lord High Constable of

Scotland, the Lord Steward of his Majesty's Household, the Teller of the Exchequer, the Speaker of the House of Commons, the Surveyor General, the Auditor of the Exchequer, the Board of Green Cloth, the Board of Works, Earl Bathurst, the War Office, &c. &c. Many were also sent, by courtesy, to different persons; and the public press was liberally supplied. The average number of tickets issued by the Lord Great Chamberlain was 3000, and by the Earl Marshal upwards of 4000. Each department had a particular place assigned, as the Hall or Abbey, equal to the number of tickets issued, allowing twenty-two inches to each person.

Amongst the subjects not the least interesting, or productive of the least anxiety, was the question of dress. It had been repeatedly announced, under the authority of the Lord Chamberlain, that the dress to be worn both by ladies and gentlemen, was to be full court costume. This notification, however, not having been announced in any official form was received with doubt; and many who knew they would receive tickets for the Hall, neglected to provide themselves in the way suggested. At length an extraordinary Gazette was published, formally confirming the statement which had been previously made. This order was seen but by few till the Tuesday preceding the Coronation, and when it was once generally known, the confusion it produced was truly comic, although to some not a little mortifying. The ladies rushed in swarms to their mantua makers, and innumerable dresses, which had pined in solitude for months before, were suddenly drawn forth, and launched into unexpected gaiety. One good effect was produced in many instances, in which heavy sums were standing in the mantua makers' books, against the fair votaries of fashion, but which were now immediately discharged, as a bribe to execute the completion of the coronation dress *in time*. Wretched indeed was, however, the fate of the poor dress makers on this occasion; torn fifty ways at once, they scarcely knew how to act, and at last were incapable of meeting one half the claims of their urgent customers, who were in consequence obliged either to brave the criticism of their acquaintance, by appearing at the Coronation in tasteless attire, or altogether to sacrifice at the shrine of fashion.

But still more distressing was the situation of the gentlemen, hundreds of whom never had the honour of wearing a court dress, or perhaps even of seeing one, but who on the occasion were resolved to make any sacrifice for the sake of testifying their loyalty. Orders innumerable, with promises of immediate payment, surprised and delighted the whole fraternity of the tailors; and the farce of the "Devil among the Tailors" was got up with great eclat in every part of the metropolis. Another class of tradesmen were not less fortunate; we allude to those convenient circulating costumaries which are to be found in sundry parts of the town, where dresses of all sorts, civil, military, and ecclesiastical, may be had at five minutes notice. It was no matter whether the dress fitted the wearer—it was a court dress, and that was sufficient. But the most comical and laughable circumstance which attended the demand for court dresses, was the metamorphosis which was produced by the shifts to which some were obliged to recur in order to appear in the proper costume. The same lawyers who but a short time before had been seen parading the cold and cheerless flags of Westminster Hall, were now to be seen adorned in all the glittering finery of the dress of a Field-marshal; the effeminate coxcomb strutted his hour in the dress of the hussar; the trading citizen in the sombre canonicals of the divine; the contemner and the despiser of courts and of court fashions, became at once the courtier in his spangled dress. The chapeau, the bag, and the sword, particularly the latter, became with many unmanageable; in some cases it was seen pendent on the right side, which was consequently the wrong one; and in many cases it intruded itself between the legs of its awkward wearer, laying him prostrate on the ground, and the lives of his Majesty's most loyal subjects were often set at hazard from the bloodless points of the citizens' swords. Indeed it came very near the humours of a masquerade, to see the bedizened lawyer or the citizen tripping along the streets in all the paraphernalia of a court; for, unlike the coronation of George III. at which the price of coaches and sedan chairs was regulated by an official order, in the present instance the most extravagant prices were asked for vehicles of the most wretched appearance, and these could not always be procured, from which untoward circumstance several of the newly created courtiers were constrained to perambulate the streets, to the infinite amusement of the crowd, and particularly of the impudent coachman, who did not fail to crack his joke at their expense, and ultimately obliged them either to dive into their own coat pockets, or into the first convenient corner in which they could conceal their blushing honours.

On the whole it was a fine field for the contemplatist, who saw in the whole of it a grand epitome of human life, in which men in general are inclined to assume a character which does not belong to them, and which they have neither talents nor education to sustain.

We must now advert to circumstances of a more official nature connected with the approaching ceremony, and the regular and formal manner in which they were promulgated, tended to dissipate the doubts which were at this time beginning to rise in the minds of the people, as to the precise day on which the ceremony would be solemnized.

In the *Gazette* of the 14th of June, it was announced that his Majesty had been pleased to appoint Peter Robert Lord Gwydir to exercise the office of Great Chamberlain of England, until a sufficient deputy to exercise the said office shall be nominated by the Baroness Willoughby, of Eresby, and the Marchioness of Cholmondeley, coheiresses of the said office, and approved by his Majesty, or until his Majesty's pleasure shall be further signified.

His lordship, in consequence of his appointment, was sworn in a member of the Privy Council.

The following gentlemen were elected to be Barons of the Cinque Ports, and two ancient towns, to perform the canopy service at the Coronation:—

Hastings—The Hon. William Henry John Scott; James Dawkins, Esq.; Edward Milward, Esq.

Sandwich—Joseph Stewart, Esq.; Charles Emmerson, Esq.; George Noakes, Esq.

Dover—E. B. Wilbraham, Esq.; Henshaw Latham, Esq.

Romney—Benjamin Cobb, Esq.; Cholmeley Dering, Esq.

Hythe—Stewart Majoribanks, Esq.; William Deedes, jun. Esq.

Rye—William Phillips Lamb, Esq.; John Dodson, Esq.

Winchelsea—H. Brougham, Esq.; Lucius Concannon, Esq.

Lord Calthorpe was appointed to carry the gold spurs at the Coronation; and the Earl of Abergavenny to execute by deputy the office of his Majesty's Chief Larderer. The Marquis of Exeter to execute the office of Lord High Almoner.

A warrant of dispensation was passed to enable the several Knights Grand Crosses of the Bath, nominated since the last installation, 1st of June, 1812, to wear the collar, mantle, and the order, as though actually and formally installed.

Government undertook to provide for each Knight Grand Cross, a superb crimson satin mantle, lined with white taffeta, and the star embroidered on the left shoulder, a black velvet hat, a sword and belt, and a pair of gilt spurs.

In like manner government provided for the Knights Commanders who attended the solemnity, a short crimson satin mantle, with the star of the second class of the Order embroidered thereon, and fastened by a gold cordon, sword and belt, black velvet hat, and a pair of spurs.

The Knight Grand Crosses who were Privy Counsellors, were not to walk in the procession in the dress of the Privy Counsellors, but in the full habit of the Order.

We have great pleasure in recording this circumstance, as by the noble achievements of those individuals in the late war, they have fully entitled themselves to this proud distinction.

It was ordered by his Majesty that the entire band of Gentlemen Pensioners should attend his Coronation; and the following is contained in a letter from a member of that honourable corps:

" The dress allotted us for the Coronation is particularly gay. The original picture exhibiting the dress was painted by Vertue, representing Lord Hunsdon in the dress, and is, I believe, now in Sherborne-castle. His Majesty has been very particular in ordering our's to be exactly like it. The jacket and short breeches are of scarlet cloth, covered with several hundred yards of narrow gold lace, and have besides one thousand two hundred small sugar-loaf buttons on each dress. The puffs or sashes are of light blue velvet; scarlet silk stockings, black shoes with rosettes; straight antique looking sword; a short mantle, edged with gold bullion, and fastened by an immense bow of gold cord on the left shoulder, something like an aiguilette; Elizabeth's ruff round the neck; and a bonnet with three white feathers, with scarlet satin puckered round the crown, and turned up in front with a gold loop. The dresses are all ready; and I am given to understand each will cost two hundred pounds. The above dress is to be worn on state occasions only, and our present one is to be worn on ordinary ones."

His Majesty was pleased to appoint the following young noblemen, elder sons of peers, to be his train-bearers:—the Marquis of Douro, son of the Duke of Wellington; Earl of Rawdon, son of the Marquis of Hastings; Earl of Brecknock, son of the Marquis of Camden; Viscount Ingestrie, son of the Earl of Talbot; Earl of Rocksavage, son of the Marquis of

Cholmondeley; Viscount Cranbourne, son of the Marquis of Salisbury; Earl of Surrey, son of the Duke of Norfolk; and the Earl of Uxbridge, son of the Marquis of Anglesea.

An important question having arisen as to the attendance of the Irish peers, not being members of either the House of Lords or Commons, but who still sat in the House of Lords of Ireland, previous to the union, the following Order in Council was inserted in the *Gazette*:—

The King's Most Excellent Majesty in Council having been pleased to command me, as Deputy Earl Marshal of England, forthwith to prepare and countersign letters to be passed under the Royal sign-manual, requiring the attendance, at the solemnity of his Majesty's Royal Coronation, of all the Peers of Great Britain; and his Majesty having been further pleased to command me to prepare such letters also for such temporal Peers of that part of the United Kingdom of Great Britain and Ireland, called Ireland, who sat and voted in the House of Lords of Ireland before the Union, or whose right to sit and vote therein, or to vote at the election of a representative Peer for Ireland has, on claim made on their behalf, been admitted, or shall, on or before the last day of the present session of Parliament, be admitted by the House of Lords of the United Kingdom, and who are not now members of the House of Commons of the United Kingdom, I do hereby request that all those Peers who, in conformity to the above regulations, are or may be entitled to assist at the solemnity of his Majesty's Royal Coronation, will be pleased forthwith to transmit their respective addresses to Sir George Nayler, Clarencieux King of Arms, at the Heralds-College, in order that their letters of summons may be forwarded without delay.

HENRY HOWARD MOLYNEUX-HOWARD,
Deputy Earl Marshal.

We have on a former occasion adverted to the duties of the Earl Marshal, a very arduous part of which consists in summoning the persons who are to take part in the procession on the day of Coronation, and in making arrangement for the issue of tickets for the Hall and Abbey. In order, therefore, to obviate a greater part of the difficulty, the following Orders in Councils were issued:—

Council-Office, Whitehall, June 27, 1821.—These are to give notice, that all such Peeresses, or Widows of Peers of the United Kingdom of Great Britain and Ireland, as intend to see the solemnity of his Majesty's Royal Coronation, in Westminster-Hall, do forthwith send their names to the Right Honourable Lord Gwydir, Deputy Great Chamberlain of England; and such of them as desire to see it in the Abbey, do send their names to the Right Honourable Lord Henry Howard Molyneux-Howard, Deputy Earl Marshal of England, to the end that places may be provided for them.

JAMES BULLER.

Heralds-College, June 30, 1821.—In pursuance of an Order in Council, bearing date the 27th day of June instant, I do hereby give notice to all Peers, Privy Councillors, and others, claiming to have tickets at the ensuing solemnity of his Majesty's Royal Coronation, that (it being necessary to know beforehand the number of persons for whom accommodation is to be provided) no tickets will be issued to any Peers, Privy Councillors, or others, who shall not have signified to me, on or before Saturday the 7th of July next, his or their intention of attending at the said solemnity.

HENRY HOWARD MOLYNEUX-HOWARD,
Deputy Earl Marshal of England.

And it was determined by the Lords of the Council, that each Peer who had signified his intention to be present shall receive five tickets; Privy Councillors, not Peers, four tickets; Knights of the Grand Cross, three tickets; Knights Commanders of the Bath, two tickets; and Clerks in Council, two tickets.

Amongst the various offices which were to be filled at the Coronation, considerable interest was used by the ladies to procure that of herb-woman to his Majesty. It was finally granted to Miss Fellows, sister to Mr. Fellowes, Secretary to the Lord Great Chamberlain, pursuant to a promise which was made to her while his Majesty was yet Prince of Wales. Sandford, who is consulted as an oracle on the subject of the coronation of the kings of England, does not specify the precise manner in which this duty is to be performed; but he represents the principal herb-woman with the royal arms embroidered on her left breast.

In consequence of her appointment, Miss Fellows received the badge which she was to wear on this solemn occasion. It was of gold, and was to be suspended from her neck by a gold chain. It bore an inscription, indicative of her office, on the one side, and the King's arms on the other, beautifully chased.

The six young ladies chosen by Miss Fellowes as her maids—Miss Garth, Miss Collier, Miss Ramsbottom, Miss Hill, Miss Daniel, and Miss Walker. Their costume was white. Miss Fellowes, in addition, wore a scarlet mantle, trimmed with gold lace. Mr. Jenkinson, of the Mary-le-bone Nursery, was engaged to furnish the flowers for the occasion, which consisted of the most choice and rare exotics.

While these preliminary matters were adjusting, a most important question began to be discussed, touching the coronation of the Queen; and a report began to be circulated that her Majesty had actually presented a memorial to the King in Council, formally preferring her claim to be crowned as Queen Consort, in like manner with her royal predecessors, as a matter of right which she was not entitled to waive. This claim resolves itself into a question of constitutional law, touching the prerogative of the crown.

It was for some time doubted that such a memorial had been presented to his Majesty, until the grant to the Duke of Clarence became the subject of parliamentary discussion, and as in a Committee of Supply, it is the privilege of the members to touch upon every subject in which the expenditure of the country is concerned, the expenses of the Coronation became the subject of investigation, and it led in consequence to a very strict examination of the grounds on which the Queen was refused a participation in the ceremonies of the Coronation.

By degrees the fact was elicited from the ministers, that a memorial had actually been presented to his Majesty, from the Queen, which was as follows:—

To the King's Most Excellent Majesty in Council assembled.

The memorial of her Majesty the Queen,

Sheweth, that your Majesty has, by your proclamation, bearing date at Carlton-house, the 9th day of June instant, declared your royal will and pleasure to celebrate the solemnity of your royal Coronation upon Thursday, the 19th day of July next, at your palace at Westminster; but that directions have not been given for the coronation of the Queen, as hath heretofore been accustomed on the like occasions.

That divers of your Majesty's subjects, by ancient customs and usages of these realms, as also in regard of divers tenures of sundry manors, lands, and other hereditaments, do claim, and are bound to do and perform divers services on the day and at the time of the coronation of the Queen Consort of these realms, as in times precedent of their ancestors, and as those from whom they claim, have done and performed at the coronation of the Queen Consort in times past.

That the Queen most dutifully claims, as of right, to celebrate the ceremony of her royal coronation; and to preserve, as well her Majesty's said right, as the aforesaid lawful rights and inheritances of others of your Majesty's subjects.

The Queen respectfully prays, that your Majesty will be graciously pleased forthwith to issue your royal proclamation, thereby to appoint the same 19th day of July next, at Westminster aforesaid, to celebrate the ceremony of her coronation as Queen Consort, and to direct that all such as by the said customs and usages and tenures are bound to do and perform the services aforesaid, do duly give their attendances accordingly at the said day and time of the coronation aforesaid, in all respects furnished as to so great a solemnity appertaineth, and answerable to the dignities and places which every one of them holdeth and enjoyeth; and further, that your Majesty will be graciously pleased to issue your royal commission under your great seal, appointing commissioners to receive, hear, and determine, the petitions and claims which shall be made to them in this behalf.

And the Queen as in duty bound shall ever pray.

It was rather a fortunate circumstance, as far as the coronation of the Queen was concerned, that the Duke of Clarence's Annuity Bill was then passing through the House, as the opposition members took the opportunity of the Bill passing through its respective stages, to enforce the claim of her Majesty to be crowned, and to extract, if possible, a categorical answer from the ministers as to the positive line of conduct which they intended to pursue respecting the claim of the Queen. Thus, when the report of the Duke's Annuity Bill was brought up, Sir R. Ferguson said, he should give his decided negative to the grant for the arrears, and at the same time wished to ask if her Majesty was to be crowned?

The Marquis of Londonderry said, an application had been made by her Majesty some days ago; but that the law officers, to whom it was referred, had not yet given their answer. As far as he was aware, there was no intention that her Majesty should participate in that ceremony.

Mr. Denman thought it extraordinary that no positive answer was given to the application of her Majesty, and that it should have remained unanswered from Monday till Saturday. Full time ought to be given to her Majesty to assert her claims before the council. He was not disposed to say any thing on the policy of a coronation taking place; but this he could safely say, that unless her Majesty participated in it, it would lose the greater part of its interest and importance.

The Marquis of Londonderry was surprised her Majesty's legal advisers should have so long stood still, and not have brought her Majesty's claim forward. His Majesty's ministers gave the best advice they could to their Royal Master, and they certainly could not advise that her Majesty should share the august ceremony. It was only as matter of favour that her Majesty could be crowned; and that favour they could not advise their Royal Master to confer.

Mr. Denman observed, it would have been very unbecoming in her Majesty's legal advisers to have put forward her claim, until it was ascertained whether the coronation would take place or not. The same appearances were seen a year ago, when it was not quite certain, whether they were for a coronation of the King or the degradation of his Royal Wife. He still complained of the delay which took place in an swering the memorials of her Majesty. Courtesy at all events should have dictated a different line of conduct, if the exalted station of a Queen of England could not command attention. He saw no reason why any delay should have occurred, when it was known what were the opinions of his Majesty's ministers. He could hope but little from the council to whom her Majesty had addressed her memorials.

The Marquis of Londonderry said, there was somewhat of mystery, if not of inattention, on the part of her Majesty's legal advisers. If she had a right, it should have been asserted before.

Mr. Scarlett wished to know if her Majesty claimed to be heard by counsel, or not? There was only one instance in which a Queen was not crowned. The wife of Charles I. was not crowned because she was a Catholic, and in the then state of the times it would have been dangerous to introduce a Popish Priest to perform the ceremony for her.

The Marquis of Londonderry begged not to be understood as giving an opinion on this subject. As a privy councillor he was bound to secrecy; but he could assure the honourable member, that any claim of her Majesty would be fully attended to.

Mr. Denman said her Majesty had sent two memorials which were not answered, in consequence of which a letter was sent this day, and as yet no reply was given to it.

The Marquis of Londonderry said, although his Majesty's ministers might have formed their opinion some time since against the right, they were still bound, when a grave application was made to give it full consideration.

Col. Davies wished to know the probable expense of the Coronation? He thought a vain, idle pageant, for it was nothing else, ought not to take place, particularly when it imposed such a burden on the people.

The Chancellor of the Exchequer replied that 100,000*l.* was provided for last session, and though something additional might be proposed next session, it would not be a very large addition.

In the House of Lords, Lord Grosvenor, on Lord Darnley's motion for an address to his Majesty on the present distresses of the country, took occasion to observe that, one source of additional expense was the approaching Coronation. It had been estimated at 100,000*l*. but it was apparent, and it had indeed since been admitted, that it would exceed that sum. He thought the measure unnecessary and injudicious, and that it ought not to have been recommended by the advisers of the Crown under present circumstances. For, even supposing that the law was clear, and declared in positive terms, that the Queen had no right to be crowned, still, as a matter of grace, he thought it was injudicious to recommend a coronation, from which she should be excluded. The ground on which her right was contested, was the single precedent of Henry VII. having been crowned alone, when it was supposed that his marriage with the Queen had been celebrated. But this ground must fail, for the marriage of that monarch had only taken place after his coronation, so that there was at the time no queen to be crowned. He had heard also, that the procession, at the approaching ceremony, was to be hemmed in on all sides by soldiers. That would be the greatest insult which could be put both upon the King and the people of this country.—It would make him appear like an Oriental despot, moving in the midst of his satraps. He should wish to see the Monarch surrounded by hosts of hearts, and not by hosts of bayonets.

On the 2nd of July, a second memorial was sent by her Majesty addressed to the King, desiring to be heard by her counsel in support of her claim; which memorial, although it carried on the face of it a great informality, was yet immediately laid before his Majesty, who was pleased to allow the prayer of the Queen, and summonses were immediately issued to the members of the Privy Council, to meet in their

Chamber at Whitehall, on the following Thursday, the 5th of July.

On the evening of the day on which the above memorial was presented, the Duke of Clarence's Annuity Bill again became the subject of discussion in the House of Commons, when Mr. Brougham entered into an explanation of the alleged delay imputed to her Majesty, in claiming to be crowned. On the 21st of May a question had been put by Mr. Monck on the subject, to which the noble marquis had replied, that there was no right so clear as that of the Crown; and that the coronation of the Queen Consort depended upon the grace and favour of the King. He (Mr. Brougham) at that time protested against the doctrine of the noble marquis. In candour, however, he must say, that he added, he had not made up his own mind on the legal question. It was not the duty of her Majesty's law officers to put in her claim immediately upon this. It was their duty to wait her orders, as they were not her responsible advisers like the ministers of the crown. Besides, as the coronation had been appointed in the preceding year, and had been postponed, it became proper to wait until there was almost a certainty of its actually taking place. The proclamation appointing the ceremony this year was dated the 9th of June; and inserted in the Gazette on the 12th. The memorial claiming her Majesty's right to be crowned, was settled at his (Mr. Brougham's) chambers eleven days afterwards, and upon a subject of such great importance he was not disposed to take any great blame to himself for a delay of eleven days. The memorial was sent in on the 25th of May, and as yet no answer had been returned to it. There was now seventeen days to intervene before the coronation, but there was ample time to alter the arrangements, and yet keep strictly within precedents. There was an instance on record, of a proclamation giving only sixteen days notice of the coronation itself; and another, of an alteration in the arrange-

T

ments being ordered only two days before the appointed day.

The Marquis of Londonderry said, he had not intended any reflection on her Majesty's legal advisers in their professional character. He had merely contrasted the rapidity with which they had expected an answer, with the slowness of their own movements in making the legal claim. The 21st of May, which had been particularly alluded to by the honourable and learned member, was not the only occasion on which the opinion of his Majesty's ministers had been intimated to the Queen. Between that day and the 21st of June, her Majesty addressed a letter to the principal minister, the Earl of Liverpool, desiring to be informed what arrangements had been made for her convenience, and who were appointed as her attendants on the approaching solemnity. An official answer had been returned, stating, that it was a right of the Crown to give or withhold the order of her Majesty's coronation, and that his Majesty would be advised not to make any order for her Majesty's participation in the arrangements. The Queen rejoined, insisting on her right, and declaring that she should attend the Coronation, unless she were absolutely prevented. A respectful, but equally peremptory answer was returned to her Majesty, repeating the legal right of the Crown, and declaring, that the former answer must be understood as amounting to a prohibition of her attendance. These proceedings clearly showed that her Majesty was fully aware of the course intended to be taken by the government. Now, with these facts before the House, he would ask whether it was not rather hard to call ministers over the coals, and blame them for the delay. Respecting the hearing of her Majesty's law officers before the Privy Council in support of the claim, he had to state to the House, that this had been asked that very morning for the first time. A memorial dated on Saturday last, had that morning been received from her Majesty addressed to the King, and desiring to be heard by her counsel in support of the claim. This, however, was informally addressed, it being addressed to the King in his Sovereign capacity, and not to the King in Council. It would have shown a want of respect to her Majesty's claim, if, when it had been formally presented, it was not referred to the legal officers of the Crown. Both applications were equally informal; but they both had been attended to. Upon the first, her Majesty had been informed that no directions would be given to include her in the arrangements; and with respect to that which had only been received this morning, he had to inform the House, that it was immediately laid before his Majesty, who had given direction that the Queen should be heard by her lawyers before the Privy Council, it being first clearly ascertained, that this was no right; but was a grace and favour. This he mentioned to show that there really had been no delay on the part of government, and to justify the course they had taken.

The public attention was now drawn for a short time from the extensive preparations for the Coronation, which were drawing rapidly to a conclusion, to the meeting of the Privy Council, in which the important question of the Queen's claim to be crowned was to be decided; and it was the general opinion that, if the claim was established, the Coronation would be postponed *sine die*.

On Thursday morning, the 5th, precisely at ten o'clock, the Privy Council assembled in their Chamber at Whitehall; upwards of forty members of the council were present, and a few minutes after ten, the memorial of her Majesty was read, and then the order in council, that her Majesty should be heard by counsel, in compliance with the prayer of that memorial.

Mr. Brougham then rose. He observed, that he had a communication to make, to which he claimed their lordships' attention. He had a very short time since heard that there was a book deposited with the Dean and Chapter of Westminster, called the "*Liber Regalis*," which was a written formula of the ceremonies to be observed at the coronation of a sovereign. Her Majesty's counsel had lost no time in applying for permission to examine this record; but their application was not attended with that courteous facility of access, which they had to acknowledge the kindness of receiving in other quarters of reference that it became necessary for them to make in behalf of her Majesty during their research. The Dean and Chapter, replied to the application of her Majesty's counsel to see the *Liber Regalis*, that they would not grant the request without legal sanction. In answer to a second application, for the purpose of knowing what they would consider as sufficient authority, they replied, that the authority they required was "the highest authority." Application was again made to them to know what they considered to be the highest authority, and the reply was "either the crown or a court of law." Application was then made to some of the members of the Privy Council, but no conclusive answer being returned, and the process by *mandamus* in a court of law being necessarily tedious, and liable to stand over until the last day of term, he had now to apply to the Council, either that their lordships would use the influence of their authority to obtain the book, or that they would allow her Majesty's claim to stand over until the process of law should obtain the desired object. His opinion was, that the Privy Council, if they were pleased to exercise it, had the authority to order the production of this book; for, on the 25th Feb. 1684, they ordered the Lord Keeper and other Commissioners of Records, to produce them before the Council, relating to the Coronation of James II.

The Lord-Chancellor said, that the book might be sent for, but it was for the learned counsel to endeavour to make out his right so far as he could do so from such other sources as he had examined, and to show that the *Liber Regalis* contained matter essential to his purpose.

Mr. Brougham said, that he had in the Cotton manuscripts seen collections stated to have been extracted from the book, and from them he assumed the book itself to be material for his purpose.

The Earl of Harrowby said they should send to the Dean and Chapter, and Mr. Brougham might go on in the mean time, subject to a future reference of his extracts with the original, if he deemed it necessary to refer to them in his argument before the arrival of the book from the Dean and Chapter.

After a short conversation as to the form of proceeding between the Lord-Chancellor, the Earl of Harrowby, and Mr. Brougham, the latter said he would, as it seemed to be the opinion of their lordships, proceed with his argument without at present delaying the Council until the arrival of the book.

Mr. Brougham then proceeded to address the Council upon her Majesty's right. He was occupied for a considerable portion of time in tracing the Saxon successions through the ceremonial history of their coronations, which were celebrated during their reigns. He pursued the same line of inquiry through the several Norman-reigns down to the reign of King John, pointing out, from the bearing of circumstances connected with the solemnized coronations, the general policy which guided them, the principle of right as it regarded the Queens, which was established by them, together with the motives and accidents which had caused any seeming interruption of the acknowledgment of that right on particular occasions. He found, that down to the time of Henry III. there had been eight coronations of Kings of England solemnized without the coronation of their Queens, and that there had been eight coronations of Queens, with or without Kings, celebrated for those Queens, alone, and without any commixture of the same solemnities performed at the time on behalf of the Kings. There had been eight Kings, including William Rufus, who died unmarried, crowned without Queens; and in the same period of time had there been eight Queens crowned without Kings. Henry III. was crowned in 1220, before he was married. Having wedded Eleanor, January 14, 1236, she was crowned alone, in about six days after, the King himself being present, to do the ceremony the more honour, not in the exercise of his power as Sovereign of the realms, but as one of the highest rank in the state; and, according to Matthew Prior, the sword of Edward the Confessor, called the Sword Curtanea, was carried before him as a token of the authority of the Constable of the Palace, the particular function of which was to prevent any thing from being done wrong in the course of the ceremony. The learned counsel then went on to refer to the subsequent reigns down to the period of Henry VII., during all which time, he contended that the right of a Queen to be crowned had been, by a variety of acts, distinctly recognised. Upon the reign and coronation of Henry VII. it would be necessary for him to make more than one observation. It was well known that that Prince held the throne by the three-fold claim of marriage, conquest, and descent. Lord Bacon remarked that he (Henry VII.) always considered descent as the principal claim, and that he considered the other two as only casualties compared with that of descent. He had, as the same writer observed, always placed descent as the shield, and conquest and marriage as his supporters.' All his adherents of the Lancaster party upheld his pretensions on the claim of descent. The King's claim *de facto* was constituted by Act of Parliament to be *de jure* even after. Not only Henry and his adherents, but that which was the only legitimate organ to which their lordships could attend, the Parliament, held the claim of descent to be the highest of the three. Henry caused himself to be crowned, however, before he made any application to Parliament, in 1485. Parliament sat a few days after. The

Act was passed which entailed the Crown, limiting the succession to Henry VII. and the direct heirs of his body. He was declared to have a full and perfect right to the crown, and no mention was made of the Princess Elizabeth, and it was kept as a matter of doubt whether she was to be Queen or not, his policy being to avoid that marriage, if it were possible. It was even said that he was in treaty for another Princess, and still he continued to defer celebrating the marriage as long as he could. He was not married till 1486. A very remarkable delay then took place in the coronation of the Queen, who was, it was to, be observed, a Princess, and the daughter of Edward IV. Great doubts were entertained, and much discontent was excited by this delay. She was attended and treated in all respects as Queen Consort. Now, the more jealous Henry had been of her pretensions being mingled with his own, the more anxious he was to avoid meeting Parliament until he had confirmed his own claim,—the more solicitous he had been to defer the marriage, the more likely he was to avoid doing any thing after, which might seem to imply even a notion of the Queen's rights with respect to the crown. She was always treated as the Queen Consort, and Lord Bacon had remarked that Henry's marriage to her had occasioned much more triumph and rejoicing than his own entry or coronation, which, his lordship further remarked, the King rather suffered than liked. The delay of her coronation was found to give great umbrage. And here he would show what were the feelings of the country, and especially of the Queen's party, on the occasion, by referring to a then living authority. Margaret of York, aunt to Elizabeth, afterwards married to the Duke of Burgundy, had these remarks among the reflections which she made upon the events of those times, " She could not," she said, " see without trouble, that Henry refused to let Elizabeth be crowned (an honour which no Queen of England had been debarred of since the Conquest), and that the birth of a son had

not rendered him at all more indulgent or just in his
conduct towards her." He could not appeal to a
better authority than that of an aged and royal woman, the aunt of the reigning Queen, the last fortress
and prop of the Lancasters, zealous of the rights which
belonged to her family, and fearful of any thing which
appeared to slight their claims. She had passed the
less active moments of her life in study and meditation
on the history of her family, conscious of all which
had transpired in the course of that history, and especially of the facts which connected her family with
the Crown. There could be no better witness to show
what had been the sense of former times, what understanding had existed respecting the rights and usages
of those times in reference to Queens of England
She maintained that Queen Elizabeth ought to be
crowned, as every other Queen Consort had been before her. Henry VII. at length yielded to public
feeling, and the Queen was crowned 25th November,
1487. Lord Bacon said that it was an old christening
which had stood long for godfathers, and his lordship
gave his readers to understand that it went much
against the King's stomach. The coronation was ordered in the very same forms and words in which two
years and eight months before the King's own coronation had been. Up to this period, from the Conquest, there had been nineteen Kings crowned. Of
these, eighteen were married before or after the coronation, and of these marriages the eighteen Queens
were all crowned. The learned counsel next applied
himself to the reign of Henry VIII. and submitted
that there was sufficient, from the State Ecclesiastical
affairs, as well as from the peculiar manner in which
Henry had got rid of one set of wives and taken another, to render it absolutely impossible for him to
force the coronation of the latter upon his people in
the then state of society. Having then done with these
cases, he was now come to a period when he was
better able to feel his way, and when the facts to which
he should have occasion to allude were more defined

and better authenticated. It would be his duty to refer their lordships to a most curious and valuable work which was in the British Museum, in the Harleian Collection. In this were contained the whole particulars of the coronation of Charles I., and the ceremonial of that occasion furnished several facts calculated to throw light upon the present question. From that it appeared, that up to a very short time preceding the coronation, the King had determined that his Royal Consort should be crowned with him. This, however, did not take place; but the grounds upon which her absence was to be accounted for were distinct and decisive. He submitted, that the Queen not being crowned with her husband arose, in a great measure, from her own indisposition—or more properly, her scrupulous aversion to be present at a ceremony performed in a religion different from her own. It was unnecessary to tell this Court, that Henrietta Maria, wife to Charles I. being a daughter of the King of France was in her religion a Roman Catholic. Her history was an eventful one, and the sufferings which she afterwards experienced, and great part of which were induced by her attachment to the tenets of that religion, proved that she was not only professedly a Roman Catholic, but that she was also a most scrupulous believer in, and uncompromising stickler for the infallibility of that religion. Charles, as the head of a Protestant State, was necessarily a Protestant, and the laws of this country required that the ceremony should be performed by the hands of a Metropolitan of the Church of England. In these times religious animosities ran very high, and Charles, whose conduct had already given the people cause to dislike him, seemed only to want this ill-omened marriage with the daughter of the King of France to aggravate that feeling, for by it, he added religious jealousy to political distrust. At all events, it would seem that the King was carried along by circumstances, and that if he did forbid his wife to be crowned with him, it was, perhaps, more in compliance with the feelings of the times, and more to allay party heats, than from any conclusions drawn from considerations of her right to assist at the ceremony. It was sufficient that she was a Papist—the people would exclude her on that ground only, and, whatever justice there was in her claims, the King did not think it advisable at that particular time to aggravate the misunderstanding between him and the people by recognising her right to be crowned with him. That he wished her to partake in the ceremony, there was no doubt, but it was possible that, for the reasons stated, he was induced to give the design up. This was possible; but it was more than probable that the Queen's own scruples of religion weighed with her on this occasion. She could not be insensible of the dislike which the people felt towards her on account of her religion; and it could not be her wish, as it certainly was not her interest, to aggravate that feeling. The nature of the ceremony too, into which so much of religious form necessarily entered, was disagreeable to her, as being inconsistent with the tenets of her faith. If, however, it was the fact, that the Queen, for certain objects, was forced and compelled to be absent from the coronation, such force and compulsion in place of weakening, materially strengthened his argument. If the Queen acted under the influence of her own feelings, it accounted safely for him; she made the objection, which was so far a waiver of her right; but the doing so could not apply to any future Queen Consort, who ought not and could not be affected by her act. The next case he came to, formed no exception to the general custom which he established, because the Queen of Charles II. was a Papist—himself a Protestant, added to which he was unmarried at the time of his coronation. He now came to the revolution, since which period all Queens Consort were invariably crowned, and he was not called on to make any observations. With respect, however, to the queen of George I. she never came to this country; she never was called queen, nor known as queen, and was further said to have been divorced by a foreign Ecclesiastical Court before her husband was crowned; it was, therefore, doubly impossible that she should be crowned; it was legally impossible if she were divorced; it was physically impossible if she never came here. With regard then to the institution of any proceedings, he humbly took it that the settled law could not be altered by them. On this point he should merely allude to a case which was argued in the House of Lords, where a person was said to have been found guilty, but never had sentence passed. On that occasion one of the learned judges said, " If a man be found guilty, and has no sentence passed on him, he must be looked upon as being as innocent as if no charge were made against him." He should be ashamed to occupy the time of their lordships in enforcing this very proper principle, for nothing was clearer than this, that the laws knew no difference between complete guilt or complete innocence.

Here the learned counsel referred to the *Liber Regalis* in the possession of the Dean of Westminster, for entries of the coronations, and on expressing his wish for its production, the court was ordered to be cleared. In less than a quarter of an hour the book was offered for his inspection. The Dean of Westminster was then asked by one of the council, if there were any other books containing any similar entry; to which he replied, there was no other, except the great Mass Book, which contained the ceremony used on those occasions. The Misal was then sent for, and counsel called in.

After some observations on the time which would be necessary for Mr. Brougham to conclude his argument, the Court was adjourned to Friday.

Accordingly the Council met again on the following morning, pursuant to adjournment, when Mr. Brougham resumed. He reminded their lordships, that he had proved this proposition as one of fact, namely, that a Queen Consort had in all ages been crowned; and that there was no instance of a married King being crowned, without his Consort partaking of the solemnity. The single case of Charles I. formed an exception, but, coupled with the reasons for its omission, it could not affect his case:—on the contrary, he contended his right to assume, that a Queen Consort had in all times been crowned. It must be manifest that one or two instances, in a long succession of ages, may exist, in which this ceremony did not take place. Supposing, however, the fact to be so—supposing the husbands of Queens Consort to be crowned, and Queens Consort not—then, according to all the rules of evidence—according to all the rules of probability on which men judge and act in common affairs—according to all the rules of strictly legal evidence, must those instances be no more than exceptions; and exceptions could not prevail against a general rule. Here there was no doubt of the right being asserted, still less of its being waived or given up. But with regard to the other exceptions, they were confined to mere omissions, to non-usual or non-claim; and if he could show that in ninety-nine cases out of a hundred the right was enjoyed when it could be so, it would be in vain to argue that in the hundredth case it was not so. Every thing was in his favour in the majority of instances, and therefore he must take the general usage and immemorial custom to be altogether conclusive as to the right of a Queen Consort's being crowned. In instances of omission, or non-enjoyment, the presumption would evidently be, that if all the circumstances producing them were known they could be satisfactorily explained. The waiver of her right, so far from showing its non-existence, merely proved the abstaining from its use for certain reasons of the party so waiving it. A long state of waiver would be a very different thing; but here there was an uniformity of enjoyment, except in the case of the wife of Charles I.; and even if he failed in explaining the grounds on which it became an exception, he could not imagine how it should affect the mass of cases the other way. It could not be denied that there were interruptions of right; but in looking to the subject of right itself there were three stages which should be adverted to; the first was simple usage; the next was where the right was contested but might nevertheless be enjoyed (and this was one of the ninety-nine cases out of the hundred which he had already put); and the third consideration was the assertion and adjudication, or a denial of right. Here he should admit that the claim and refusal would be more fatal to the right than the mere admission of its existence coupled with a denial, if its exercise would be in its favour. But in this case the enjoyment was uniform, and the interruption casual; there were ninety-nine cases one way, and the hundredth the other, and it would surely be an inversion of all reasoning to say that the hundredth should prevail against the ninety-nine! There were, however, instances where interruption was attempted, and where it failed. Henry II. was crowned without the Princess his wife, on which she complained to her family, and the remonstrance was attended with the effect she wished, and she had a coronation. There was also another instance of attempted interruption in the case of the wife of Henry VII.: he thought to debar her of being crowned; but that failed, and sooner or later she was crowned. Now, he asked, in what other way could any right be proved than that in which he had proved the right of a Queen Consort to be crowned? How could the Court of Claims sit to adjudicate, and in fact adjudicate, except on the very same evidence on which he relied? For instance, no one denied the claim of the Barons of the Cinque Ports to perform certain offices at the Coronation, but why and how? From custom—from usage; from that custom and that usage which carried his case much farther back than theirs. He should like to hear any man say, if the Barons had not preferred their claim that their omission to do so would be a forfeiture of the right, in virtue of which they might have claimed? It would be monstrous to say so, and to act on such a doctrine would be a violation of every legal and every christian principle. Here there was custom, here was enjoyment countervailing interruption and omission; and why should one exception, and only one, countervail the claim of the Queen Consort to be crowned, where the common practice was in her favour? The Queen Consort had a distinct, substantive, independent right of being crowned, and the performance of a coronation was considered as essential for her as for the King, if history were to be credited. There were numerous instances in which Queens were separately crowned—instances which were undenied: while there was only one solitary instance in which, either with or without the husband, a Queen was not crowned. The wife of Henry III. was crowned alone, as were the wives of Edward III. and Richard II. These Coronations showed the independence and substantiveness of the Queen's right, and were not at all performed as accessaries to the Coronation of the King. The uniformity of its performance was so remarkable, that even where a King married the second time, the second wife had a Coronation performed, at which the King to show his respect for her usually attended. This showed at all events a something (and if he could not explain why he did not think it made at all against his argument) —he repeated that it certainly showed a something which rendered it necessary to perform the ceremony independent of the King—he bearing no part in it, as actually occurred in some of the cases he had so often mentioned. He was not exactly prepared to show by what tests it could be demonstrated, that the Coronation of a Queen Consort was not accessary on that of the King—nor did he think himself at all bound to do so. This, however, appeared evident, that they never enjoyed this right at the mere will and pleasure of the other party; that they had a part in the same ceremony was true, but that they had a distinct ceremony was also true. There were beside substantive and independent rights held by others in virtue of certain offices performed by them at the Queen's Coronation; and of the right to which they might be deprived, if such ceremony should not take place.—It was exactly the same with respect to the Coronation of the King—a ceremony, the origin of which was lost in the remoteness of antiquity. But in consequence of certain duties to be performed at that ceremony, other persons held distinct rights, the exercise of which they would be denied, unless in the event of its performance. These were the only grounds, independent of principle, which could be assigned for a King's Coronation at all taking place. There was an old-established custom to sanction it, and other persons enjoyed other rights by virtue of its performance; but beyond these there were no authority for its occurring. The King's Coronation he took to be for the satisfaction of the realm, not the gratification of the individual. The Coronation of the Queen was exactly on the same footing. The Sovereign, as such, being a creature of the law, these ceremonies were but creatures also, and the King's high office was only given him to exercise its rights for the benefit of the realm. Those who were prepared to say the Queen's Coronation depended on the will and pleasure of the King, could only get rid of it by admitting that it is no more than an empty ceremony, an insignificant pageant; it must be so if it depended solely on an individual's will. The chapter of a King's rights, as a private individual, was small indeed. The law drew out the acts of a Sovereign from that condition, and lawyers were astute to bring out his public, rather than his natural capacity. How then, he asked, could the Coronation be taken as a personal act? Why was the Sovereign to be crowned at all, except on immemorial usage, all the Kings of England having been crowned, with the exception of Edward V. to whom the ceremony was physically impossible? Immemorial custom as strongly pleaded for the Coronation of a Queen Consort as for a King her husband—and yet they were now to be told that the King had a right at his mere will and pleasure of preventing his Queen from participating in that ceremony? A Coronation did not always tread closely on an accession, and if it could be delayed for a year or two, there could not be that necessity for it, which he had no doubt he should hear stated at the other side. He had mentioned the rights held by other persons in consequence of the Coronation of the Queen Consort, and whether those rights were great or little, the law bestowed on them an equal consideration. After some further legal arguments in support of his proposition, the learned counsel proceeded to remark, that the question for decision was one strictly of law, and happy he was that he had to address able lawyers, amongst others, on the subject. The facts which had lately occurred had a tendency to interrupt the peace, and agitate the temper of society. With that agitation an assembly like that he now addressed had nothing to do; their views should be directed to after times, when all agitation had ceased on the subject, and the judgment of that Court would remain alone to explain to them the reasons of an otherwise unintelligible decision. As we now calmly considered and contemplated the Saxon records, undisturbed by Norman jealousy or prejudices, posterity will then sit in fearful judgment on the character of the lawyers of the 19th century. They will (said he) look to their judgment with the anxiety which the importance of the question demands. May they look to it with that confidence which their great names are calculated to inspire!

Mr. Denman next addressed the Council in a most powerful and eloquent speech. The ceremony of the coronation, he said, was a religious ceremony—a solemn compact between the King and his people. In a free country like this, much of authority depended on the recollections which the people entertained of their Sovereigns, and their predecessors in the kingly dignity. The recollection constituted a part of the pride and property of the subject, who felt there was a just dignity in seeing these rights upheld in all the splendour of their antiquity. Every government must suffer a proportionate, and no small loss, as it possessed less of the sacred protecting influence of this principle. Such had been the deep toned reflections of a traveller of celebrity; who in his research through the States of America, during its most flourishing period, felt constantly the loss his condition sustained from the absence of all recollections connected with antiquity or the past. Such, too, had been the feeling of that extraordinary individual, whose death had only just been announced, who with powers unrivalled, great energy of mind, and supported by the achievement of acts, which were more illustrious and felicitous than ever before immortalized a soldier's name, still felt that he was unable, without a reference to the recollection of the past, to found a nobility, which he had the prudence to perceive was necessary to a monarchy in France. The justice of this inference might be proved from the sentiment of our own poet; when he said in a popular work—

" This is the English, not the Turkish court,
Not Amurath succeeds to Amurath,
But Harry, Harry."

The law of Kings in this respect was custom. There was no law to convene the subjects of the realm to witness the imposition of the crown on the Royal brow. Selden, in his work, called " Titles of Honour," thought these distinctions not unworthy of the application of his great talents. In page 190, speaking of the Coronation of the Emperors, he says; he shall be on his elevation to the dignity, crowned, *si forte non habuerit uxorem;* distinctly adding, *Si uxorem habuerit, eam necesse est coronari, conduci in ecclesiam, et debet prosterni ante altaria,* &c. The prerogative and rights of the Queen, were traced by this very able author through several Saxon institations to the ordinance of Ethelwolf, which, for reasons of policy, deprived the consort of the King of the title and style of Queen, and confined it to that of *conjux*. This exception, however, which proved the rule, never prevailed except in that King's time. Throughout this work one monition was constant and unvarying, namely, that no departure should ever be attempted with respect to the ancient observances and customary forms on such extraordinary occasions. His learned friend's research had reached through the kingly history from William I. to the present time. He should recur to the principle on which rested the recognition of the Royal quality of a Queen. He, in the next place, should advert to her as the mother of those heirs who were in future to reign over the subject. There had, in early times, been always great disputes as to the succession—a misfortune which was rendered the more frequent, owing to the habits of Kings in those days, as well as by the custom of bethrothing illustrious young persons together at a very early age, who were afterwards permitted to dissent from these engagements at a more mature period of life. These disputes also not unfrequently arose out of the interference of the church, whilst it was Catholic, as to the validity of marriages contracted within certain degrees of consanguinity. So Mathew Paris in his history stated, that in the case of Arbysa the Archbishop interposed, and protested before King John she was not his lawful wife. That marriage was annulled. Considerable doubts, too, had prevailed with respect to the connexion of Charles II. with Mrs. Waters, whom it was supposed he had married, which would have legitimated his son the Duke of Monmouth. The public were never satisfied until the King publicly disclaimed such a marriage. The case of George I. would suffice to show that where a Monarch of another country came over to this country with a wife to assume the Royal authority, that it was necessary a public Coronation should take place to set the matter at rest for ever. The cases of twenty-seven Queens of England all crowned with their husbands, if previously married, bore most strongly on this question. There was but one exception, namely—that of Henrietta Maria, the Consort of Charles I. William the Conqueror, was crowned alone, his Duchy being in Normandy; William II. died unmarried; Henry I. was crowned with his wife; Henry II. was thrice crowned, at London, Lincoln, and Warwick, at each of his sons' births; Richard was crowned in Cyprus with his Queen Bellingeria; Henry III. was crowned alone; all the other Monarchs up to Henry VIII. were similarly crowned with their wives, if they were married; this last was certainly no very desirable precedent to quote as to the treatment of a royal wife. Besides, such was the unsettled state of things about this time, that it may very fairly be doubted whether, after the death of Anne Boleyn, any one dared to say there was any church in this country, or not, at the hazard of their lives. Three out of four of this King's wives were his own subjects; the fourth, Anne of Cleves, was so glad to be separated from him, that she acceded to a proposition to be considered and addressed as his sister. The case of Henrietta Maria was one of great peculiarity; she was a Papist, and came into England at a period when that religion was peculiarly obnoxious and detested, and when all the laws against Popish recusants were in full vigour and malignancy: for Charles I. to have issued a proclamation for her being crowned, would have brought on himself all the weight of unpopularity, and in the minds of the public have excited unappeasable alarm. His acquiescence in the popular prejudice should not be taken as a precedent against the present claim, where all the precedents, save this, were on the opposite side. The custom of the realm was part of the common law of the land, to which even the King himself was subject. "*Nihil aliud potest rex, quam quod de jure potest.*" Lord Coke had said that a King could not create a King within the realm, as in the case of Beauchamp, created King of the Isle of Wight by Henry VI. Nothing, in fact, but an act of the Legislature could alter the law of the land. The Coronation was a solemnity in which his Majesty took an oath to observe the laws and customs of this realm. It should not, therefore, be slightly altered, and it would be indeed dangerous to say, that the King had it in his power to exclude the highest subject in the land, and rob the ceremony of some of its most imposing features by doing so. Her Majesty founded her right to be crowned upon custom, and if custom was not secure there was nothing secure in the country. " The Crown itself," continued Mr. Denman, " is supported by custom. Why do we now submit to a King, or to the government of a King ? Because at all times a King had subsisted in this country; because time beyond memory proves that a kingly government had been the practice of England. Nothing, therefore, can be more dangerous than a separation of the privileges and rights which custom has interwoven with the very nature and existence of those institutions. Why do Juries daily decide upon the properties and lives of their fellow men ? Why do the Peers assemble in the House of Lords, or the Commons in their House? Or why do the King, Lords, and Commons legislate for us and the people of this kingdom ? It is because custom, long fixed established custom, has sanctioned all these institutions. If custom be destroyed, away with titles, dignities, offices, property, and all that is valuable to us as subjects and as men. Prescriptive right alone preserves us from anarchy and confusion. I say not this to derogate from the value of those possessions, but to add to their support; to prove that they are founded upon the surest grounds, the soundest principles that guide the human heart. But without the consequences, it is impossible that we should enjoy the benefit of the principles ; if we admit the premises, we must also admit the deductions. Remove, therefore, the landmarks of custom, and away with all the grounds of allegiance and obedience; all the pillars of society will be shaken, and we shall be plunged amidst the ruin of all the institutions into that state of confusion which we all deprecate and which we all abhor." That case was so strong, that in no court of justice could it be got over. The claim which her Majesty had put forth was in self-defence; she could not forego it without sacrificing her honour, which was dearer to her than life. Had she been contented to purchase tranquillity with the loss of that honour, she might have done so: she might have retired into peace and obscurity; but that magnanimity which had always regulated her conduct, which was peculiar to her character, prohibited such an act. Her case was now in the hands of their lordships, and there he placed it with confidence. Her Majesty looked forward to their decision with equal confidence, and without suspicion; for under all circumstances she was prepared to submit to it with cheerful resignation.

After Mr. Denman had concluded, Mr. Brougham stated that he had certain documents to lay before the Court; which were received, on condition that they should, if required, be compared with the original, and proved to be correct.

Lord Harrowby then stated, that the Court had agreed to adjourn to to-morrow morning at 10 o'clock, when the Attorney and Solicitor-General were to be heard, in reply to the arguments which had already been advanced at the bar.

The Council met pursuant to adjournment. The Chamber was again crowded to excess.

The Attorney-General said, that it was his duty to show their lordships that the claim, as one of right, which had been so strenuously asserted and attempted to be proved by the Queen's Attorney-General, that her Majesty, as Queen Consort, had a legal right to enjoy the ceremony of the Coronation, was not only not a legal right, but one altogether derivative and permissive. The claim, he was prepared to contend, was altogether unfounded. He could find no traces

of it extant, as a legal right, in any of the recognised
authorities, where it doubtless would be found if it
had the legal foundation ascribed to it. He could
not find it mentioned in the works of the legal or constitutional writers who had set forth or touched upon
the privileges of the Queen Consort. The grounds
(or rather the single ground) upon which her Majesty's claim has been put, was that of usage—and it
was said by the Queen's Attorney-General, that long-
continued usage established both legal and constitutional right. But if he proved that here the usage
was not original, but derivative, then there was an end
at once to the claim set up on the ground of usage.
His (the Attorney-General's) arguments must be necessarily long and protracted, but he entreated, at the
outset, that their lordships would attend to him,
while he showed, in the first instance, how the ceremony of the Coronation was constructed, how it was
used both for a King and for a Queen, and how the
very nature of the ceremony itself precluded the existence of the claim of right asserted on the part of a
Queen Consort. If they attended to all the parts
composing the ceremony of the Coronation, they
would clearly find, that the allotted part to the Queen
Consort was an honour intended for her by the King,
and not one which was inherent in her own dignity.
In illustration of this part of his argument, he should
have to call their lordships' attention to the ceremony
of the King's Coronation, and then, as separate from
it, to that of the Queen Consort. They could then
examine how far the ceremonies supported the right
now claimed on the ground of usage. Their lordships
had heard from the Queen's Attorney-General an elaborate and accurate detail of the probable origin of
the ceremony of the coronation, and that it originally
sprung from the elective title of the early monarchs
to the crown. The Coronation, as it stood when
more solemnly regulated and prescribed, was, no
doubt, intended to be somewhat of a political act, that
is, the solemn covenant on the part of the King, with

all the solemnity of an oath, that he should uphold the rights and liberties of the people; and the people on the other hand, by their assent, ratified and confirmed the King's title to the throne. It was, therefore, so far as the King was concerned, a political act, from which no minister would advise a Sovereign to abstain; but with respect to the Queen, it had no political character, but must be altogether considered as a mere political ceremony. The Queen had no political character: she was not recognised as such by any legal writer, ancient or modern. There was not, in fact, any political character assigned to her in the state. Why, therefore, have any ceremony to connect or confirm any compact between her and the people, when the law did not recognise her character in any political manner. She could in fact, as Queen Consort, do no political act; and Lord Coke, in Caloin's case, asserted, that even with respect to the King, the ceremony was merely voluntary upon his part, for that the right of inheritance actually descended to the King upon the death of his predecessor, and that he then became fully and absolutely King, without any *ex post facto* act. The Coronation of the King therefore was, according to Lord Coke, a mere ordinance, and no necessary or essential recognition of his right to the throne by hereditary descent—and Lord Coke adds, that it was so settled by the twelve judges at the time, that the King's right was integral and complete without the Coronation, or any outward solemnity. The opinion of Lord Coke upon that point was fully adopted by Lord Hale. If such were the mature and legal construction of the act before the statute of William and Mary, how did that statute affect the case, so as to give a new principle to the Coronation?. If it did not, as he contended, by a reference to the statute, so far as the King's ceremony was concerned, then as to Queen's *a fortiori*, it could make no alteration. Indeed, the whole of the ceremony of the Queen's Coronation was an adjunct to the King's, and not a distinct solemnity recognising any right to enjoy it on the part of the Queen Consort.. It was in vain to plead that there were tenures and rights held by persons which were dependant upon the Coronation of the Queen Consort; so there were upon the King's; but nobody would assert that if there were no Coronation, those rights would be forfeited—they were only to be performed if the Coronation took place; if it did not, and the King refrained from the Coronation, then, of course, there could be no forfeiture of the rights or tenures: so the argument founded upon them went for nothing. The longest passage respecting the ceremony of a Coronation was to be found in Selden: it was the most elaborate detail of all the matters connected with the ceremony. Mr. Selden referred, in his chapter of " Honours," to the time of the Roman Emperors; and his argument, so far as it bore upon the question of a Queen Consort, was entirely with his (the Attorney-General's) view of the present case. He particularly alluded to the remarks upon the title of Augusta being conferred upon the wives of the Roman Emperors, but clearly and uniformly showing that that, as well as all other honours. assigned the Empresses, were conferred by the will and pleasure of their imperial husbands. Referring to the general historical argument of the Queen's Attorney-General, and his narrative of the long series of Coronations which had undoubtedly taken place, it still remained to be proved how far the solemnities respecting the Queens, from the Saxon annals downwards, took place as a matter of right. In Selden it would be found that the ceremony respecting the Queen was called " her Consecration," and clearly done by order of the King; the words were after stating what was to be done by " *reverendissima pater,*" and then " *postulamus reginam,*" all this the bishop was to do " by order of the King." In fact, he could not too often contend that the Queen Consort, as of right, had just the same claim to demand the Coronation of the King, as she had that of herself. He should now come to the Scottish Act of Parliament of James I. which had been quoted by the Queen's Attorney-General. Now, upon reference to that act, it was clear that James I. owing to the troubled state of the times, and being about to leave Scotland, was most anxious to confer upon his Queen the ceremony of the Coronation.

The whole order emanated from the desire of the King himself. It was from him the letters of fidelity were ordered to be " prometted" to the Queen. He again asserted that, according to the construction of the ceremony in Selden, and Pinkerton, no claim of right could be made out for the Queen. Among the old law writers, Bracton was, perhaps, the most copious upon the prerogatives of the Queen; but he did not, in the slightest degree, hint to her having any right to the Coronation; he did not enumerate any one part of that ceremony as appertaining to her legal rights. Bracton had stated her being in law *a femme sole*; he had stated her claims to the *aura reginæ*; but he was wholly silent about Coronation prerogatives. He had a long chapter, *De Coronation a Regis*, but not a word as a matter of right *De Coronation a Reginæ*. The Attorney-General then followed Mr. Brougham through his series of historical precedents. He would, he said, first advert to the case of William the First, whose wife was not crowned at the time; why not? Because the King did not think it right, so to order it, though he did subsequently. Did not that clearly show the right to be in the King? Rufus, not being married, furnished no case. Then Stephen, why was not his wife crowned with him? He was married at the time of his Coronation: and yet her's did not take place for some time afterwards. Why was that delay, if the Queen could claim as of right? He then adverted to the circumstance of Prince Henry's Coronation, in Henry the Second's lifetime; and said that that proved nothing, although Louis of France remonstrated, for unless the Princess could have demanded her husband's Coronation, during his father's life-time, how could she have

Y

any claim to demand her own. There was every reason why the wife of Henry VII. should be crowned. There was a strong party in the country anxious to put forward and support the York interest, through which Henry was considered to derive his best title to the throne; and even under such strong circumstances in favour of his Queen being crowned, he refused it for a considerable time. Now Bacon's words on that subject should be looked to with the closest attention, inasmuch as they clearly showed that that Coronation was nothing more than a mere ceremony. He referred their lordships to Bacon's Works, vol. 3, quarto edition, in which they would find that great man say, " that Henry's conduct to the Yorkists alienated his subjects from him, and that, even after a son was born to him, he did not vouchsafe his Queen the honour of a matrimonial crown. It was not until two years afterwards that the troubles and contentions of the times taught him what he ought to do." Now he asked, if the Queen had a right to be crowned, would the word " vouchsafe" have been used? Most decidedly not. If the right existed, he would have been bound to have her crowned. Bacon continued to give the reasons why Henry " vouchsafed" a Coronation—namely, " because of the heart-burnings and contentions which had arisen, in consequence of his depressing the friends of the York party. And wishing to give contentment to his people in the ceremony of a Coronation, he resolved that no further delay should occur. There again their lordships would find the Coronation called nothing more than a ceremony, and they would also see, that its being granted or not, depended altogether on the will and pleasure of the Sovereign. Bacon was not merely an historian, but an able lawyer, and if the Queen had a right to be crowned, it is pretty manifest that he would not altogether have omitted to notice it. All the attempts which were made at the other side to explain this circumstance had totally failed; while in support of his argument, he required no other authority to show those two leading points; first, that the Queen had no right to be crowned; and secondly, that her Coronation was merely a matter of ceremony. Henry VIII. had only two wives crowned, and four who were not crowned—and as far as that case went—what was to be said of uniform usage? and the more so when it was considered how often the practice was interrupted from time to time. His first Queen and Anne Boleyn were the only two of Henry's consorts who were crowned. Lady Jane Seymour, who was the mother of his son, (for which he was so anxious)—she who was one of his greatest favourites, was not crowned; and if the ceremony of a Coronation were necessary as a public recognition of the Queen, what reason was there in that case, of all others, that it should not have been performed? It was either a right or not a right: if it were a right, it could not be abstained from; if it were not a right, it was nothing more than a ceremony, and depended on the will of the Sovereign. If it were a right, and connected, as it was said to be, with the rights of the people, it could not be waived as it had been on so many different occasions. Some reasons were advanced by his learned friends, as explanatory of the causes that prevented four of Henry's Queens from being crowned, such as the disturbed state of the church, and other matters; but if the Coronation of a Queen were a right in her, and not a ceremony, the disturbed state of the church was no sufficient reason. He could well apprehend how the disturbed state of the church, and attachment to Anne Boleyn, would operate on the mind of the Sovereign to prevent the Coronation of his favourite wife Lady Jane Seymour; but it could only have been done so, in consequence of its depending on his free-will to have it performed or not. If it were a right, he contended that no motives of expediency or state policy could have prevented it. Now as to Charles I. though Rushworth gave a very precise account of the solemnity of his Coronation, he was totally silent as to the Queen; and no writer had since stated that she was crowned. There was, it was true, in the Harleian Collection, an account of her Coronation; but it was evidently drawn up prospectively—for a something to be done—but not for any thing which was passed and had been done. It said, amongst other things, that two thrones were to be erected, one for the King; and one below that, and of a smaller size, for the Queen: some of the Queen's dresses were also described; but no man, who looked attentively at the record, could deny its being written before the event. From some curious manuscript letters preserved in the British Museum, it would appear that the Coronation was described as having taken place on a Thursday; that the King went to Westminster Church by water; but that the Queen was not crowned. On the contrary, the letters went on to say, that she stood at a window, in the neighbourhood, looking on, while her ladies were frisking and dancing in the room. Taking all the accounts together, there could be no doubt that the wife of Charles I. was never crowned. If it were in the breast of the King to say whether the Coronation should or should not take place, *cadet questio*, the question fell all at once to the ground. It was probable enough, that she objected to certain parts of the ceremony; but if she had the independent right which was now contended for, she could not have waived it; and that especially, because it would be involving the rights of others. The ground of waiver could not exist as to a public right; and if it were so, it was decisive against the claim which was now put forward. With respect to the uniformity on which such force was laid, it proved nothing, if the being crowned was not a right, while the deviations did every thing to put an end to the question of right; and the Coronation of a Queen Consort became mere matter of discretion in the Monarch. Charles II. was not married till after his own Coronation. Some doubt was thrown upon the fact of his having been ever married by a Protestant bishop; but though the historians of the times were silent as to the transaction, he found from a newspaper, called " The King's Intelligence," published in 1662, that the King was married at Portsmouth, by Gilbert, Bishop of London. The " Mercurius Politicus," another paper published at the same time, also corroborated the fact. If this were the case then, there was an end to his wife's objections to share his Coronation. For, if she had no scruple at being married by a Protestant, she could have no objection to be crowned by a Protestant. There were in her case peculiar circumstances, which rendered it very necessary she should be crowned, and if it were a matter of right it would most certainly have been performed. The fact however was, she never had the ceremony of a Coronation performed for her. Talking of the usage in these cases,—four of the wives of Henry VIII. were not crowned; the wife of Charles I. was not crowned, neither was the wife of Charles II., nor of George I.: these then were some instances where Queens Consort were not crowned since the time of Henry VII., and so far against the usage, he had a majority of cases. In seven instances the ceremony was not performed, in six instances it was—and this was the real current of the usage. Such deviations evidently made against the right which his learned friends contended for; and got rid of the inference arising from usage, on which alone the right was founded. The forms used in the Coronation also showed, that the crowning of Queens Consort was entirely at the discretion of their royal husbands. The case of Edward II. as related in Rymer, was referred to; but, although the writ of summons required the presence of those summoned in honour of his wife and himself, the ceremony itself took no notice of that fact. The term *ordinabimus* would not have been used in the mandate of the King, if it were not the will of the King; and very nearly the same phraseology was to be found in all our modern proclamations. " We have resolved" was always used, from the time of Charles I. to the present day, following as nearly as possible the old forms which were adopted. All this showed that the Coronation proceeded from the King, and did not exist as a matter of right in the Queen. The *Liber Regalis* was considered by his learned friend as a very valuable instrument to show the ceremonies of the Coronation; but he asked him, did he therefore mean to contend there was any fixed or settled ceremonial for all Coronations? The law knew no fixed ceremony—it was subject to the revision of the head of the church, directed by an order of council. It was also said by his learned friend, that certain offices were holden in consequence of the Coronation of the Queen; but he replied to that, that they were by no means dependant on that event. These tenures were not granted of the Queen, but of the King, and the services for which they were given might be dispensed with by the King. With respect to the offices, the same observation might be made. If the ceremony were not performed, these persons would not be called on; if it were performed, as he had just said, the King could dispense with their attendance. Looking again to the general language of the proclamations, it abundantly appeared to him, that the right of having a Coronation only existed in the Sovereign. With respect to the prize act, which was referred to, it had no analogy to the present case; besides, it here appeared that the Queen claimed to be crowned on a particular day. He had argued against the existence of the right at any time, and hoped by this time that he had satisfied their lordships no such right existed. He was afraid he had not done the case that justice which its importance required. But the fact was he found himself as others who argued cases in the courts of law did, namely, that of finding a greater difficulty in arguing a clear case than one of perplexity. And if he failed of throwing any additional light upon the subject, he hoped it would be attributed to its proper cause. His learned friend, the Queen's Attorney-General, had certainly delivered to their lordships a most able and historical detail, with the main facts of which he coincided ; but with the conclusions drawn from which he totally differed. The claim now made, was made for the first time ; and if it were of such great importance to her and to the people, it was strange to find no law writer mention a syllable on the subject. It was not attempted to be supported by any statuary enactments—by any dictum of law—by any passage in any able text writer—but depended entirely for its support on usage, and usage only. Though the Queen was high both in dignity and privilege, it should not be forgotten that she was still no more than a subject. The Queen had no political character which required that she should be known or recognised at the Coronation ; and, on all these grounds, he had no hesitation in saying, her Majesty had no claim of right to be present at that ceremony.

The Solicitor-General said, that coinciding as he did with the opinions just delivered by his learned friend,—having given their opinions together upon the subject before, having consulted the same documents and pursued the same inquiry, it would be impossible to expect that he should throw any additional light upon it. The only argument used in support of this claim was that of uninterrupted use and enjoyment; but when looking to the right claimed, their lordships should be satisfied of the circumstances under which the use and enjoyment were said to give it. The learned counsel for the Queen should have shown when this right was claimed, and exercised as such ; and also, that it was not conferred by the grace and favour of the crown. The case of right of way and common, which was introduced, rather made against than for the claim now asserted, because it might have been a hostile right or an act of usurpation. Even a case might arise out of the very ceremonial, which rested on the same principle as the present claim—he alluded to the case of persons summoned to attend the Coronation. But would it be said, because certain persons usually were summoned, it was absolutely necessary they should now be called? If this claim were admitted, these persons must be called; if it were not necessary they should be so called, this claim must then of necessity be refused. Beside this, the language of the proclamations, which scarcely varied since the time of Charles I., all tended to show that the right of having a Coronation performed, was altogether at the will and discretion of the King. "We have decreed" is the language which they used —and how this could be reconciled with the substantive independent right of the Queen, he was totally at a loss to imagine. Were the Privy Council to take the usage by itself to support the right, or draw the inference of right from usage in connexion with the circumstances compounded with it? The latter appeared to him to be the course which their lordships ought to pursue; and in doing so, then they would have to consider whether it was a right enjoyed by licence and authority from the crown, or an adverse right claimed independently of the crown. In the very outset of the case, there was one circumstance which afforded strong evidence that negatived the right in respect of usage; he alluded to the necessity of a royal proclamation. The force of this was felt by his learned friend, Mr. Brougham, who endeavoured to evade it with great dexterity, and at the same time to misapply it in favour of his own argument; for he said that when once the right was established, the proclamation must issue as a matter of course. This was a complete fallacy. His learned friend the Attorney-General and himself reverted to this circumstance, merely for the purpose of showing in what manner the right was enjoyed, namely—by permission, by consent, by authority, and by the command of the Sovereign; and for the purpose of showing that the proclamation was to be taken, in connexion with the usage, to establish the right. It really appeared to him that the case, when considered, resolved itself into a dry, technical point of law (though surrounded by circumstances of great splendour and pomp), and must be treated as all courts of justice treated such questions. The claim, in this case, was founded upon uniform usage, and unless it was clearly established that such an usage existed, the claim must fall to the ground. The authority of Lord Bacon, already referred to—a great and learned lawyer, a contemporary historian of the times of which he wrote, and perfectly conversant with the subject of which he treated, was decisive to show that the Queens Consort had no right, as matter of usage, to be crowned; but that when she was crowned, it was a matter of grace and favour conceded to her by her royal husband. Another concurrent authority to the same point, was Leland's Collectanea, in the Cotton manuscripts of the British Museum. His learned friend, after all his industry and research upon the historical part of the case, completely failed in making out the uniform usage on which he relied. Under the Saxon line, the privilege of Coronation had long existed before it was communicated to the Queens Consort. According to the authority of Selden, it did not take place at all until after the tenth century, and then proceeded entirely from the King, as matter of grace and favour. This was perfectly manifest from reference to every instance from the time of the Norman Conquest. William the Conqueror was married at the time he came to the throne. The Queen of Stephen was not crowned with him; but it was said by his learned friends, that there was a necessity and a convenience why Stephen should be crowned alone. Why this very assertion was an argument in favour of the view he took of the case, for if this was an inherent right in Matilda, no necessity or convenience could deprive her of it. Henry II. was married when he came to the throne, and he was not crowned until a very considerable period after his accession, because he considered that he held by so strong a title that there was no necessity for hastening his Coronation. Their lordships would always keep in view, that this claim was founded upon uniform and immemorial usage. The fact was, that Henry II.

came to the throne in December, 1154, and he was not crowned until 1158, and his Queen was not crowned until 1159. The argument founded upon immemorial usage, in this instance therefore completely failed. Then as to the instance of Prince Henry, the Coronation of his Princess took place in consequence of the remonstrance of Lewis, who thought that the abstaining to crown his daughter with her husband was a reflection upon his own Royal dignity, and therefore the ceremony took place, but only in the light of favour and grace. So much then as to that historical fact. As to the case of John, he was married at the time of his Coronation, but his wife, Elizabeth of Gloucester, was not crowned with him. It was said, however, that the reason why she was not crowned, was, because John was then seeking the hand of Isabella of Angouleme in marriage. That was not the fact, because the thoughts of his courtship with that Princess were not entertained until a whole year after his Coronation. He was crowned in the month of May, 1199, and it was not until the month of May, 1200, that his attachment for Isabella began. It was said that there were some doubts as to the validity of John's marriage with his first wife, but history proved that he lived with her nine years afterwards. From the period of the Conquest, therefore, there were four Kings who were married at the time of their respective Coronation, and not one of their four Queens was crowned with her consort. These were facts too stubborn, even for his learned friend's ingenuity, great as it was, to grapple with. He should add nothing more to what had been said by the Attorney-General as to the case of Henry VII. It was quite clear that that monarch delayed his marriage as long as policy and expediency would suggest. That brought him to the reign of Henry VIII. and the learned solicitor repeated all the observations made by his learned coadjutor, upon the different marriages of that monarch, to show that the argument in support of the right in respect of uninterrupted usage was not bottomed in fact. It was no sufficient reason why Henry VIII. did not crown Lady Jane Seymour, his favourite wife, as it had been said, that the church was then in a disturbed and distracted state; for never were the clergy of this country in so abject a state of tyranny and thraldom as at that time, when the Monarch took upon himself, with his own hand, to alter the Mass-book; and nothing could have been more easy for him than to command the performance of the august ceremony. The solution of the difficulty, therefore, resorted to by his learned friends, availed them nothing. Next as to the case of Charles I.; it was perfectly certain that his wife Henrietta was not crowned with him. If that Queen was entitled to be crowned, as a matter of right, she could not have waived it; but being a matter in the pleasure of the King, it was quite easy to assign a sufficient reason for her not being crowned. The learned Solicitor-General, in the remainder of his argument, followed precisely the course adopted by his learned coadjutor, and contended that the usage relied upon having completely failed in proof, and being directly contrary to the opinions of the ablest lawyers and historians who had written upon the privileges of the Queens Consort of these realms, the claim set up by her present Majesty must be disallowed.

Mr. Brougham after retiring for a few minutes, with the permission of the council, then replied to the arguments of the Attorney and Solicitor-General in a very able and eloquent address, which we regret we are unable to give in detail. His learned friends were mistaken in supposing that he relied upon the necessity of a proclamation issuing, as evidence of the Queen's right to be crowned. He had merely mentioned it by way of anticipating the argument which might be drawn from it on the other side, and of rebutting the presumption which would probably be raised upon it. He contended that the language of the usual proclamation on such occasions was merely the mode of allowing the right, which was to be considered as *ex debitum justitia*, and not *ex gratia*. The like language was used in writs of error and other writs, which of right belonged to the subject. In this point of view, the proclamation was to be considered merely as a writ of coronation, conferring no favour on the Queen, but giving her that which she had a right to demand. He then reinforced many of the arguments which he had used in opening her Majesty's case, for the purpose of contrasting them with what had been urged on the other side, and contended, that he had not been removed from the ground on which he originally stood. The honourable and learned gentleman then proceeded to submit, that no instance had been adduced in which a Queen had claimed her right to be crowned, and in which that claim had been refused; and unless such an instance could be adduced, he apprehended the position for which he had been contending remained unshaken. The contrary doctrine which had been laid down, was a mere asumption, without a scintilla of proof. Whether the question of right were admitted or not, there still remained the question of expediency, upon which he had not ventured to offer a single remark. It would be for those to whom he addressed himself to decide, whether in point of propriety, and he humbly conceived it would be all but criminal to refuse, they would hesitate to advise the Sovereign to conform to established usage—or whether they would advise him to be the first monarch to set an example, under such circumstances, of omitting so to do.

At the conclusion of the learned gentleman's reply strangers were ordered to withdraw; after which it was announced that the Council had adjourned to Tuesday morning at ten o'clock, on which day they will decide on the question at issue.

The neighbourhood of Whitehall was crowded all the afternoon by persons anxious to know whether the Council had formed their determination.

The anxiety of the public was now upon the

stretch, to ascertain the decision of the Privy Council on her Majesty's claim, as on that decision rested the positive determination of the time when the ceremony of the Coronation of her Majesty was to take place.

Tuesday, at ten o'clock, the Privy Council re-assembled at the Cockpit, Whitehall. The several passages leading to the Council Chamber were thronged with persons who were desirous of hearing the proceedings, but they were informed that strangers would not be admitted; even the Counsel and Solicitors were excluded. Besides the Lords of the Council, Mr. Buller, the Clerk, only was present. It soon afterwards became necessary to remove the strangers from the passages immediately contiguous to the Cockpit, to enable the Members of the Privy Council to pass to the Chamber.

Amongst the Lords of the Council present were—the Duke of York, the Archbishop of Canterbury, Lord Harrowby (President), the Marquis of Londonderry, the Earls of Liverpool, Lauderdale, and Donoughmore, Lord Sidmouth, Sir H. Russell, the Lord-Chancellor, Sir T. Plomer (the Master of the Rolls), the Chief Justices of the King's Bench and Common Pleas, Chief Baron Richards, the Hon. F. Robinson, &c.

At a quarter past ten o'clock, the Council proceeded to the consideration of the case. Mr. Buller was desired to take in the documentary evidence adduced by Mr. Brougham on behalf of the Queen; the Records brought from the Tower, the *Liber Regalis*, and several other ancient volumes. The doors continued closed, and strangers were not allowed to remain in the adjoining rooms and passages.

The Attorney and Solicitor-General, Mr. Brougham, Mr. Denman, and Mr. Williams, were in attendance in anti-rooms, but they were not in their Barrister's costume.

It will be recollected, that the Memorial was addressed " To the King's most excellent Majesty in Council assembled;" so that in the event of the

Lords in Council coming to any decision, judgment could not be given till it had the approbation of the King. Arrangements, however, were made to forward the result to his Majesty, for his sanction, immediately that any opinion was pronounced, in order that no unnecessary delay might take place in the promulgation of the decision.

At eleven o'clock his Majesty's Attorney and Solicitor-General were called into the Privy Council; but Mr. Brougham still remained in the anti-room.

The King's Law Officers remained with the Council till about a quarter past eleven. They then withdrew.

The Privy Council continued its sitting till half-past eleven, when it adjourned. No communication was made, or could be made, for the reason previously stated, to the Queen's Law Agents, of any decision that had been come to; but it was understood that the Marquis of Londonderry and the Earl of Liverpool were to convey to his Majesty the judgment of the Privy Council on the subject.

DECISION OF THE PRIVY COUNCIL
In regard to the Queen's Claim to be Crowned.
(OFFICIAL.)

At the Court at Carlton House, the 10th July, 1820, present, the King's Most Excellent Majesty in Council.

Whereas, there was this day read at the Board, a Report from a Committee of the Lords of his Majesty's Most Honourable Privy Council, in the words following, viz:—

"Your Majesty having been pleased, by your Order in Council of the 3d of this instant, to refer unto this Committee the several Memorials of her Majesty the Queen claiming a right to be crowned on the same day and at the same place which has been appointed for the Coronation of your Majesty, and praying to be heard by Counsel in support of the said Claim; the Lords of the Committee, in obedience to your Majesty's said order of reference, have accordingly heard her Majesty's Attorney and Solicitor-General in support of her Majesty's said Claim, and having also heard the observations of your Majesty's Attorney and Solicitor-General thereupon, their Lordships do agree humbly to report to your Majesty, their opinions, that as it appears to them that the Queens Consort of this realm are not entitled of right to be crowned at any time, her Majesty the Queen is not entitled as of right to be crowned at the time specified in her Majesty's Memorials."

His Majesty having taken this said Report into consideration, has been pleased, by and with the advice of his Privy Council, to approve thereof.

(Signed) C. C. GRENVILLE.

On the receipt of this official notice of the Privy Council, her Majesty despatched the following letter to Lord Sidmouth:

"*Brandenburgh House, July* 11, 1821.

"MY LORD,—I have received your Lordship's Letter of yesterday, to Lord Hood, conveying to me the Report of the Committee of Council on my Memorial to the King in Council, claiming my right to be crowned; and as I find the Committee positively denies that right which I have claimed, and which all Queens Consort have enjoyed (without one exception arising from the will of the Sovereign), I consider it necessary to inform your Lordship, that it is my intention to be present at the Ceremony on the 19th, the day fixed for his Majesty's Coronation, and I therefore demand that a suitable place may be appointed for me.

(Signed) "CAROLINE R."

"To the Right Hon. Lord Viscount Sidmouth."

The following reply was immediately forwarded to the Queen without a signature:

"*Whitehall, July* 12, 1821.

"MADAM,—I have laid before the King your Majesty's letter to me of the 11th of this month, in which it is stated that your Majesty considers it necessary to inform me, that it is your Majesty's intention to be present at the ceremony of the 19th, the day fixed for his Majesty's Coronation, and you therefore demand that a suitable place may be appointed for your Majesty; and I am commanded by the King to refer your Majesty to the Earl of Liverpool's letter to your Majesty of the 7th of May last, and to acquaint your Majesty that it is not his Majesty's pleasure to comply with the application contained in your Majesty's letter.

Letter alluded to in the foregoing :

"*Fife House, 7th May,* 1821.

" Lord Liverpool has received the King's commands, in consequence of the last communication of the Queen to Lord Liverpool of the 5th inst. to inform the Queen, that his Majesty having determined that the Queen shall form no part of the ceremonial of his Coronation, it is therefore his Royal Pleasure, that the Queen shall not attend the said ceremony."

To the above letter her Majesty replied :—

"*Brandenburgh House, July* 13, 1821, *five o'clock, P. M.*

" MY LORD,—I have this instant received a letter, dated Whitehall, July 13th, without any signature. I therefore consider it as anonymous, and shall treat it as such till I hear from your Lordship. CAROLINE R.

" To the Right Hon. Lord Viscount Sidmouth."

The omission of the signature of Lord Sidmouth was eagerly seized upon by a particular party, and converted into a premeditated insult upon her Majesty. It was, however, purely accidental. The letter was taken off his lordship's table, and folded up under the idea that it was signed as usual. Immediately upon it being returned by the Queen, his lordship's signature was affixed, and the letter again forwarded to her Majesty.

Lord Hood then wrote to the Duke of Norfolk, as Earl Marshal of England, informing him that it was her Majesty's intention to be at Westminster Abbey at half past 8 o'clock in the morning of the 19th, and requested him to have persons in attendance, to conduct her Majesty to her seat. The Duke of Norfolk in his answer, referred her Majesty to the acting Earl Marshal, Lord Howard of Effingham, who, after laying the subject before Lord Sidmouth, informed the Queen that he could not comply with her Majesty's commands to appoint a place for her at the Coronation. Her Majesty then wrote a letter to the Archbishop of Canterbury, in which she informed him of her desire to be crowned some days after the

King, and before the arrangements were done away with, so that there might be no additional expense. The Archbishop in his answer, represented with great humility, that he could not stir a step in the ceremony, except in consequence of orders from the Sovereign.

Then baffled, disappointed, and defeated in all her attempts, to become either a participant, or even a spectator of the ceremonies of the Coronation, her Majesty drew up a formal protest and remonstrance to his Majesty, which was accordingly forwarded on the 17th. It was as follows:—

CAROLINE R.

TO THE KING'S MOST EXCELLENT MAJESTY.

The Protest and Remonstrance of Caroline, Queen of Great Britain and Ireland.

Your Majesty having been pleased to refer to your Privy Council the Queen's memorial, claiming as of right to celebrate the ceremony of her Coronation on the 19th day of July, being the day appointed for the celebration of your Majesty's royal Coronation, and Lord Viscount Sidmouth, one of your Majesty's Principal Secretaries of State, having communicated to the Queen the judgment pronounced against her Majesty's claim,—in order to preserve her just rights, and those of her successors, and to prevent the said minute being in after-times referred to, as deriving validity from her Majesty's supposed acquiescence in the determination therein expressed, the Queen feels it to be her bounden duty to enter her most deliberate and solemn protest against the said determination; and to affirm and maintain, that by the laws, usages, and customs of this realm, from time immemorial, the Queen Consort ought of right to be crowned at the same time with the King's Majesty.

In support of this claim of right her Majesty's law officers have proved before the said Council, from the most ancient and authentic records, that Queens Consort of this realm have, from time immemorial, participated in the ceremony of the Coronation with their royal husbands. The few exceptions that occur demonstrate, from the peculiar circumstances in which they originated, that the right itself was never questioned, though the exercise of it was from necessity suspended, or from motives of policy declined.

Her Majesty has been taught to believe that the most

valuable laws of this country depend upon, and derive their authority from custom; that your Majesty's royal prerogatives stand upon the same basis: the authority of ancient usage cannot, therefore, be rejected without shaking the foundation upon which the most important rights and institutions of the country depend. Your Majesty's Council, however, without controverting any of the acts or reasons upon which the claim made on the part of her Majesty has been supported, have expressed a judgment in opposition to the existence of such right. But the Queen can place no confidence in that judgment, when she recollects that the principal individuals by whom it has been pronounced were formerly her successful defenders; that their opinions have varied with their interest, and that they have since become the most active and powerful of her persecutors; still less can she confide in it when her Majesty calls to mind that the leading members of that Council, when in the service of your Majesty's Royal Father, reported in the most solemn form, that documents reflecting upon her Majesty were satisfactorily disproved as to the most important parts, and that the remainder was undeserving of credit. Under this declared conviction, they strongly recommended to your Majesty's Royal Father to bestow his favour upon the Queen, then Princess of Wales, though in opposition to your Majesty's declared wishes. But when your Majesty had assumed the kingly power, these same advisers, in another minute of council, recanted their former judgment, and referred to and adopted these very same documents as a justification of one of your Majesty's harshest measures towards the Queen— the separation of her Majesty from her affectionate and only child.

The Queen, like your Majesty, descended from a long race of Kings, was the daughter of a sovereign house connected by the ties of blood with the most illustrious families in Europe; and her not unequal alliance with your Majesty was formed in full confidence that the faith of the King and the people was equally pledged to secure to her all those honours and rights which had been enjoyed by her royal predecessors.

In that alliance her Majesty believed that she exchanged the protection of her family, for that of a royal husband, and of a free and noble-minded nation. From your Majesty, the Queen has experienced only the bitter disappointment of every hope she had indulged. In the attachment of the people she has found that powerful and decided protection which has ever been her steady support and her unfailing consolation. Submission from a subject to injuries of a private nature may be matter of expedience—from a wife it may be matter of necessity—but it never can be the duty of a Queen to acquiesce in the infringement of those rights which belong to her constitutional character.

The Queen does therefore repeat her most solemn and deliberate protest against the decision of the said Council, considering it only as the sequel of that course of persecution under which her Majesty has so long and so severely suffered, and which decision, if it is to furnish a precedent for future times, can have no other effect than to fortify oppression with the forms of law, and to give to injustice the sanction of authority. The protection of the subject, from the highest to the lowest, is not only the true but the only legitimate object of all power; and no act of power can be legitimate which is not founded on those principles of eternal justice, without which law is but the mask of tyranny, and power the instrument of despotism.

Queen's House, July 17.

This may be said to be the close of all official correspondence between her Majesty and the King's Ministers; and the public were in some degree left in doubt as to the line of conduct which her Majesty intended to pursue. Some information was, however, given on the subject by Alderman Wood on Tuesday the 10th, when, on a motion being made in the House of Commons that the House do adjourn,

Mr. Hume said he thought the House ought not to separate without expressing some opinion upon the manner in which the Queen was treated by the ministers. If the noble lord were present, he would ask whether it was the intention of ministers to persevere in their course of persecution towards her.—If he knew any thing of the spirit and character of her Majesty, he believed, and indeed he had reason to be strong in that belief, that she would go to the Coronation. If her determination to be present at the ceremony should cause any interruption of the public peace, ministers must impute it to their own conduct towards her Majesty. For his part he was anxious to take all possible means to prevent so dangerous a consequence, and he therefore now gave notice, that next day he would move an humble address to his Majesty, that his Majesty might be graciously pleased to take such measures as to him should seem fit, with a view to provide for the peace and tranquillity of the capital, in consequence of her Majesty's resolution to attend the Coronation.

Mr. Butterworth regretted that such a motion should be made in the present state of the House; he hoped her Majesty would not be so ill advised as to risk the peace of the country, and what little credit she might still have left, by interfering in the august ceremony of his Majesty's Coronation.

Mr. Alderman Wood.—The honourable member is entirely mistaken, if he supposes, that in the conduct which her Majesty will pursue on the present occasion, she will be influenced by any advice, or act under any other suggestions than those of her own dignified mind. Her Majesty has the spirit to protect her rights, and to maintain the dignity with which the laws and the constitution have invested her. With regard to the expressions which the honourable member has permitted himself to use, I trust, even for his own sake, that they were dropped in the warmth of debate, and that he is not prepared to defend them. Is it decorous, or manly, or consistent in that honourable member to talk of " the little credit which her Majesty may still have left in the country," when, if he were to poll the opinions of his constituents, he would find ninety-nine out of a hundred indignant at the wrongs which her Majesty has sustained, and firm supporters of her cause. I have no hesitation in declaring, that whatever may be the decision of the tribunal before which her Majesty's claim is now pending, and a favourable one can scarcely be anticipated, it is her Majesty's decided intention to attend at the ceremony of the Coronation.

Mr. Butterworth repeated, that he hoped her Majesty would not be so ill advised as to interfere in the ceremony.

Accordingly on the following day, the 11th, the

day appointed for the prorogation of parliament, the Speaker had no sooner taken the chair, than Mr. Hume rose to make the motion of which he had given notice on the preceding day. The peace of the country he said, was connected with the Coronation of her Majesty. The members of that House were now within eight days of the Coronation, and yet they were in complete ignorance of the situation which the first subject of the realm was to occupy in that ceremonial. The Coronation of her Majesty was a question which occupied a large portion of the public attention, and he felt satisfied that nothing less than the performance of that ceremony would quiet and satisfy the public mind. He had heard to-day with much regret, but not with surprise, that the Privy Council had decided against her claim of right to be crowned. He did not mean to impugn the decision of the Privy Council, but he certainly must say that he differed widely from the opinion delivered by them. He thought that the Queen had just as good a right to be crowned as the King had; and with that view he should move an address to his Majesty, praying that the Queen might be permitted to a participation in the honours of the Coronation. He protested against those acts which would go to exclude her Majesty from the ceremony, conscious, as he was, that they would be looked upon by the country as most oppressive. He would tell the noble lord (Londonderry) that the time was now come which afforded an opportunity of doing away, by a kind attention to her Majesty, the impression which former acts of injustice towards her had left on the public mind. He could assure that noble lord that his object was not to create discontent, but to avoid it by conciliatory measures; he wished, above all things, to prevent such an irritation of the public mind as was manifested in the course of last session. He would advise the noble lord not to allow her Majesty to be further degraded. Surely they would not exhibit to the public such a spectacle as that of turning the Queen away from the Coronation altogether. This was the fittest opportunity that could be given to his Majesty of doing that as a matter of grace and favour, which his Privy Council had informed him could not be claimed as a right. The honourable member concluded by moving, " That an humble address be presented to his Majesty, praying, that he will be graciously pleased to issue his Royal Proclamation for the Coronation of her Majesty, thereby consulting the true dignity of the crown—the tranquillity of the metropolis, and the general expectations of the people."

Mr. Hume had not commenced the reading of his resolution, ere the Black Rod was heard at the door, and before he had concluded he was called to order by the Speaker.

The Black Rod then informed the House that the Lords bearing his Majesty's Commission were in the House of Peers, whither the Speaker immediately repaired, attended by a great number of members.

We shall now revert to the circumstances immediately connected with the ceremony of the Coronation; one of the most important of which were the military arrangements, which formed so striking a contrast with those which were adopted at the Coronation of George III. at which no other troops were employed than those which constituted the Guard of Honour; on the contrary, a few days preceding the Coronation of George IV. troops were seen directing their march from all quarters to the metropolis, and there was not a village in the vicinity which did not show the " plumed helm," or " the neighing war-horse." We will not pretend in this instance to decide whether it was the turbulent disposition of the times, or the extraordinary attachment to military show, which prompted the strong accession of the soldiery, but by the people it was regarded with a most jealous eye, and by some members of the House of Commons, particularly the Marquis of Tavistock, who made it the subject of a substantive motion.

The following was the disposition directed to be

made of the military, under a printed order from the office of the Commander-in-Chief:—

Horse Guards, July 16, 1821.

The following are the Disposition, Strength, and Stations, of the Guards and Picquets for the Ceremony of the King's Coronation:—

1st Life Guards.
2d Ditto.
Royal Horse Guards.
2d Dragoons.
9th Lancers.
10th Royal Hussars.
14th Light Dragoons.

} The Cavalry Duties are to be taken by the Corps named in the Margin, under the Command of Major General Lord Edward Somerset, K. C. B.

Stations.	Officers.	Men.	
King's Guard	3	60	
Palace Yard, outside of Platform	3	60	Patrole to meet those from Tothill-street.
Space between the western door of the Abbey, and the end of Tothill and Prince's-street	3	60	Patrole along the Platform, to meet those of Palace-yard.
Smith-square, Saint John's Church	4	100	Patrole from House of Lords, College-st. Bowling-st. to Tothill-st. meet and patrole from the Riding-house at Pimlico; also along Vauxhall-road to Pimlico, to meet Patrole from Riding-house.
Riding House, Pimlico	4	100	Patrole York-st. Tothill-st. to Dean's-yard, meet Patrole from Smith-sq. to Pimlico and Vauxhall-road; meet Patrole from Smith-square.
Horse Guards	4	100	Patrole Park, Parliament-st. to Great George-st. Delahay-st. Charles-st. King-st.
			Patrole Park, Cockspur-st. to meet Patrole from

Carlton Palace	4	100	Horse Guards, Pall-mall, St. James's-st. Piccadilly, and Constitution-hill; to meet Patrole from Hyde Park.
Hyde Park Barracks	3	60	Detach 1 officer, 20 men, to Hyde Park-corner; Patrole Piccadilly and Constitution-hill; to meet Patrole from Carlton Palace; Patrole Park-lane and Park, to meet Patrole from King-st. Barracks.
King-street Barracks	4	100	Patrole Park-lane & Park, to meet Patrole from Hyde Park-corner; Patrole Portman-sq. Manchester-sq. Cavendish-sq. Oxford-st. to meet Patrole from Regent's Park.
Regent's Park Barracks	4	100	Patrole Portland-rd. Tottenham-st. Gray's Inn-lane, Pentonville; meet Patrole from King-street Barracks.
To be cantoned at Bow, &c.	8	200	To be at the disposal of the Lord Mayor, for the use of the City, if required.
Marsh-gate, Westminster-bridge	4	100	Patrole Lambeth to Vauxhall-bridge, Surrey road, to meet Patrole from Blackman-street.
Blackman-street	4	100	Patrole to Blackfriars and Waterloo Bridges, Surrey-road, and meet Patrole from Blackman-st.
Champion's Guard	Serjt.	Pri. 12	To escort the King's Champion from Hill-st. Berkley-sq. to Westminster Hall.
	52	1253	
Light Horse Volunteers			The Corps of Volunteers and Yeomanry specified in the margin, having tendered their services on the day of the King's Coronation,

Eastern Berks. ⎫
1st Bucks. ⎪ Yeomanry.
2d ditto. ⎬
Surrey. ⎪
Honourable Artillery Company.

of which his Majesty has been graciously pleased to accept, they are to be stationed at the following places, and their Commanding Officers will be pleased to put themselves in communication with Major-General Lord Edward Somerset.

Light Horse Volunteers - Old Palace Yard.
Hon. Artillery Company - Parliament-street.
1st Bucks Yeomanry - Kensington.
2d Ditto - - - Wandsworth, &c.
Surrey Ditto - - - Camberwell, &c.
Eastern Berks Yeomanry - Windsor.

Grenadier Regiment {1st Batt., 2d Do., 3d Do.}
Coldstream Regt. {1st Batt., 2d Do.}
Third Regiment 2d Batt.

The Foot Guards, as per margin, commanded by the Hon. Col. Brand, will take the following Duties, viz :—

STATIONS.	Officers.	Rank & File.	
Picquet in Portman-street Barracks -	4	100	
Ditto in King's Mews - -	8	200	
Ditto in Knightsbridge Barracks -	4	100	
King's Guard - - -	3	100	
Tilt Yard, augmented to - -	4	100	
Dean's Yard - - -	2	40	
Storey's Gate - - -	1	30	
Opposite North Gate of Westminster Abbey	1	20	
Speaker's Yard - - -	4	100	{ Guard of Honour.
Hyde-Park Corner - - -	1	30	
Stable Yard - - - -	1	30	
Foot of Westminster Bridge, Westminster side - - - -	1	30	
King-street and near Great George-street	1	20	
West Door of Abbey - -	2	60	
Guards - - - -	37	960	

Brought over	37	960	
East End and Door of Abbey	1	30	
Abingdon-buildings	1	30	
Steps leading to Painted Chamber	1	30	To at-
At Great Gate, Westminster Hall	—	S. P.	tend the
Exchequer Coffee-house	—	1 12	Orders
Head of Cannon-row	—	1 12	of the
Platform leading from the Champion's Stable	—	1 12	Lord High
King's Stairs, Old Palace-yard	—	1 12	Cham-
Passage by St. Margaret's Church	—	1 12	berlain.
Entrance to Little George-street from Great George-street	—	1 12	
Total of Guards	40	1122	
Platform	—	1500	
General Total	40	2622	

The infantry to parade in St. James's park at one o'clock in the morning: the cavalry to proceed to their respective posts by the most convenient routes; and all the guards, cavalry as well as infantry, to be at their respective stations by two o'clock.

Exclusive of the guards and detachments above enumerated, two companies of grenadiers are to be stationed in the Abbey, and the platform along which the procession is to proceed from Westminster-hall to the Abbey, will be occupied by a single rank on each side for its whole extent.

When the procession appears, both in going to, and returning from the Abbey, the men to be shouldered, silent and steady, and on the appearance of his Majesty at the flank of each division, arms will be presented, and all the music, drums, &c. to strike up at once, and continue until his Majesty has passed the division to which they are attached.

In order to effect this arrangement for receiving his Majesty's procession, the troops occupying the platform will be divided into three divisions, each commanded by a field officer, and occupying the opposite sides of the platform, with a portion of the bands, drums, &c. attached to each.

As there may be difficulty in procuring victuals for the troops throughout the day, the commanding officers of the different corps will make arrangements, in order that their men may carry with them bread, cheese, and cold-meat.

The detail regarding these several duties, and the allotment of corps to their respective stations, are left—for the cavalry to the arrangement of Major-General Lord E. So-

merset, and for the infantry to the Honourable Colonel Brand.
By his Royal Highness the Commander-in-Chief's Command.
H. TORRENS, Adjutant-General.

Public curiosity and interest heightened to the most ardent intensity during several days preceding the Coronation, produced a sensation during the whole of the night, of Wednesday, the 18th, which for animation and bustle, gave to the still season of rest the cheerful life of day; and the metropolis, as if by one simultaneous consent, had agreed to postpone even the most necessitous demands to that respect and attention due to the splendid celebration of the national Jubilee. The rattling of carriages, the busy hum of men, and the cheerful note of preparation marked the night as the continuation of day. As early as one o'clock on the morning of the 19th, Westminster, the scene of this magnificent pageant, presented a spectacle, which confounded the senses. Even at that hour, those whose happy lot destined them to seats in the Abbey and the Hall, had commenced their approach to the scene of celebration. From Charing Cross, as the conveying centre to the metropolis, two streams of carriages were observed directing their course through the passages respectively marked out the one appropriated to the visitors of the Abbey, and the other to those of the Hall. Through the grey mist of morning, the gay apparel of the inmates was visible, and excited sensations not to be described. The streets were crowded with foot passengers, hastening to the common centre of attraction, some eager to secure their seats on the different platforms, and others anxious to gain some standing place convenient for view. All distinction of persons or of rank seemed to be confounded in a desire to reach the grand object of attraction; judges, peers, bishops, commanders, naval and military; the citizens, accompanied by their daughters in their richest attire, were all in the gradual progress to the scene of splendour.

His Majesty having expressed his intention to sleep in the mansion of the Speaker of the House of Commons, on the night previous to the Coronation, preparations were accordingly made for his reception. These, however, were of a very economical nature; in fact, very little addition was made to the furniture of the suite of rooms, which included the Speaker's levee rooms, set apart for his use. His Majesty's own couch bed was brought from Carlton-house, and placed in the tapestry-room, looking over the Thames. Furniture, however, had been ordered as usual on the Coronation of a King of England, as it is the perquisite of the Lord Great Chamberlain.

On Wednesday evening, the 18th, a Guard of Honour marched into the Speaker's yard, preparatory to the arrival of his Majesty, and about the same time a troop of Cuirassiers took up their station along the platform in New Palace-yard, in Bridge-street, in Parliament-street, and in Little Bridge-street. The crowd, even at this time, was beyond all calculation. At about half-past eight o'clock, his Majesty arrived in his carriage at the Speaker's house, and was received by that right honourable gentleman, by the Lord Chancellor, Lord Stowell (late Sir William Scott,) the Marquis of Londonderry, Lord Sidmouth, and some other officers of state.

His Majesty was conducted to the suite of rooms prepared for his reception, and subsequently supped with the Speaker. On retiring to rest, the Lord Great Chamberlain, and Mr. Fellowes, his secretary, took their station on one side of his Majesty's chamber, and the Usher of the Black Rod on the other. Here they remained till morning.

On the same day a grand rehearsal of all the duties to be performed by the State officers, took place both in Westminster Hall and the Abbey. Each person who had a part to perform, was provided with a printed form of his duties, and went through them precisely in the same manner as the succeeding day.

A rehearsal of the duties of the Champion also took

place in Westminster Hall, Mr. Dymocke being dressed in his full costume, and being accompanied by the Marquis of Anglesea on one side, and Lord Howard of Effingham on the other.

All the decoration of the outer platform being completed, the carpenters proceeded to close up that part which had been left open for the passages of carriages, and placed it in the same state with the rest. The boards which closed the sides of the platform were then removed, and the whole was cleansed and swept. A strong body of constables were on the spot to preserve order. While these arrangements were going on on the outside, great progress was made within. All the private dining-rooms were placed in their proper order, and the tables properly decorated. Every guest had his napkin, knife, fork, spoon, goblet, wine-glasses, and water-carafe; the tables were in fact set out in the most comfortable style. The spoons were of Prince's metal, with the crown and George IV. engraved on the handle.

In the course of the evening an immense quantity of fresh fruit for the desert, with salad, bread and fresh butter, was delivered at the kitchens, and in all quarters there were indications of the near approach of the solemn ceremony. At this period too, hundreds of well-dressed persons were seen battling with the crowd to get to their respective lodgings, which they had engaged for the occasion. In many cases this task was accomplished with difficulty, from the prodigious crowd which was every where assembled.

The morning was ushered in by discharges of artillery in the Park, and from a man-of-war brig, and other boats stationed in the river. In consequence of the orders issued for the accommodation of those who came in carriages, and the limitation of the hours at which the visitors were to obtain admittance to the Abbey and Hall, the throng of carriages by six was extremely great; and at that hour there was a complete stoppage for a considerable time. Long before this hour many of the company, impatient of the ordinary delay of setting down at the doors, got out of their carriages, and hastened to their places of destination through the crowd. The intermixture of waving plumes, glittering diamonds, and splendid costumes, with the assembled multitude gave a singularly striking appearance to the scene. Many of the nobility attired in their Coronation robes, were obliged from the same cause to alight before their carriages arrived at the barrier leading to the Hall, and the contrast of their splendid robes and coronets, with the surrounding groupes, formed a most singular but striking scene. Many peers had indeed procured lodgings in the vicinity, and had thereby acquired the means of assuming and throwing off with all practicable speed the trappings and ornaments of their respective rank and functions.

Every moment some object of attraction was presented to the view of the gazing multitude. The splendid, and, in some instance, grotesque dresses of those who were to form a part of the grand procession excited wonder and admiration; of the latter description were the dresses of the pursuivant gentlemen pensioners, the attendants of the lords spiritual, and many others which were formed after the model of the earliest times. Most of the persons of this description being pedestrians, afforded the spectators a full opportunity of observing their appearance.

About six o'clock two or three of the royal carriages arrived, conveying some of his Majesty's household. By this time many other persons connected with the ceremonials of the Hall had also arrived. Amongst others, the royal band of gentlemen pensioners, the royal band of musicians, &c. &c. At this time nothing was more impressive than the order and quietness which every where prevailed. Never was a more gratifying sight beheld than the display of assembled beauty, elegance, and wealth, on the different Pavilions round the platform and the vicinity. It is due to the acting Lord Great Chamberlain, Lord Gwydir, and his deputy, Mr. Fellowes, who were on duty in the Hall the whole of the preceding night, to state, that their arrangements were admirably adapted to insure admission to the respective places appropriated for spectators, and to afford the utmost accommodation to every person whose duty it was to attend in the Hall throughout the day. Lord Gwydir and his deputy were both personally superintending the arrangements, and most active in facilitating the necessary accommodation for the visitors, many of them of the highest rank, who arrived at the Hall at day-break. A considerable number of ladies arrived at 3 o'clock; and the gentlemen attendants, who were dressed in scarlet frock coats with blue sashes, were every where on the alert to usher the respective parties to the seats provided for their tickets. While yet

"A paly light as of the morning shone"—

and before the rays of the sun had illuminated the Hall with its morning lustre—

"The gothic imagery of darker shade"

was brilliantly relieved by the presence of groupes of splendidly dressed ladies, who before 4 o'clock, occupied the principal seats of the galleries, and "made the temple bright" by the display of their beauty, and the sparkling brilliancy of their decorations. At that hour the arrival of different official attendants, in dresses, all of them brilliant, but some of them fantastical, began to develop some of the chivalrous pomp attending the Coronation ceremony; several yeomen of the guard in their full dress, and bearing their ornamented partisans entered and paraded the Hall; many of the military officers on duty in Palace-yard also made their appearance, and several persons elegantly attired in Spanish costume; these, together with a few of the gentlemen pensioners in their costly dress, a few heralds and trumpeters, who sauntered about the Hall thus early to survey the scene, presented a varied and interesting combination, as remarkable for the novel variety as for the splendour of the dresses of those composing the several groupes. The first set of official personages who entered in form were the Barons of the Cinque Ports, with their canopy. They were attired in richly embroidered dresses, and attended by eight gentlemen in plain full dress, who practised, as bearers, the duty of supporting the canopy along the area of the Hall; it was of straw colour silk, richly embroidered with gold, the frame studded with silver ornaments, and the supporting rods of silver richly embossed; it had a light and elegant appearance. The cornice was composed of the four orders, in their proper colours, on a silver ground—namely, the Knights of the Garter, the Knights of the Bath, the Knights of the Thistle, the Knights of St. Patrick, together with their proper stars. The whole was supported by silver staves, and a silver gilt bell was suspended over each staff. The inside of the canopy was lined with silver tabby plain, with a double heading of silver gymp. There was a deep silver twine edge at the bottom.

At about half-past five in the morning, the members of the corporations of the cities of London, Oxford, and Dublin, mustered at the foot of Blackfriars Bridge, where the state barge, manned by watermen in scarlet liveries, with silver badges and velvet caps, and commanded by the Water Bailiff and Mr. Searle, was in waiting to receive them. The Lord Mayor was received with much warmth of congratulation by the numerous crowd of citizens who had assembled to view the preparations. His lordship was dressed in a superb court dress of purple and white satin, with a brilliantly embroidered robe of scarlet to correspond, and had on a velvet cap, surmounted by a plume of black ostrich feathers, turned up with a loop of brilliants; he appeared in excellent spirits.

His lordship was attended by the Sword-bearer, with the City Sword, the Common Crier, who bore the City Mace, the Water Bailiff and his lordship's Chaplain acting as the Common Hunt, an office which has long been obsolete, but which formerly was one of the greatest importance in the city, inasmuch as he was intrusted with the care and command of the hounds that were kept by the corporation. These four officers were attired in new state robes, and attended his lordship as his esquires. Sheriffs Waithman and Williams followed, in their state robes.

The aldermen who were present were, Sir Richard Carr Glynn, Aldermen Wood, Brown, Sir C. Flower, Sir J. Shaw, Magnay, Birch, Sir John Perring, Bridges, Cox, Annesley, Garratt, Venables, Atkins, Scholey, Joshua Jonathan Smith, Christopher Smith, and Thomas Smith. The aldermen were dressed in full embroidered court dresses, with their scarlet robe and gold chains, and had on black velvet caps surmounted with plumes of three ostrich feathers. They were received with various testimonies of public opinion by the crowd. Aldermen Atkins and Bridges received peculiar tokens of remembrance. The Recorder and Remembrancer were also present. The following were the twelve citizens who attended as masters of the twelve companies of the livery. But two of them, however, are masters for the present year; the whole were nominated last year, and have retained their appointment, notwithstanding the attempts made by the Common Council and the present masters to oust them. They were,

Sir Charles Price, Bart. Master of the Ironmongers' Company.

R. H. Sparks, Esq. of the Merchant Tailors' Company.

Thomas Day Frampton, Esq. of the Grocers' Company.

Richard Ryland, Esq. of the Fishmongers' Company.

Thomas Moore, Esq. of the Vintners' Company.

The other seven gentlemen were:—Stephen D. Totton, Esq. John Butts, Esq. J. Griffin, Esq. W. Seward Hall, Esq. J. Randall, Esq. J. Farley, Esq. D. Whalley, Esq.

A considerable crowd assembled about her Majesty's house, in South Audley-street, soon after four o'clock. As soon as it was ascertained that her Majesty's coach was making ready in the yard, the crowd, both in South Audley-street and in Hill-street, became very great. The wall opposite to her Majesty's house in Hill-street was soon covered with spectators, who announced to the crowd below each successive step of preparation. " The horses are to"—" every thing is quite ready"—" the Queen has entered the coach,"—were the gradual communications, and they were received with the loudest cheers. Lady Anne Hamilton arrived a few minutes before five, and was most cordially and respectfully greeted. Soon after five, the gate was thrown open, and a shout was raised—" The Queen!" " The Queen!" The Queen immediately appeared in her coach of state, drawn by six bays. Lady Hood and Lady Anne Hamilton sat opposite to her Majesty. Lord Hood followed in his own carriage. Her Majesty looked extraordinarily well; and acknowledged, with great dignity and composure, the gratulations of the people on each side of her coach. The course taken was, through Great Stanhope-street, Park-lane, Hyde Park-corner, the Green Park, St. James's Park, Birdcage-walk, and by Storey's-gate, along Prince's-street, to Dean's-yard. The crowd accumulated immensely along this line: the soldiers every where presented arms with the utmost promptitude and respect; and a thousand voices kept up a constant cry of " The Queen," " The Queen for ever!" not unmingled, however, with cries of a contrary character. Her Majesty first went to the Dean's-yard Gate, but finding that the entrance for persons of rank was at Poet's Corner, she directed her coach to drive thither. The coachman accordingly followed the line of the platform to New Palace-yard, but he there found that there was no thoroughfare. He drove on, however, opposite to Westminster Hall Gate, and there stopped. Lord Hood now alighted, to inquire for the means of getting through to the Abbey, and having found an open gate leading to the Speaker's house, in which, by the bye, his Majesty then was, he went back to her Majesty, and requested her to alight. Her Majesty did accordingly alight. While her Majesty remained in the carriage, a crowd assembled about her, and gave her repeated cheers, which were answered by an expression of different sentiments from the galleries and windows. Her Majesty seemed to be a good deal agitated, but she bowed with great condescension to her friends.

Her Majesty when she alighted, was accompanied by Lady Hood and Lady Hamilton, and leaned upon the arm of Lord Hood. On reaching the door, however, the mistake was discovered, and the group returned. Her Majesty was now surrounded by a great number of persons, who followed her along the side of the platform till she reached the steps by which persons having peers' tickets were permitted to ascend. There she instantly mounted, followed by her suite, and leaning on Lord Hood. On reaching the platform, the soldiery were drawn across the passage, and an officer advanced and asked for the tickets. Lord Hood said, he had authority to be there, and at the same time took a paper from his pocket. On presenting it, without examination, her Majesty was permitted to pass. She then crossed the platform, and descended on the other side. As she proceeded, several constables went before her, and the populace surrounded her on all sides. The constables and mob having led the way towards the passage leading to the kitchen, her Majesty followed ; but the gate being shut, and an explanation given of the place at which she had arrived, Lord Hood said her Majesty's desire was not to go into the Hall, but to go to Poet's Corner, with the view of gaining admission to the Abbey. Thither she was instantly conducted, through an opening in the covered way. On arriving at the place where tickets were received, Lord Hood demanded admission for the Queen.

The door-keeper said, that his instructions were to admit no person without a Peer's ticket.

Lord Hood.—" Did you ever-hear of a Queen being asked for a ticket before? This is your Queen."

The door-keeper said that his orders were general, and without any exceptions. He had never been in a similar situation before, and could say nothing as to the propriety or impropriety of refusing her Majesty admission.

Lord Hood.—" I present to you your Queen, do you refuse her admission?"

Her Majesty added, that she was his Queen, and desired to be permitted to pass.

The door-keeper repeated that his orders were peremptory—and said, however reluctant he might be, he could not suffer her Majesty to pass without a ticket.

Lord Hood.—" I have a ticket."

Door-keeper.—" Upon producing it I will permit you to pass."

Lord Hood then took from his pocket one ticket for the Abbey, for a Mr. Wellington, which he tendered to the door-keeper.

The door-keeper said that it would admit but one individual.

Lord Hood then asked her Majesty if she would enter alone?

Her Majesty hesitated—upon which

Lord Hood asked, whether there had not been some preparations made for her Majesty's reception.

The door-keeper answered in the negative.

Lord Hood.—" Then I am to understand you refuse your Queen admittance to Westminster Abbey?"

The door-keeper said he was ready to admit her Majesty with a ticket, but not without.

After a short consultation with her Majesty, as to whether she would go into the Abbey alone, or not—her Majesty declined—and it was resolved, having been refused admission to the cathedral church of Westminster, that she should return to her carriage.

As she turned round to quit the spot, some persons in the door-way burst into a vulgar laugh of derision. Her Majesty looked at them contemptuously; and Lord Hood observed, that in such a place he expected to have met with decorous conduct at least towards a Sovereign—instead of that she had been denied her indubitable right, and been treated, not only in an ill-mannered, but in an unmanly way.

Her Majesty then turned about, and passed through a group of fashionable women who were going to the Abbey with tickets, but who did not take the slightest notice of her. Her Majesty was followed by a crowd to the platform, some of whom were approving and some disapproving her conduct. On entering her carriage, there was considerable disapprobation, intermingled with cries of "shame, shame," "off, off;" but other parts of the populace repeated the cries of "the Queen, the Queen," with great enthusiasm. Her Majesty was elegantly dressed in a muslin slip, on a petticoat of silver brocade. She wore a small purple scarf, and had a splendid diamond bandeau on her head, with feathers. Lady Hamilton and Lady Hood were likewise elegantly dressed, and seemed to participate in all the feelings of her Majesty. Lord Hood was in a court dress, and in the little he said, spoke with firmness, but with politeness.

The knowledge of her Majesty's presence drew forth a great number of the persons who had assembled to take part in the procession. The grotesqueness of their dress as they appeared on the leads of the committee rooms of the House of Commons, had a most singular appearance. Some of them joined in the cry of "shame" against her Majesty.

At 6 o'clock their Royal Highnesses the Duchesses of Gloucester, Kent, and Clarence, and the Princess Feodore, daughter of the Duchess of Kent, entered their box, with a large retinue of ladies. About the same time the Prince and Princess Esterhazy, and a number of foreigners of distinction, entered their box at the opposite side. The foreign ambassadors and their suite were chiefly in military costume, and decorated with orders. The richness and variety of the foreign uniforms made the box allotted to the foreign embassies the most brilliant in the hall. At twenty minutes before seven o'clock the Yeomen of the Guard entered in due form, and at that time the arrivals of peers and peeresses at Palace-yard became so rapid, that the gates were constantly thrown open; they were however rather suddenly closed while a number of privileged persons seemed to be in the act of producing their tickets entitling them to ingress. At half-past seven o'clock, a number of gentlemen, dressed in mulberry-brown frock coats with lace ruffs and white sashes, entered; they were the attendants upon the acting Earl Marshal, and bore gold wands with the emblazoned arms of the Duke of Norfolk, the hereditary Earl Marshal. The Gentlemen Pensioners entered at the same time, and the Heralds laid their maces of office, and the swords of state, at the top of the peers' dining table, on the western side of the hall. The different attendants were then called to their respective places, the military, heralds, and other personages, who had throughout the morning moved backwards and forwards in detached bodies, began to separate and assume more regular order, and every appearance denoted the near approach of the solemn ceremonies of the day. Before eight o'clock most of the persons who had to walk in the procession assembled in the following places, viz:—

In the House of Lords—Their Royal Highnesses the Dukes of the blood-royal in their robes of estate, having their coronets, and the Field-Marshals their batons, in their hands. The Peers in their robes of estate, having their coronets in their hands. His Royal Highness the Prince Leopold, in the full habit of the order of the Garter, having his cap and feathers in his hand. The Archbishops and Bishops, vested in their rochets, having their square caps in their hands.

In his place near the bar—The Gentleman Usher of the Black Rod.

In the space below the bar of the House of Lords—The Train-bearers of the Princes of the blood-royal. The at-

The Assembling of Attendants.

tendants on the Lord High Steward, on the Lord-Chancellor, the Lord High Constable, and on the Lord Chamberlain of the Household. The Gentlemen-Ushers of the White and Green Rods, all in their proper habits.

In the Painted Chamber, and adjacent rooms near the House of Lords—The Lord Chief Justice of the King's Bench; the Master of the Rolls; the Vice-Chancellor; the Lord Chief Justice of the Common Pleas; the Lord Chief Baron; the Barons of the Exchequer, and Justices of both benches; the gentlemen of the Privy Chamber; the Attorney and Solicitor-General; Sergeants at Law; Masters in Chancery; the Lord Mayor, Aldermen, Recorder, and Sheriffs of London; King's Chaplains, having dignities; six Clerks in Chancery.

In the chamber formerly the House of Lords—The Knights Grand Crosses of the order of the Bath, in the full habit of the order, wearing their collars, their caps and feathers in their hands. The Knights Commanders of the said order, in their full habits; their caps and feathers in their hands. The officers of the said order, in their mantles, chains, and badges.

In the chamber formerly called the Prince's-chamber, or Robing-room, near the former House of Lords—The Treasurer and Comptroller of the Household; the Vice-Chamberlain; the Marquis of Londonderry, in the full habit of the order of the Garter, having his cap and feathers in his hand; the Register of the said order, in his mantle with his book; Privy Councillors, not being peers or knights grand crosses of the Bath; Clerks of the Council in ordinary.

In his Majesty's Robing-chamber, near the south entrance into Westminster-hall—The Trainbearers of his Majesty; Master of the Robes; Groom of the Robes.

In the room of the Chairman of Committees adjoining the House of Lords—Lords and Grooms of the Bedchamber. The Keeper of the Privy Purse; Equerries and Pages of Honour; Gentlemen Ushers and Aides-de-Camp.

In the witness room adjoining the House of Lords—Physicians, Surgeons, and Apothecaries.

In the House of Commons and the lobbies—Officers of the band of Gentlemen Pensioners with their corps, and the Serjeant at Arms; the officers of the Yeomen of the Guard, with their corps.

In the lobby between the House of Lords and the Painted Chamber—The Kings, Heralds, and Pursuivants of Arms.

In Westminster-hall, at the lower end, near the great north door—The sixteen Barons of the Cinque Ports, in their proper habits, with the canopy.

In Westminster-hall, near the north door—The Knight Marshal and his two officers, in their proper habits.

In Westminster-hall, at the lower end—His Majesty's band.

Without the north door of Westminster-hall—All who were to precede the Knight Marshal in the procession.

Soon after eight o'clock Mr. Fellowes led into the hall Miss Fellowes, who afterwards preceded the procession on the royal platform, as his Majesty's herb-woman; she was attended (as her maids) by Miss Garth, Miss Collier, Miss Ramsbottom, Miss Hill, Miss Daniel, and Miss Walker. The ladies were very elegantly dressed in white muslin with flowered ornaments. Shortly after, three large ornamented baskets filled with flowers were brought in and placed near the ladies, who were, until the procession moved, accommodated with chairs at the extremity of the hall. At a quarter past eight o'clock the doors were closed; the canopy-bearers were arranged at the foot of the royal platform, and the Heralds commenced their arrangements for marshalling the procession in the hall. The King's Sergeants, Lens, Vaughan, Onslow, Pell, entered in their scarlet robes; the Knights of the Bath, and the Knights Commanders of the Bath, followed, in the collars and habits of their order, were divided by the Heralds, and filed off at each side of the hall behind the Peers' tables. The Judges next entered, the Chief Baron, Mr. Baron Garrow, Mr. Justice Richards, Mr. Justice Bayley, and Mr. Justice Park. The other Judges also entered, but apparently without a rigid attention to their respective orders of rank. Chief Justice Dallas, the Vice-Chancellor (Sir John Leach), the Master of the Rolls (Sir Thomas Plumer), and the Lord Chief Justice of the Court of King's Bench, successively entered, and were arranged without the Peers' table. Privy Councillors not Peers were next arranged: among them were the Right Honourable George Canning, Mr. Bragge Bathurst, Sir C. Long, the Chancellor of the Exchequer in his robes of office, Mr. Sturges Bourne, Mr. Charles Grant (Secretary for Ireland), Mr.

Robert Ward, Mr. Huskisson, Mr. Frederick Robinson, Mr. Wallace, Mr. Beckett, Lord George Beresford, Lord Yarmouth: the Barons, eighteen in number, next entered—the newly created Baron Stowell (late Sir William Scott), and Baron Maryborough (late Mr. Wellesley Pole), entered the Hall first. There were but forty-nine present. Next came the Bishops, fifteen attended; the Viscounts, nineteen in number. The Earls were more numerous, about seventy or eighty; but the Hall now became so crowded that there was a difficulty in counting them accurately. The Marquisses and Dukes, and lastly the great Officers of State, Archbishops, and Members of the Royal Family, entered. The Marquis of Londonderry soon after entered in the full robes of the Order of the Garter. On the royal platform their Royal Highnesses the Dukes of York, Clarence, Sussex, Cambridge, and Gloucester, and Prince Leopold, in their full robes, as Knights of the Garter, separated at each side of the throne. His Grace the Duke of Wellington, with his gold staff as Lord High Constable, stood near the table in front of the throne, attended by his page. The Lord-Chancellor, the Duke of Montrose (the Master of the Horse), Marquis of Hertford (Lord Chamberlain), the Earl of Harrowby (President of the Council), the Earl of Westmorland (Lord Privy Seal), were also arranged near the table. The Heralds immediately proceeded to call over the names of the Peers assembled in the Hall. The names were called over twice in succession by two Heralds, and the Peers arranged in the area of the Hall in front of the Privy Councillors, Judges, and other official personages. This ceremony occupied from nine o'clock until twenty minutes before ten, and while the Peers were arranging in the centre of the Hall, the Dean and Prebendaries of Westminster entered the great gate from Palace-yard, and formed in a close compact body immediately within the Hall. The whole arrangements for

2 D

the procession were then completed. The Lord Mayor, Sheriffs, and Corporation of London, with the civic regalia, and Corporation of Oxford, were assigned their respective places, and a pause of about twenty minutes then took place.

During the arrangements the Deputy Lord Great Chamberlain waited upon the King, and carried to his Majesty his shirt and other apparel; and, together with the Lord Chamberlain of the Household, dressed his Majesty. Having performed this duty, he repaired to the House of Lords, and came from thence into the Hall, walking amongst the Peers.

At nine o'clock the King's band, in rich uniform, took their seats in the music gallery.

The scene at this moment was perhaps one of the most magnificent it was possible for the human imagination to conceive. Soon after nine his Majesty quitted the Speaker's house, and coming by the Speaker's passage into the lobby of the House of Commons, proceeded through the subsequent passages to his room behind the throne.

At this moment their Royal Highnesses the Dukes of York, Clarence, Sussex, Cambridge, and Gloucester, were assembled on the royal platform, together with Prince Leopold, the Lord High Constable, the Deputy Marshal, and other distinguished individuals. The Royal party were attended by their pages and train-bearers.

Every thing being duly arranged, the platform was cleared, with the exception of the Royal Dukes; the Great Officers of State, with the Duke of Wellington at their head, as Lord High Constable, proceeded to his Majesty's apartment.

The buzz of moving about now subsided, and a solemn stillness pervaded the Hall; every eye was turned towards the throne, in anxious expectation to see the illustrious Sovereign who was to contribute and support the most interesting part in the most splendid of all ceremonials. The Heralds at Arms alone were active in arranging the various orders of nobility and persons of rank in such parts of the Hall as would enable them to join in the procession.

At ten o'clock precisely the King entered the Hall, preceded by the Great Officers of State, and took his seat in the chair of state, at the head of the royal table. His Majesty was most splendidly attired, and wore a plume of ostrich feathers, surmounted by a black heron's plume.

The King wore his hair in thick falling curls over his forehead, and it fell behind his head in a similar shape. He took his seat with an air of majesty, but in a somewhat hurried step, and appeared for the moment oppressed by the imposing solemnity of the scene which for the first time met his eye. His Majesty with great affability then bowed to the Peers who stood on each side.

The moment the King entered, the whole of the persons in the gallery rose, and kept standing during the time his Majesty continued in the Hall; the trumpets struck up the air of "God save the King."

At this moment a gun was fired from the man of war stationed off Cotton Gardens, to announce to the metropolis the commencement of the august solemnity.

The Deputy Lord Great Chamberlain, the Lord High Constable, and the Deputy Earl Marshal, ascended the steps, and placed themselves at the outer side of the table.

The Lord High Steward, the Great Officers, Deputy Garter, and Black Rod, then arranged themselves near the chair of state; the royal trainbearers on each side of the throne.

The Lord Chamberlain, assisted by officers of the Jewel Office, then brought the sword of state to the Lord High Constable, who delivered it to the Deputy Lord Great Chamberlain, by whom it was laid upon the table; then Curtana, or the sword of mercy, with the two swords of justice, being in like manner presented, were drawn from their scabbards by the Deputy Lord Great Chamberlain, and laid on the table before his Majesty; after which the gold spurs were delivered, and also placed on the table. Immediately after, a procession, consisting of the Dean and Prebendaries of Westminster, in their surplices and rich copes, proceeded up the Hall, from the lower end thereof, in manner following:—

PROCESSION WITH, AND DELIVERY OF THE REGALIA.

Sergeant of the Vestry, in a scarlet mantle.
Children of the King's chapel, in scarlet mantles, four abreast.
Children of the choir of Westminster, in surplices, four abreast.
Gentlemen of the King's chapel, in scarlet mantles, four abreast.
Choir of Westminster, in surplices, four abreast.
Sub-Dean of the Chapel Royal.
Two Pursuivants of Arms.
Two Heralds.
The two Provincial Kings of Arms.
The Dean of Westminster, carrying St. Edward's crown on a cushion of cloth of gold.
First Prebendary of Westminster, carrying the orb.
Second Prebendary, carrying the sceptre with the dove.
Third Prebendary, carrying the sceptre with the cross.
Fourth Prebendary, carrying St. Edward's staff.
Fifth Prebendary, carrying the chalice and patina.
Sixth Prebendary, carrying the Bible.

In the procession they made their reverences, first at the lower end of the Hall, secondly about the middle, where both the choirs opening to the right and left formed a passage, through which the Officers of Arms passed, and opened likewise on each side, the seniors placing themselves nearest towards the steps: then the Dean and Prebendaries having come to the front of the steps, made their third reverence. This being done, the Dean and Prebendaries being come to the foot of the steps, Deputy Garter preceding them (he having waited their coming there), ascended the steps, and approaching near the table before the King, made their last reverence. The Dean then presented the crown to the Lord High Constable, who delivered it to the Deputy Lord Great Chamberlain, and by him it was placed on the table before the King. The rest of the regalia was severally delivered by each Prebendary, on his knee, to the Dean, by him to the Lord High Constable, by him to the Deputy Lord Great Chamberlain, and by him laid on the table. The regalia being thus delivered, the Prebendaries and Dean returned to the middle of the Hall.. His Majesty having commanded Deputy Garter to summon the nóblemen and bishops who were to bear the regalia, the Deputy Lord Great Chamberlain, then taking up the several swords, sceptres, the orb, and crown, placed them in the hands of those by whom they were to be carried.

First—St. Edward's Staff was delivered to the Marquis of Salisbury.

Second—Lord Calthorpe, as Deputy to the Baroness Grey de Ruthyn, received the Spurs, which are elaborately worked; they have no rowels, but terminate in an ornamental point, being of that kind which are denominated prick spurs.

Third—The Sceptre with the Cross was resigned to the Marquis Wellesley.

Fourth—The Pointed Sword of Temporal Justice was delivered to the Earl of Galloway..

Fifth—The Sword of Spiritual Justice was received and borne by the Duke of Northumberland. This sword is pointed, but rather obtuse. The length of the blade appeared about three feet and a half; the breadth an inch and a half; the handle is covered with gold wire. The length of the cross, which is plain steel gilt as before, seemed about eight inches.

Sixth—The Curtana, or sword of Mercy, was given to the Duke of Newcastle. This sword was the principal, in dignity, of the three swords borne naked befóre the King. It is a broad bright sword, of which the length of the blade is thirty-two inches, the breadth almost two inches; the handle, which is covered with fine gold wire, is four inches long, and the pommel an inch and three quarters, which with the cross, is plain steel gilt; the length of the cross is almost eight inches. The scabbard belonging to it is covered with a rich brocaded cloth of tissue, with gilt ornaments.

Seventh—The Sword of State was delivered to the Duke of Dorset. This is a large two-handed sword, having a splendid scabbard of crimson velvet, decorated with gold plates of the Royal Badges in order as follow:—At the point is the Orb or Mound, then the Royal Crest of a Lion standing on an Imperial Crown; lower down, are a Portcullis, Harp, Thistle, Fleur-de-lis, and Rose; nearer the hilt is the Portcullis repeated; next are the Royal Arms and Supporters; and, lastly, the Harp, Thistle, &c. occur over again. The handles and pommel of the sword are embossed with similar devices, and the cross is formed of the Royal supporters, having a rose within a laurel on one side, and a fleur-de-lis on the other.

Eighth—The Sceptre with the Dove, to the Duke of Rutland.

Ninth—The Orb, to the Duke of Devonshire.

Tenth—St. Edward's Crown, to the Marquis of Anglesea, as Lord High Steward.

The noble marquis, on ascending the platform to receive the Crown, was about to apologize to his Majesty for his inability to walk backward down the steps, on account of his having lost a leg; but he was interrupted by his Majesty, who graciously allowed him to get down in the best manner he was able, without thinking of adhering to the accustomed ceremonial.

Eleventh—The Patina, to the Bishop of Gloucester.

Twelfth—The Chalice to the Bishop of Chester.

Thirteenth—The Bible, to the Bishop of Ely.

The Bishops of Oxford and Lincoln, who were appointed to support his Majesty, were then summoned by the Deputy Garter, and ascending the steps, placed themselves on each side of the King.

When these ceremonies, which lasted about three quarters of an hour, were performed, some of them not as rapidly as they might have been, owing to the

The Coronation Procession of King George the Fourth.

tardy appearance of some of the Peers who were at the end of the Hall when the heralds summoned them to the platform to assist in the performance of their respective duties, the procession set out at eleven o'clock from Westminster Hall to the Abbey in the following order, the anthem, " *O Lord, grant the King a long life,*" &c. being sung in parts, in succession with his Majesty's band playing, the sounding of trumpets, and the beating of drums, until the arrival in the Abbey.

ORDER OF THE PROCESSION.

The King's Herb Woman with her six Maids, strewing the way with herbs.
Messenger of the College of Arms, in a scarlet cloak, with the arms of the college embroidered on the left shoulder.
The Dean's Beadle of Westminster, with his staff.
The High Constable of Westminster, with his staff, in a scarlet cloak.
Two household fifes with banners of velvet fringed with gold, and five household drummers in royal livery, drum-covers of crimson velvet, laced and fringed with gold.
The Drum-major, in a rich livery, and a crimson scarf fringed with gold.
Eight Trumpets in rich liveries; banners of crimson damask embroidered and fringed with gold, to the silver trumpets.
Kettle-drums, drum-covers of crimson damask embroidered and fringed with gold.
Eight Trumpets in liveries, as before.
Sergeant Trumpeter with his mace.
The Knight Marshal, attended by his officers.
The Six Clerks in Chancery.
The King's Chaplains having dignities, four and four.
The Sheriffs of London.
The Aldermen and Recorder of London.
Masters in Chancery.
The King's Sergeants at Law.
The King's Ancient Sergeant.
The King's Solicitor-Gen.   The King's Attorney-Gen.
Gentlemen of the Privy Chamber.
Sergt. of the Vestry of the Chapel Royal.   Sergt. Porter.
Children of the choir of Westminster, in surplices.
Children of the Chapel Royal, in surplices, with scarlet mantles over them.

Choir of Westminster, in surplices.
Gentlemen of the Chapel Royal, in scarlet mantles.
Sub-Dean of the Chapel Royal, in a scarlet gown.
Prebendaries of Westminster, in surplices and rich copes.
The Dean of Westminster, in a surplice and rich cope.
Pursuivants of Scotland and Ireland, in their tabards.
His Majesty's Band.
Officers attendant on the Knights Commanders of the Bath, in their mantles, chains, and badges.
Knights Commanders of the Bath, not Peers.
Officers of the Order of the Bath, in their mantles, chains, and badges.
Knights Grand Crosses of the Bath (not Peers), in the full habit of their Order, caps in their hands.
A Pursuivant of Arms, in his tabard.
Barons of the Exchequer, and Justices of both Benches.

| The Lord Chief-Baron of the Exchequer. | The Lord Chief-Justice of the Common Pleas. |
| The Vice-Chancellor. | The Master of the Rolls. |

The Lord Chief-Justice of the King's Bench.
The Clerks of the Council in Ordinary.
Privy Councillors, not Peers.
Register of the Order of the Garter.
Knights of the Garter (not Peers), in the full habit and collar of the Order, caps in their hands.
His Majesty's Vice-Chamberlain.

| Comptroller of his Majesty's Household. | Treasurer of his Majesty's Household, bearing the Crimson Bag with the medals. |

A Pursuivant of Arms, in his tabard.
Heralds of Scotland and Ireland, in their tabards and collars of SS.
The STANDARD OF HANOVER, borne by the Earl of Mayo.
Barons, in their robes of estate of crimson velvet, their coronets in their hands.
A Herald, in his tabard and collar of SS.

| STANDARD OF IRELAND, borne by Lord Beresford. | STANDARD OF SCOTLAND, borne by the Earl of Lauderdale. |

The Bishops of England and Ireland, in their rochets, caps in their hands.
Two Heralds, in their tabards and collars of SS.
Viscounts, in their robes of estate, their coronets in their hands.
Two Heralds, in their tabards and collars of SS.
THE STANDARD OF ENGLAND, borne by Lord Hill.
Earls, in their robes of estate, their coronets in their hands.
Two Heralds, in their tabards and collars of SS.
THE UNION STANDARD, borne by Earl Harcourt.

Marquisses, in their robes of estate, their coronets in their
hands.
The Lord Chamberlain of his Majesty's Household, in his
robes of estate, his coronet in his hand, attended by an
Officer of the Jewel-office in a scarlet mantle, with
a crown embroidered on his left shoulder, bearing a cushion, on which were placed the
Ruby Ring and the Sword to be girt
about the King.
The Lord Steward of his Majesty's Household, in his robes
of estate, his coronet in his hand.
THE ROYAL STANDARD, borne by the Earl of Harrington.

King of Arms of the Ionian Order of St. Michael and St. George, in his tabard, crown in his hand.	Gloucester King of Arms, in his tabard, crown in his hand.	Hanover King of Arms, in his tabard, crown in his hand.

Dukes, in their robes of estate, their coronets in their hands.

Ulster King of Arms, in his tabard, crown in his hand.	Clarencieux King of Arms, in his tabard, crown in his hand.	Norroy King of Arms, in his tabard, crown in his hand.
The Lord Privy Seal, in his robes of estate, coronet in his hand.		The Lord President of the Council, in his robes of estate, coronet in his hand.

Archbishops of Ireland.
The Archbishop of York, in his rochet, cap in his hand.
The Lord High Chancellor, in his robes of estate, with his
coronet in his hand, bearing his purse, and attended by
his Pursebearer.
The Lord Archbishop of Canterbury, in his rochet, cap in
his hand.
Two Sergeants at Arms.

THE REGALIA.

St. Edward's Staff, borne by the Marquis of Salisbury.	The Gold Spurs, borne by the Lord Calthorpe.	The Sceptre with the Cross, borne by the Marquis Wellesley.
The third Sword, borne by the Earl of Gallo- way.	Curtana, borne by the Duke of New- castle.	The second Sword, borne by the Duke of Northum- berland.

2 E

The Procession.

Two Sergeants at Arms.

Usher of the Green Rod.   Usher of the White Rod.

The Lord Mayor of London, in his gown, collar, and jewel, bearing the city mace.   The Lord Lyon of Scotland, in his tabard, carrying his crown and sceptre.   Garter Principal King of Arms, in his tabard, bearing his crown and sceptre.   Gent. Usher of the Black Rod, bearing his rod.

The Deputy Lord Great Chamberlain of England, in his robes of estate, his coronet and his white staff in his hand.

His Royal Highness the Prince Leopold, in the full habit of the Order of the Garter.

His Royal Highness the Duke of Gloucester, in his robes of estate, carrying in his right hand his baton as Field Marshal, and in his left his coronet.

His Royal Highness the Duke of Cambridge, in his robes of estate, &c.

His Royal Highness the Duke of Sussex, in his robes of estate, &c.

His Royal Highness the Duke of Clarence, in his robes of estate, &c.

His Royal Highness the Duke of York, in his robes of estate, &c.

The High Constable of Ireland, in his robes, coronet in his hand, with his staff.   The High Constable of Scotland, in his robes, coronet in his hand, with his staff.

Two Sergeants at Arms.

The Deputy Earl Marshal, with his staff.   The Sword of State, borne by the Duke of Dorset.   The Lord High Constable of England, in his robes, his coronet in his hand, with his staff; attended by a Page, carrying his baton of Field Marshal.

Two Sergeants at Arms.

A Gentleman carrying the staff of the Lord High Steward.   The Sceptre with the Dove, carried by the Duke of Rutland.   St. Edward's Crown, carried by the Lord High Steward.   The Orb, carried by the Duke of Devonshire.   A Gentleman carrying the coronet of the Lord High Steward.

The Patina, borne by the Bishop of Gloucester.   The Bible, borne by the Bishop of Ely.   The Chalice borne by the Bishop of Chester.

THE KING,

Twenty Gentlemen Pensioners, with the Standard Bearer.

Supporter: Lord Bishop of Oxford.

in the royal robes, wearing a cap of estate, adorned with jewels, under a canopy of cloth of gold, borne by 16 Barons of the Cinque Ports. His Majesty's train borne by 8 eldest sons of Peers, assisted by the Master of the Robes, and followed by the Groom of the Robes.

Supporter: Lord Bishop of Lincoln.

Twenty Gentlemen Pensioners, with the Lieutenant.

Captain of the Yeomen of the Guard.   Gold Stick of the Life Guards in waiting.   Captain of the Band of Gentlemen Pensioners.

Lords of the King's Bedchamber.
The Keeper of his Majesty's Privy Purse.
Grooms of the King's Bedchamber.
Equerries and Pages of Honour.
Aides-de-Camp.
Gentlemen Ushers.
Physicians, Surgeons, Apothecaries.
Ensign of the Yeomen of the Guard.   Lieutenant of the Yeomen of the Guard.
His Majesty's Pages in full state liveries.
His Majesty's Footmen in full state liveries.
Exons of the Yeomen of the Guard.   Yeomen of the Guard.   Exons of the Yeomen of the Guard.
Gentlemen Harbinger of the Band of Gentlemen Pensioners.
Clerk of the Cheque   Clerk of the Cheque
to the Yeomen of the Guard.   to the Gentlemen Pensioners.
Yeomen of the Guard.

As soon as the procession made its appearance from Westminster Hall, the soldiers stationed along the platform shouldered arms, and observed the greatest silence and steadiness. On the advance of his Majesty to the flank of each division, arms were presented, and all the music, drums, &c. struck up at once, and continued playing until his Majesty had passed the division to which they were attached.

The troops occupying the platform were divided into three divisions, each commanded by a Field Officer.

While the procession was moving from the lower part of the Hall, his Majesty called several of the youthful pages to him, and conversed with them successively for some time, with that dignity and urbanity which his Majesty unites in so pre-eminent a degree. His Majesty afterwards conversed with the Duke of York, who, on leaving the platform to join the procession, made his obeisance in a singularly graceful manner.

His Majesty, in descending the steps, called on a noble peer near him to assist him, and then proceeded under the canopy, at twenty minutes before eleven o'clock. His Majesty walked with a firm step, and appeared quite cheerful.

Immediately after the departure of the procession from the Hall, the members of the royal family were conducted behind the throne by W. D. Fellowes, Esq. and through the House of Lords to Poets' Corner, and from thence into their box in the Abbey.

The foreign ministers were conducted in the like manner to their box, and the peeresses and others, having peers' tickets, took the same course.

At thirty-five minutes before ten the clangor of the trumpets gave notice to the spectators without that the procession was moving from Westminster Hall, and very soon afterwards Miss Fellowes, attended by her six maids, were seen scattering flowers on the blue cloth, with which the centre of the platform was carpeted. Miss Fellowes and her maids appeared to have studied their parts most attentively. As the procession moved forward, the crowd was dazzled with its splendour. As is customary on such occasions, popular feeling was manifested on different individuals who have appeared on the political arena as they passed along the platform. Alderman Wood received strong marks of affection and good will; but they were not unmixed with symptoms of disapprobation. One or two voices exclaimed "no Wood!" to which an Hibernian labourer responded with laughable effect, "No wood! If there was no wood, what would you do for scaffolding?" Mr. Sheriff Waithman and Mr. Sheriff Williams were noticed very favourably. The Marquis of Londonderry was received with alternate cheers and hisses. His lordship acted on the old adage, "that those who win may laugh;" and, turning round to his auditors, treated them with that convulsion of features which naturalists tell us distinguishes man from the brute creation. Lord Hill, by whom the standard of England was borne, received the most enthusiastic applause, which he answered by repeated obeisance. The Duke of Sussex and Prince Leopold of Saxe-Cobourg, the latter of whom carried himself with peculiar dignity, were greeted in the most affectionate manner. The Duke of Clarence did not escape observation, and whether it was in consequence of his conduct during the late investigation in the House of Lords, or his recent application to parliament for money, cannot be determined; but, that observation was not of the most friendly character.

His Majesty was now seen approaching at the distance. All minor objects of curiosity were forgotten, and every eye was directed to the Royal Person.

We shall now give a brief description of the Abbey, as it appeared at the entrance of his Majesty:—

About four o'clock in the morning the gates of the Abbey were thrown open. A large concourse of persons had collected themselves in the area (formerly the church-yard) between the north door of the building and the Guildhall of Westminster; but a comparatively small proportion only were provided with tickets of admission. About two hundred individuals entered the Abbey, cheered by a merry peal from the steeple of St. Margaret's, and a little annoyed by the occasional jeers of the less fortunate spectators. Costume varied widely. One gentleman appeared in a full court suit, and his next neighbour in great coat and trowsers. Military gear was a good deal affected, particularly by those who had no title to assume it; and naval uniforms were sprinkled here and there. The front row of the vaulted gallery was rapidly occupied (principally by handsome and well-dressed females), but not the slightest confusion occurred. Each ticket contained the number of the particular box in which the holder was destined to sit; and all the boxes were provided with locks, to guard against the entrance of unauthorized visiters. The space immediately behind the gallery formed an extensive and commodious lobby, through which the company lounged at their leisure, awaiting the commencement of the spectacle. Agents attended from some of the most considerable confectioners in town; tables were set out under proper superintendence; and ices, fruit, wine, sandwiches, and " such savoury messes" were to be obtained, of good quality, and upon reasonable terms. From five o'clock until eight, the numbers in the lower parts of the Abbey gradually increased, and the pages and ushers of the rod, dashing about in their gay uniforms, gave motion and sprightliness to the scene. At half-past eight, a flourish of trumpets was heard, and THE PROCESSION WITH THE REGALIA marched out of the Abbey.

From half-past eight to ten (spite of the novelty of the ceremony, and the *piquant* circumstance of having been compelled to get up at two o'clock in the morning to behold it) something like *ennui* began to show itself in the demeanour of the expectant fair ones; soon after ten, however, loud and continued music in the distance gave a fillip to half-slumbering curiosity, and at ten minutes before eleven (looking down the Abbey as from the east, behind the organ) Miss Fellowes, with her six tributary herb-women, heading the grand procession, appeared at the western gate. The cavalcade halted, for a few moments at that point, apparently to give time for the rear to come up, and lively music (fifes and drums, and flourishes of trumpets alternately) filled up the interim. After a short pause, the procession again put itself in motion. The herb-woman with her maids and the sergeant porter remained at the entrance within the west door: the drums and trumpets filed off to the gallery over the entrance door. The Abbey at this moment began rapidly to fill. The Peeresses, (their natural attractions heightened by every aid which art or fancy could supply, their dresses sparkling with jewels, and their white feathers waving in in the wind) thronged into the seats appointed for them (immediately below the choir); and ranged in rows, to the number of one hundred and fifty-five, without a single creature of the grosser sex to disturb the uniformity or break the delicacy of the scene; with robes of every colour, various as the rainbow, and plumes of hues almost as many, their box showed like a bed of summer flowers, in which the rose, the tulip, and the violet, the snow-drop, and the bright blue-bell, displayed, contending, each its pride of beauty, and all insisted on pre-eminence. The procession continuing its course, the choirs of the Chapel Royal, and of Westminster, proceeded with his Majesty's band, to the organ gallery: some little confusion occurred in the filing off of the different bands; but the difficulty was quickly at an end; and, upon the entrance of the King into the aisle, a hundred instruments, and twice a hundred voices, rang out their notes at once; and the loud anthem, attended with the applauding shouts of the spectators, echoed to the very roof of the Abbey. The box of the Foreign Ministers presented, at his Majesty's entrance, a peculiarly glittering appearance. It afforded specimens of the costume of every country in amity with Great Britain, from the splendid uniform of Prussia or France, to the plain chintz gown and dark beard of a gentleman whose name we could not learn, but who stated himself to be the nephew of the Persian ambassador, and claimed, in right of such relationship, to be seated with the ministers of foreign courts. The cavalcade continued its course.

The Prebendaries and Dean of Westminster filed off to the left, about the middle of the nave, and there awaited the King's coming into church; when they again fell into the procession next before the Kings of Arms who preceded the great officers.

That part of the procession preceding the Knight Commanders of the Bath, the Knights Grand Crosses of the said Order, and their Officers, the Clerks of the Privy Council in Ordinary, the Privy Councillors, the Register of the Garter, Vice Chamberlain, Comptroller and Treasurer of his Majesty's Household, and Peers, were conducted to their seats by the Officers of Arms.

The Prebendaries of Westminster went to their places near the altar.

The Sergeants at Arms went to their places near the Theatre.

The standards were delivered by the bearers of them to Pages at the entrance of the choir, to be resumed and borne in the return.

The Princes of the Blood Royal were conducted to their seats as Peers.

The Prince Leopold sat in the Royal Box.

The Barons of the Cinque Ports bearing the canopy, and the Gentlemen Pensioners, remained at the entrance of the Hall.

The King ascending the Theatre, passed on the south side of the Throne to his chair of state, on the east side thereof, opposite the altar, and after his private devotion (kneeling down upon the faldstool) took his seat. His Majesty appeared distressed almost to fainting. It was with uneven steps and evident difficulty that he made his way up the aisle. The heat was indeed so great, that a lady in one of the galleries fainted, and was obliged to be removed from the building, and the weight of the state cloak alone, which had seven supporters, might have overpowered a man in the most vigorous bodily health. His Majesty being seated, the two bishops, his supporters, stood one on each side. The noblemen bearing the four swords on his right hand, the Deputy Lord Great Chamberlain, and the Lord High Constable on his left, the Great Officers of State, the Deputy Earl Marshal, the Dean of Westminster, the Noblemen bearing the Regalia, Trainbearers with Deputy Garter, the Lord Lyon, the Lord Mayor of London, and Black Rod, standing about his chair.

Whilst his Majesty was passing through the body of the church, and through the choir, up the stairs to the Theatre, the following Anthem was sung:—

ANTHEM I.

Psalm cxxii. verses 1, 5, 6, 7. " I was glad when they said unto me, we will go into the House of the Lord. For there is the seat of judgment, even the seat of the House of David. O pray for the peace of Jerusalem; they shall prosper that love thee. Peace be within thy walls, and plenteousness within thy palaces. Glory be to the Father, and to the Son, and to the Holy Ghost. As it was in the beginning, is now, and ever shall be, world without end. Amen."

The important business of the day commenced with the Recognition, which was then performed, the King being seated, the Archbishop turned to the east part of the Theatre; then, together with the Lord-Chancellor, Lord Great Chamberlain, Lord High Constable, and Earl Marshal (Garter King at Arms preceding them), went to the other three sides of the Theatre, in the order, south, west, and north, and at each side addressed the people in a loud voice; the King at the same time stood up by his chair, turned and showed himself to the people at each of the four sides of the Theatre, while the Archbishop spoke as follows:—

" Sirs—I here present unto you King George the Fourth, the undoubted King of this Realm: wherefore all you that come this day to do your homage, are ye willing to do the same?"

This was answered by the loud and repeated acclamations of the persons present, expressive of their willingness and joy, at the same time they cried out—"God save King George the Fourth."

Then the trumpets sounded.

This being finished, the following Anthem was sung. Psalm lxxxix. verse 14, the King resuming his seat,

"Let thy hand be strengthened, and thy right hand be exalted. Let Justice and Judgment be the preparation of thy seat, let mercy and truth go before thy face.—Allelujah."

THE FIRST OBLATION.

The Archbishop in the mean time went to the altar and put on his cope, and placed himself at the north side of the altar; as did also the bishops who took part in the office.

The officers of the wardrobe, &c. here spread carpets and cushions on the floor and steps of the altar.

And here, first the Bible, patina, and cup, were brought and placed upon the altar. The King then, supported by the two Bishops of Durham and Bath, and attended by the Dean of Westminster, the Lords carrying the Regalia before him, went down to the altar and knelt upon the steps of it, and made his first oblation, uncovered.

Here the pall, or altar-cloth of gold, was delivered by the Master of the Great Wardrobe to the Lord Great Chamberlain, and by him, kneeling, it was presented to his Majesty. The Treasurer of the Household then delivered a wedge of gold of a pound weight to the Lord Great Chamberlain, which he, kneeling, delivered to his Majesty. The King then (uncovered) delivered them to the Archbishop.

The Archbishop received them one after another (standing) from his Majesty, and laid the pall reverently upon the altar. The gold was received into the bason; and, with like reverence, was placed upon the altar.

Then the Archbishop said the following prayer, the King still kneeling:—

" O God, who dwellest in the high and holy place, with them also who are of an humble spirit; mercifully look down upon this thy humble servant, George our King, here humbling himself before thee at thy footstool, and graciously receive these oblations which, in humble acknowledgment of thy sovereignty over all, and of thy great bounty to him in particular, he hath now offered up unto thee, through Jesus Christ, our only Mediator and Advocate. Amen."

When the King had thus offered and fulfilled his commandment, and had repeated—" Thou shalt not appear before the Lord thy God empty," he went to his chair set for him on the south side of the altar, and knelt at his faldstool, and the Litany commenced, which was read by two bishops, vested in copes, and kneeling at a faldstool above the steps of the Theatre, on the middle of the east side; the choir read the responses.

In the mean time the lords who carried the Regalia, except those who bore the swords, approached the altar, and each presented what he carried to the Archbishop, who delivered them to the Dean of Westminster, who placed them on the altar. They then retired to the places and seats appointed for them.

The bishops, and the people with them, then said the Lord's Prayer.

The Communion service was read, the people kneeling, made the responses to the ten commandments, which were delivered by the Archbishop.

Then the Archbishop, standing as before, said the following collect for the King:—

" Let us pray.—Almighty God, whose kingdom is everlasting and power infinite: Have mercy upon the whole church, and so rule the heart of thy chosen servant George our King and governor, that he (knowing whose minister he is) may above all things seek thy honour, and glory; and that we and all his subjects (duly considering whose authority he hath) may faithfully serve, honour, and humbly obey him, in thee and for thee, according to thy blessed word and ordinance, through Jesus Christ our Lord, who with thee and the Holy Ghost, liveth and reigneth ever one God, world without end. Amen."

The following epistle was then read by one of the bishops:—

1 Pet. ii. 13.—" Submit yourselves to man for the Lord's sake; whether it be to the King as supreme; or unto Governors as unto them that are sent by him for the punishment of evil-doers, and for the praise of them that do well. For so is the will of God, that, with well-doing, ye may put to silence the ignorance of foolish men. As free, and not using your liberty for a cloak of maliciousness, but as the servants of God. Honour all men. Love the brotherhood. Fear God. Honour the King."

The Gospel was then read by another bishop, the King and the people standing.

St. Matth. xxii. 15.—" Then went the Pharisees, and took counsel how they might entangle him in his talk. And they sent out unto him their disciples, with the Herodians, saying Master, we know that thou art true, and teachest the way of God in truth, neither carest thou for any man, for thou regardest not the person of men; Tell us therefore, What thinkest thou? Is it lawful to give tribute unto Cæsar, or not? But Jesus perceived their wickedness, and said, Why tempt ye me, ye hypocrites? Show me the tribute money. And they brought unto him a penny. And he saith unto him, Whose is this image and subscription? They say unto him, Cæsar's. Then saith he unto them, Render therefore unto Cæsar the things which are Cæsar's: and unto God, the things that are God's. When they had heard these words, they marvelled, and left him and went their way."

Then the Archbishop read the Nicene Creed, the King, and the people standing as before.

" I believe in one God the Father," &c. &c.

At the end of the Creed, the Archbishop of York preached the sermon in the pulpit placed against the pillar at the north-east corner of the Theatre. The King listened to the same, sitting in his chair on the south side of the altar, over against the pulpit.

The King was uncovered during the offering and the service that followed; when the sermon commenced, he put on his cap of crimson velvet, turned up with ermine, and continued so to the end of it.

The text on which the right reverend prelate addressed his congregation was taken from 2 Samuel, chap. xxiii, verses 3, and 4. " The God of Israel said, the Rock of Israel spake to me, he that ruleth over men must be just, ruling in the fear of God ; and he shall be as the light of the morning when the sun riseth, even a morning without clouds ; as the tender grass springing out of the earth by clear shining after rain." He began by stating that this text was deserving of the most serious consideration at the hands of the audience he was addressing, not merely on account of its being the declaration of a dying King, but also the inspiration of a divine prophet. He then entered into a dissertation upon the mutual advantages which accrue both to the governor and the governed from good government.

After some general observations on the wisdom of that advice to a King which was contained in the text, his Grace called the attention of his august congregation to the important event which brought them together. It was, he said, the solemnization of a great compact, and ought therefore to be the ratification of a lasting peace amongst the King and his people. His Majesty would now show all his affection for his subjects, and they in return would express their gratitude and unbounded devotion to him; but it was the part of the King to insure the people's regard by pledges that he would sustain the religion and morality of the country by his own example, and that he would not undermine them by giving encouragement to the profligate and unworthy.—His duty it was, by his declarations, to convince the disaffected, that if they calculated upon success from their dark machinations, they should expect nothing but disappointment. And it behoved royalty to be strenuous in giving examples of purity in its own person, for its high situation would not save it from falling. The scripture constantly warned men " who were exalted to take care lest they should fall." The King, though raised much above men, should never forget that he was human; he should never forget that his virtues formed one of the strongest ties between him and his people. The gratitude and respect of the subject rested upon the virtues of the Monarch, and their respect for him was in the same proportion as his virtues were conspicuous. That the attachment of the people to the King was always commensurate to the degree of virtue in the latter, was a proposition too plain to be demonstrated. Every page in history proved that people were neither regardless of the character of their Sovereign, nor blind to his merits. The records of every nation showed that were the Prince was just, indulgent, and merciful, the people were loyal, obedient and submissive. It was in the power of Kings to do those under them incalculable benefits. He might give to weakness the security of strength, and take from pride the insolence of security. In every government, however regulated, much remained with the Prince, and the sword of mercy, which was always at his side, was the brightest ornament of his throne. He might repress disorders; he might extinguish domestic feuds; he might allay party divisions; he might, by the magic of his power, reconcile conflicting passions. It was, therefore, true that " He that ruleth over men *must be* just, ruling in the fear of God; and that he shall be as the light of the morning when the sun riseth, even a morning without clouds." But it was not necessary that a Prince should be just towards his own subjects alone, he should be so towards the whole world. The duties of a Sovereign, if duly considered, might then be divided into two heads—first, those principles of just government which a Prince ought to exercise towards his subjects—and secondly, that by which he ought to be directed in his intercourse with foreign nations. In this latter, too many Princes were forgetful of the great rules of right, thinking, that if they kept within the bounds of ostensible propriety, they were not amenable at the bar of conscience. But this was a mistake, the same faith which one individual required from another, was due from nation to nation, and an infraction of it was as little justifiable in one case as in the other. It was not true that there ought to be one system of law for individuals and another for nations; in too many cases when nations were concerned, the greatest infractions of faith might have been committed by the breach of promises, and the greatest injustice by the extent of conquests. But a Prince to be just should never forget that he ought to be universally just, and that his conduct ought to be alike to individuals and to nations. It was in the infraction of the principle that the danger lay, and as much was to be apprehended from that when committed against a collected body of men as against an individual. In many cases, however, the Prince was not the blameable party—he had too often found it necessary to sacrifice his feelings, and perhaps, his better sense and more correct judgment, to national arrangements. He was not blameable, therefore, in every case from without; but he certainly was responsible for what he did at home. Our prudence—our morality, and our devotion to the cause of religion, were proverbial amongst other nations, and the virtues of our present King seemed to secure a permanency to that feeling. But the example of the Ruler was most material to the continuance of this feeling; and if morality once came to be discountenanced by the Sovereign, it was in vain to talk of the influence of the law as a remedy. When the whole mass of the people became corrupted by bad example, the law would be very inefficient in producing a reform. But it was no argument against a strict adherence to morality to say, that the State was successful abroad. A State might certainly succeed though its sources were corrupted; but was prosperity happiness? It ought, therefore, to be the object of every good Ruler to give strength to right, and to give to every subject, as far as human means would permit him, protection in his greatest difficulties. Nothing was a stronger symptom of a bad Prince than his raising bad men to his favour. A Prince ought to choose such men as he knew were not only attached to his particular interest, but also devoted to the best interests of the country. There never was a Prince yet who had shown a mild disposition towards his people, but more particularly those who had cultivated their good will, that had not been relieved by their gratitude. And in the present case the country had great reason to hope that his Majesty would fulfil all the expectations which had been entertained of him. The House of Hanover, to which he belonged, had long been remarkable for its attachment to religion, and the interest which religion acquired from their example. The late King had laid claim to the gratitude of this country, which ought not to be quickly forgotten, and it was a consolation to see his son and worthy successor treading in the same steps. And, indeed, the past conduct of his Majesty had given every reason to hope the best from him for the future. The Sovereign was now about to receive the Imperial Crown of his ancestors, and it was consoling to think that he was not totally unused to the cares of Royalty. When his Majesty came to the head of affairs in this country, he found it involved in an expensive and ruinous war, but it was owing to his steadiness that we got through it with such glorious results. And it should be remembered, that in making peace, though we had so great advantages, yet no terms were asked as if we were conquerors. It ought, therefore, to be the prayer of all to beseech GOD to put the Sovereign into a situation where he should not be forgetful of all that is expected from him. The Right Rev. Prelate commenced preaching thirty-five minutes after twelve, and ended at eight minutes before one o'clock.

On his Majesty's right hand stood the Bishop of Durham, and beyond him, on the same side, the lords that carried the swords. On his Majesty's left hand stood the Bishop of Bath and Wells, and the Lord Great Chamberlain.

On the north side of the altar sat the Archbishop in a purple velvet chair; the bishops were placed on forms along the north side of the wall, betwixt the King and the pulpit. Near the Archbishop stood Garter King at Arms. On the south side, east of the King's chair, nearer to the altar, stood the Dean of Westminster, the rest of the bishops who took part in the church service, and the Prebendaries of Westminster.

THE OATH.

When the sermon ended, the Archbishop went to the King, and standing before him (his Majesty, on Thursday, the 27th of April, 1820, in the presence of the two Houses of Parliament, made and signed the Declaration) administered the Coronation Oath, first asking the King—

"Sir; is your Majesty willing to take the oath?"
The King answered :—" I am willing."

The Archbishop then ministered these questions; and the King, having a copy of the printed form and order of the Coronation service in his hands, answered each question severally, as follows :—

Arch. "Will you solemnly promise and swear to govern the people of this United Kingdom of Great Britain and Ireland, and the dominions thereto belonging, according to the Statutes in Parliament agreed on, and the respective laws and customs of the same?"

King. "I solemnly promise so to do."

Arch. "Will you to your power cause law and justice, in mercy, to be executed in all your judgments?"

King. "I will."

Arch. "Will you to the utmost of your power maintain the laws of God, the true profession of the Gospel, and the Protestant reformed religion established by law? And will you maintain and preserve inviolably the settlement of the united church of England and Ireland, and the doctrine, worship, discipline, and government thereof, as by law established within England and Ireland, and the territories thereunto belonging? And will you preserve unto the bishops and clergy of England and Ireland, and to the united church committed to their charge, all such rights and privileges, as by law do, or shall appertain to them, or any of them?

King. "All this I promise to do."

Then the King arising out of his chair, supported as before, and assisted by the Lord Great Chamberlain, the Sword of State being carried before him, went to the altar, and there being uncovered made his solemn oath in the sight of all the people, to observe the premises; laying his right hand upon the Holy Gospel in the great Bible, which was before carried in the procession, and was now brought from the altar by the Archbishop, and tendered to him as he kneels upon the steps, saying these words :—

"The things which I have here before promised, I will perform and keep. So help me God."

Then the King kissed the book, and signed the oath.

THE ANOINTING.

The King having thus taken his oath, returned again to the chair, and kneeling at his faldstool, the Archbishop began the hymn Veni, Creator Spiritus, and the choir sang it out.

ANTHEM II.

"Come, Holy Ghost, our souls inspire,
And warm them with thy heav'nly fire.
Thou who th' anointing spirit art,
To us thy sevenfold gifts impart.
Let thy bless'd unction from above
Be to us comfort, life, and love.
Enable with celestial light
The weakness of our mortal sight;
Anoint our hearts and cheer our face,
With the abundance of thy grace:
Keep far our foes, give peace at home;
Where thou dost dwell, no ill can come:
Teach us to know the Father, Son,
And Spirit of both, to be but one,

"That so through ages all along,
This may be our triumphant song;
In thee, O Lord, we make our boast,
In thee, O Lord, we make our boast,
Father, Son, and Holy Ghost."

This being ended, the Archbishop said this prayer:

" O Lord, Holy Father, who by anointing with oil didst of old make and consecrate Kings, Priests, and Prophets, to teach and govern thy people Israel: Bless and sanctify thy chosen servant George, who by our office and ministry is now to be anointed with this oil, and consecrated King of this realm: Strengthen him, O Lord, with the Holy Ghost the comforter: Confirm and establish him with thy free and princely spirit, the spirit of wisdom and government, the spirit of counsel and ghostly strength, the spirit of knowledge and true godliness, and fill him, O Lord, with the spirit of thy holy fear, now and for ever. Amen."

This prayer being ended, the choir sang:

ANTHEM III.

" Zadok the priest, and Nathan the prophet, anointed Solomon King; and all the people rejoiced and said, God save the King, Long live the King, May the King live for ever. Amen. Hallelujah."

In the mean time the King rising from his devotions, went before the altar, supported and attended as before.

The King sat down in his chair placed in the midst of the area over against the altar, with the faldstool before it, wherein he was anointed. Four Knights of the Garter held over him a rich pall of silk, or cloth of gold; the Dean of Westminster took the ampulla and spoon from off the altar, poured some of the holy oil into the spoon, and with it the Archbishop anointed the King, in the form of a cross.

1. On the crown of the head, saying,
" Be thy head anointed with holy oil, as Kings, Priests, and Prophets were anointed."
2. On the breast, saying,
" Be thy breast anointed with holy oil."
3. On the palms of both the hands, saying,
" Be thy hands anointed with holy oil:

"And as Solomon was anointed King by Zadok the Priest, and Nathan the Prophet, so be you anointed, blessed, and consecrated King over this people, whom the Lord your God hath given you to rule and govern, in the name of the Father, and of the Son, and the Holy Ghost. Amen."

Then the Dean of Westminster laid the ampulla and spoon upon the altar, and the King kneeling down at the faldstool, and the Archbishop standing on the north side of the altar, said this prayer or blessing over him:—

"Our Lord Jesus Christ, the Son of God, who by his Father was anointed with the oil of gladness above his fellows, by his holy anointing pour down upon your head and heart the blessing of the Holy Ghost, and prosper the works of your hands; that by the assistance of his heavenly grace you may preserve the people committed to your charge in wealth, peace, and godliness; and after a long and glorious course of ruling this temporal kingdom wisely, justly, and religiously, you may at last be made partaker of an eternal kingdom, through the merits of Jesus Christ our Lord. Amen."

This prayer being ended, the King arose, and sat down again in his chair, and the Dean of Westminster wiped and dried all the places anointed, with fine linen, or fine bombast wool, delivered to him by the Lord Great Chamberlain.

The investiture then commenced, and the spurs were brought from the altar by the Dean of Westminster, and delivered to a nobleman thereto appointed by the King, who, kneeling down, presented them to his Majesty, who forthwith sent them back to the altar.

Then the lord who carried the Sword of State, returned the said sword to the officers of the Jewel House, which was thereupon deposited in the traverse in King Edward's chapel; he received thence, in lieu thereof, another sword, in a scabbard of purple velvet, provided for the King to be girt withal, which he delivered to the Archbishop; and the Archbishop laying it on the altar, said the following prayer:—

"Hear our prayers, O Lord, we beseech thee, and so direct and support thy servant King George, who is now to be girt with this sword, that he may not bear it in vain; but may use it as the minister of God, for the terror and punishment of evil-doers, and for the protection and encouragement of those that do well, through Jesus Christ our Lord. Amen."

Then the Archbishop took the sword from off the altar, and (the bishops assisting, and going along with him) delivered it into the King's right hand, and he holding it, the Archbishop said:—

"Receive this kingly sword, brought now from the altar of God, and delivered to you by the hands of us the bishops and servants of God, though unworthy."

The King stood up, the sword was girt about him by the Lord Great Chamberlain, and then the King sitting down, the Archbishop said:—

"Remember him of whom the Royal Psalmist did prophesy, saying, 'Gird thee with thy sword upon thy thigh, O thou most mighty, good luck have thou with thine honour, ride on prosperously, because of truth, meekness, and righteousness;' and be thou a follower of him. With this sword do justice, stop the growth of iniquity, protect the holy church of God, help and defend widows and orphans, restore the things that are gone to decay, maintain the things that are restored, punish and reform what is amiss, and confirm what is in good order: that doing these things, you may be glorious in all virtue: and so represent our Lord Jesus Christ in this life, that you may reign for ever with him in the life which is to come. Amen."

Then the King, rising up, ungirded his sword, and going to the altar, offered it there in the scabbard, and then returned and sat down in his chair: And the chief peer offered the price of it, namely, a hundred shillings, and having thus redeemed it, received it, from off the altar by the Dean of Westminster, and drew it out of the scabbard, and carried it naked before his Majesty during the rest of the solemnity.

THE INVESTING WITH THE ARMILL AND ROYAL ROBE, AND THE DELIVERY OF THE ORB.

Then the King arising, the Dean of Westminster

took the Armill from the Master of the Great Wardrobe, and put it about his Majesty's neck, and tied it to the bowings of his arms, above and below the elbows, with silk strings: the Archbishop standing before the King, and saying:—

"Receive this Armill as a token of the divine mercy embracing you on every side."

Next the robe royal, or purple robe of state, of Cloth of Tissue, lined or furred with ermine, was by the Master of the Great Wardrobe delivered to the Dean of Westminster, and by him put upon the King, standing; the crimson robe which he wore before being first taken off by the Lord Great Chamberlain: the King having received it, sat down, and then the orb with the cross was brought from the altar by the Dean of Westminster, and delivered into the King's hand by the Archbishop, pronouncing this blessing and exhortation:—

"Receive this imperial robe and orb, and the Lord your God endue you with knowledge and wisdom, with majesty and with power from on high; the Lord clothe you with the robe of righteousness, and with the garments of salvation. And when you see this orb set under the cross, remember that the whole world is subject to the power and empire of Christ our Redeemer. For he is the Prince of the Kings of the Earth; King of Kings, and Lord of Lords: so that no man can reign happily, who deriveth not his authority from him, and directeth not all his actions according to his laws.*

INVESTITURE PER ANNULUM ET BACULUM.

Then the Master of the Jewel House delivered the King's ring to the Archbishop, in which a table jewel was enchased; the Archbishop put it on the fourth finger of his Majesty's right hand, and said:—

---

* In Ashmole this address is as follows:—"Receive this pall which is formed of four corners, to let this understand that the four corners of the world are subject to the power of God, and that no man can happily reign upon earth who hath not received his authority from Heaven."

"Receive this ring, the ensign of kingly dignity and of defence of the Catholic faith; and as you are this day solemnly invested in the government of this earthly kingdom, so may you be sealed with that spirit of promise, which is the earnest of an heavenly inheritance, and reign with him who is the blessed and only Potentate, to whom be glory for ever and ever. Amen."

The King delivered his Orb to the Dean of Westminster, to be by him laid upon the altar; and then the Dean of Westminster brought the sceptre and rod to the Archbishop; and the Lord of the Manor of Worksop (who claimed to hold an estate by the service of presenting to the King a right hand glove on the day of his Coronation, and supporting the King's right arm whilst he holds the sceptre with the cross) delivered to the King a pair of rich gloves, and on any occasion happening afterwards, supported his Majesty's right arm, or held his sceptre by him.

The gloves being put on, the Archbishop delivered the sceptre, with the cross, into the King's right hand, saying:—

"Receive the royal sceptre, the ensign of kingly power and justice."

And then he delivered the rod, with the dove, into the King's left hand, and said:—

"Receive the rod of equity and mercy; and God, from whom all holy desires, all good counsels, and all just works do proceed, direct and assist you in the administration and exercise of all those powers he hath given you. Be so merciful, that you be not too remiss; so execute justice, that you forget not mercy. Punish the wicked, protect the oppressed; and the blessing of him who was ready to perish shall be upon you; thus in all things following his great and holy example, of whom the Prophet David said, 'Thou lovest righteousness and hatest iniquity; the sceptre of thy kingdom is a right sceptre;' even Jesus Christ our Lord. Amen."

THE PUTTING ON OF THE CROWN.—

The Archbishop, standing before the altar, took the crown into his hands, and laying it again before him upon the altar, said:—

"O God, who crownest thy faithful servants with mercy and loving kindness, look down upon this thy servant George our King, who now in lowly devotion boweth his head to thy Divine Majesty; and as thou dost this day set a crown of pure gold upon his head, so enrich his royal heart with thy heavenly grace; and crown him with all princely virtues, which may adorn the high station wherein thou hast placed him, through Jesus Christ our Lord, to whom be honour and glory, for ever and ever. Amen."*

Then the King sat down in King Edward's chair, the Archbishop, assisted with other bishops, came from the altar; the Dean of Westminster brought the crown, and the Archbishop taking it of him, reverently put it upon the King's head. At the sight whereof the people, with loud and repeated shouts, cried— "God save the King," and the trumpets sounded, and by a signal given, the great guns at the Tower were fired.

The noise ceasing, the Archbishop rose and said:—

"Be strong and of good courage; observe the commandments of God, and walk in his holy ways: fight the good fight of faith, and lay hold on eternal life; that in this world you may be crowned with success and honour, and when you have finished your course, you may receive a crown of righteousness, which God the righteous judge shall give you in that day."

Then the choir sung this short anthem:—

ANTHEM IV.

"The King shall rejoice in thy strength, O Lord: exceeding glad shall he be of thy salvation. Thou hast presented him with the blessings of goodness, and hast set a crown of pure gold upon his head. Hallelujah. Amen."

As soon as the King was crowned, the Peers, &c. put on their coronets and caps.

THE PRESENTING OF THE HOLY BIBLE.

The Dean of Westminster took the Holy Bible, which was carried in the procession, from off the altar,

---

* This prayer is called *Benedictio Coronæ* in the early rituals; and the *Liber Regalis* directs that after it is said, the archbishop shall sprinkle the crown with holy water, and cense it, before placing it on the king's head.

KING GEORGE THE FOURTH,

In his Coronation Robes.

and delivered it to the Archbishop, who, with the rest of the bishops going along with him, presented it to the King, first saying these words to him :—

"Our Gracious King; we present unto your Majesty this book, the most valuable thing that this world affordeth. Here is wisdom; this is the royal law; these are the lively oracles of God. Blessed is he that readeth, and they that hear the words of this book; that keep, and do, the things contained in it. For these are the words of eternal life, able to make you wise and happy in this world, nay wise unto salvation, and so happy for evermore, through faith which is in Christ Jesus; to whom be glory for ever. Amen."

Then the King delivered back the Bible to the Archbishop, who gave it to the Dean of Westminster, to be reverently placed again upon the holy altar.

THE BENEDICTION, AND TE DEUM.

And now the King having been thus anointed and crowned, and having received all the ensigns of royalty, the Archbishop solemnly blessed him, and all the Bishops standing about him, with the rest of the Peers, with a loud and hearty Amen.

" The Lord bless and keep you : the Lord make the light of his countenance to shine for ever upon you, and be gracious unto you : the Lord protect you in all your ways, preserve you from every evil thing, and prosper you in every thing good. Amen.

" The Lord give you a faithful senate, wise and upright counsellors, and magistrates, a loyal nobility, and a dutiful gentry ; a pious and learned and useful clergy ; an honest, industrious and obedient community. Amen.

" In your days may mercy and truth meet together, and righteousness and peace kiss each other ; may wisdom and knowledge be the stability of your times, and the fear of the Lord your treasure. Amen.

" The Lord make your days many, and your reign prosperous ; your fleets and armies victorious ; and may you be reverenced and beloved by all your subjects, and ever increase in favour with God and man. Amen.

" The glorious Majesty of the Lord our God be upon you : may he bless you with all temporal and spiritual happiness in this world, and crown you with glory and immortality in the world to come. Amen.

"The Lord give you a religious and victorious posterity to rule these kingdoms in all ages. Amen."

Then the Archbishop turned to the people and said—

"And the same Lord God Almighty grant that the clergy and nobles assembled here for this great and solemn service; and together with them all the people of the land, fearing God, and honouring the King, may by the merciful superintendency of the Divine Providence, and the vigilant care of our gracious Sovereign, continually enjoy peace, plenty, and prosperity, through Jesus Christ our Lord, to whom, with the Eternal Father, and God the Holy Ghost, be glory in the church, world without end. Amen."

The blessing being thus given, the King sat down in his chair, vouchsafed to kiss the Archbishop and Bishops assisting at his Coronation, they kneeling before him one after another.

Then the choir began to sing *Te Deum*, and the King went up to the Theatre on which the throne is placed, all the bishops, great officers, and other peers, attending him, and then he sat down and reposed himself in his chair, below the throne.

ANTHEM V.—TE DEUM.

"We praise thee, O God; we acknowledge thee to be the Lord

"All the earth doth worship thee: the Father everlasting.

"To thee all angels cry aloud: the heavens, and all the powers therein.

"To thee Cherubin and Seraphin: continually do cry,

"Holy, holy, holy: Lord God of Sabaoth.

"Heaven and earth are full of the majesty of thy glory.

"The glorious company of the Apostles: praise thee.

"The goodly fellowship of the Prophets: praise thee.

"The noble army of Martyrs: praise thee.

"The holy Church throughout all the world, doth acknowledge thee:

"The Father of an infinite Majesty;

"Thine honourable, true, and only Son;

"Also the Holy Ghost: the Comforter.

"Thou art the King of glory: O Christ.

"Thou art the everlasting Son of the Father.

"When thou tookest upon thee to deliver man : thou didst not abhor the virgin's womb.

"When thou hadst overcome the sharpness of death : thou didst open the kingdom of heaven to all believers.

"Thou sittest at the right hand of God : in the glory of the Father.

"We believe that thou shalt come to be our judge.

"We therefore pray thee, help thy servants : whom thou hast redeemed with thy precious blood.

"Make them to be numbered with thy saints : in glory everlasting.

"O Lord save thy people : and bless thine heritage.

"Govern them : and lift them up for ever.

"Day by day we magnify thee.

"And we worship thy name : ever world without end.

"Vouchsafe, O Lord : to keep us this day without sin.

"O Lord have mercy upon us : have mercy upon us.

"O Lord let thy mercy lighten upon us : as our trust is in thee.

"O Lord in thee have I trusted : let me never be confounded."

THE INTHRONIZATION.

The *Te Deum* being ended, the King was led to his throne by the archbishops and bishops, and other peers of the kingdom. And being inthronized or placed therein, all the great officers, those that bore the swords, and the sceptres, and the rest of the nobles, stood round about the steps of the throne, and the Archbishop standing before the King, said—

"Stand firm, and hold fast, from henceforth, the seat and imperial dignity which is this day delivered unto you in the name, and by the authority of Almighty God, and by the hands of us the bishops and servants of God, though unworthy; and as you see us to approach nearer to God's altar, so vouchsafe the more graciously to continue to us your royal favour and protection. And the Lord God Almighty, whose ministers we are, and the stewards of his mysteries, establish your throne in righteousness, that it may stand fast for evermore, like as the sun before Him, and as the faithful witness in heaven. Amen."

THE HOMAGE.*

The exhortation being ended, all the peers present

---

* The doing of homage to our kings, though it now forms a part of

did homage publicly and solemnly unto the King upon the Theatre, and in the mean time the Treasurer of the Household threw among the people medals of gold and silver, as the King's princely largess or donative.

The Archbishop first knelt down before his Majesty's knees, and the rest of the bishops knelt on either hand, and about him; and they did their homage together, for the shortening of the ceremony, the Archbishop saying:—

"I Charles Archbishop of Canterbury [and so every one of the rest, I, N. Bishop of N. repeating the rest audibly after the Archbishop] will be faithful and true, and faith and truth will bear, unto you our Sovereign Lord and your heirs Kings of the United Kingdom of Great Britain and Ireland. And I will do, and truly acknowledge the service of the lands which I claim to hold of you, as in right of the church. So help me God."

Then the Archbishop kissed the King's left cheek, and so the rest of the bishops present after him.

After which the other peers of the realm did their homage in like manner, the dukes first by themselves, and so the marquisses, the earls, the viscounts, and the barons, severally; the first of each order kneeling before his Majesty, and the rest with and about him, all putting off their coronets, and the first of each class beginning, and the last saying after him:—

"I, N. Duke, or Earl, &c. of N. do become your liege man of life and limb, and of earthly worship, and faith and truth I will bear unto you, to live and die, against all manner of folks. So help me God."

The peers having done their homage, they stood all together round about the King; and each class or degree going by themselves, or (as it was at the coronation of King Charles the First and Second) every peer one by one, in order, put off their coronets, singly ascended the throne again, and stretching forth

the Coronation ceremony, was not in old times connected with it, being frequently performed on the day following the Coronation. In the time of Richard I. it was on the day subsequent to the Coronation; in the reigns of John and Henry III. it was in the same week.

their hands, touched the crown on his Majesty's head, as promising by that ceremony, to be ever ready to support it with all their power, and then every one of them kissed the King's cheek.

While the peers were thus doing their homage, and the medals thrown about, the King delivered his sceptre with the cross to the Lord of the Manor of Worksop, to hold; and the other sceptre, or rod, with the dove, to the Lord that carried it in the procession.

And the bishops that supported the King in the procession also eased him, by supporting the crown, as there was occasion.

THE FINAL ANTHEM.

While the medals were scattered, and the homage of the Lords performed, the choir sung this anthem, with instrumental music of all sorts, as a solemn conclusion of the King's Coronation.

ANTHEM VI.

"Blessed be thou, Lord God of Israel, our Father, for ever and ever. Thine, O Lord, is the greatness and the power, and the victory, and the majesty; for all that is in the heaven and the earth are thine. Thine is the kingdom, O Lord; and thou art exalted as head over all. Both riches and honour come of thee, and thou reignest over all; and in thine hand is power and might; and in thine hand it is to make great, and to give strength unto all. Now, therefore, our God, we thank thee, and praise thy glorious name."

At the end of this anthem the drums beat, and the trumpets sounded, and all the people shouted, crying out,—

"God save King George the Fourth,
"Long live King George,
"May the King live for ever."

The solemnity of the King's Coronation being thus ended, the Archbishop left the King in his throne, and went down to the altar.

THE COMMUNION.

Then the Offertory began, the Archbishop reading these sentences:—

"Let your light so shine before men that they may see your good works, and glorify your Father which is in Heaven."

"Charge them who are rich in this world, that they be ready to give, and glad to distribute; laying up in store for themselves a good foundation against the time to come, that they may attain eternal life."

The King descended from his throne, supported and attended as before, and went to the steps of the altar, and knelt down there.

At first the King offered bread and wine for the Communion, which was brought out of King Edward's Chapel, and delivered into his hands, the bread upon the paten, by the Bishop that read the Epistle, and the wine in the chalice by the Bishop that read the Gospel, were by the Archbishop received from the King, and reverently placed upon the altar, and decently covered with a fair linen cloth, the Archbishop first saying this prayer:—

"Bless, O Lord, we beseech thee, these thy gifts, and sanctify them unto this holy use, that by them we may be made partakers of the body and blood of thine only begotten Son Jesus Christ, and fed unto everlasting life of soul and body: And that thy servant King George may be enabled to the discharge of his weighty office, whereunto of thy great goodness thou hast called and appointed him. Grant this, O Lord, for Jesus Christ's sake, our only Mediator and Advocate. Amen."

Then the King kneeling, as before, made his second oblation, offering a mark weight of gold, which the Treasurer of the Household delivered to the Lord Great Chamberlain, and he to his Majesty. And the Archbishop came to him, and received it in the bason, and placed it upon the altar. After which the Bishop said:—

"O God, who dwellest in the high and holy place, with them also who are of an humble spirit; look down mercifully upon this thy servant George, our King, here humbling himself before thee at thy footstool; and graciously receive these oblations, which in humble acknowledgment of thy sovereignty over all, and of thy great bounty to him in particular, he has now offered up unto thee, through Jesus Christ, our only Mediator and Advocate. Amen."

The Benediction. 229

Then the King returned to his chair, and knelt down at his faldstool, the Archbishop said:—

"Let us pray for the whole state of Christ's church militant here on earth.

"Almighty and everliving God, who by the holy Apostle hast taught us to make prayers and supplications, and to give thanks for all men: We humbly beseech thee most mercifully to receive these our prayers which we offer unto thy Divine Majesty; beseeching thee to inspire continually the universal church with the spirit of truth, unity, and concord: and grant that all they that do confess thy holy name, may agree in the truth of thy holy word, and live in unity and godly love. We beseech thee also to save and defend all Christian Kings, Princes, and Governors; and especially thy servant George our King, that under him we may be godly and quietly governed: and grant unto his whole council, and to all that are put in authority under him, that they may truly and indifferently minister justice, to the punishment of wickedness and vice, and to the maintenance of thy true religion and virtue. Give grace, O heavenly Father, to all Bishops and Curates, that they may both by their life and doctrine set forth thy true and lively word, and rightly and duly administer thy holy sacraments: and to all thy people give thy heavenly grace, and especially to this congregation here present, that with meek heart and due reverence they may hear and receive thy holy word, truly reserving thee in holiness and righteousness all the days of their life. And we most humbly beseech thee of thy goodness, O Lord, to comfort and succour all them who in this transitory life are in trouble, sorrow, need, sickness, or any other adversity. And we also bless thy holy name, for all thy servants departed this life in thy faith and fear; beseeching thee to give us grace so to follow their good examples, that with them we may be partakers of thy heavenly kingdom. Grant this, O Father, for Jesus Christ's sake, our only Mediator and Advocate. Amen."*

---

* We give the following Benediction, which was delivered on this occasion at the Coronation of George III., and we leave it to our readers to draw the comparison. There is something beautiful and sublime in the following:

"Almighty God give thee of the dew of heaven, and of the fat of the earth, and abundance of corn and wine. Let the nations serve thee, and the tribes worship thee, and let him be blessed that blesseth thee; and God shall be thy helper.

"Almighty God bless thee with the blessing of heaven above, on the mountains and hills, and with the blessings of the earth beneath;

THE EXHORTATION.

"Ye that do truly and earnestly repent you of your sins, and are in love and charity with your neighbours, and intend to lead a new life, following the commandments of God, and walking from henceforth in his holy ways; draw near with faith, and take this holy Sacrament to your comfort; and make your humble confession to Almighty God, meekly kneeling upon your knees."

THE GENERAL CONFESSION.

"Almighty God, father of our Lord Jesus Christ, maker of all things, judge of all men; we acknowledge and bewail our manifold sins and wickedness, which we from time to time most grievously have committed, by thought, word, and deed, against thy divine Majesty, provoking most justly thy wrath and indignation against us. We do earnestly repent, and are heartily sorry for these our misdoings; the remembrance of them is grievous unto us; the burden of them is intolerable. Have mercy upon us, have mercy upon us, most merciful father; for thy son our Lord Jesus Christ's sake, forgive us all that is past, and grant that we may ever hereafter serve and please thee, in newness of life, to the honour and glory of thy name, through Jesus Christ our Lord. Amen."

THE ABSOLUTION.

"Almighty God our heavenly Father, who of his great mercy hath promised forgiveness of sins to all them that with hearty repentance, and true faith, turn unto him; have mercy upon you, pardon and deliver you from all your sins,

---

with the blessings of corn and wine, and fruit; and let the blessings of the Fathers Abraham, Isaac, and Jacob, be established upon thee, through Jesus Christ our Lord. Amen.

"Bless, O Lord, the virtuous carriage of this King, and accept the work of his hands; replenish his realm with the blessings of heaven, of the dew of the water, and of the deeps. Let the influence of the sun and moon drop down fatness upon the high mountains, and the clouds rain plenty on the valleys, that the earth may abound with all things. Let the blessings of him that appeared in the bush descend upon his head, and the fulness of his blessing, fall on his children and posterity. Let his feet be dipped in oil, and his horn exalted as the horn of an Unicorn,* with which he may scatter his enemies from off the face of the earth. The Lord that sitteth in heaven be his defender for ever and ever, through Jesus Christ our Lord. Amen."

* A learned dissertation on the horn, as an emblem of power, may be found in Paschalius *Coronarium, lib.* x. *p.* 674 (4to. 1610).

The Prayer of Address.

confirm and strengthen you in all goodness, and bring you to everlasting life, through Jesus Christ our Lord. Amen."

After which was said—

"Hear what comfortable words our Saviour saith unto all that truly turn to him.

'Come unto me, all that travail and are heavy laden, and I will refresh you.' St. Matt. xi. 28.

'So God loved the world, that he gave his only begotten Son to the world, and that all that believe in him, should not perish, but have everlasting life.' St. John iii. 16.

"Hear also what St. Paul saith,

'This is a true saying, and worthy of all men to be received, that Christ Jesus came into the world to save sinners.' 1st Tim. i. 15.

"Hear also what St. John saith,

'If any man sin, we have an advocate with the Father, Jesus Christ the righteous, and he is the propitiation for our sins.' 1st John ii. 1.

After which the Archbishop proceeded, saying :—

Arch. "Lift up your hearts."
Answ. "We lift them unto the Lord."
Arch. "Let us give thanks unto our Lord God."
Answ. "It is meet and right so to do."

Then the Archbishop turned to the Lord's table, and said :—

"It is very meet, right, and our bounden duty, that we should at all times, and in all places, give thanks unto thee, O Lord, Holy Father, Almighty everlasting God :

"Who hast at this time given us thy servant our sovereign King George to be the Defender of the Faith, and the protector of thy people :

"Therefore with angels and arch-angels, and with all the company of heaven, we laud and magnify thy glorious name, evermore praising thee, and saying, holy, holy, holy, Lord God of hosts, heaven and earth are full of thy glory. Glory be to thee, O Lord, most high. Amen."

THE PRAYER OF ADDRESS.

"We do not presume to come to this thy table, O merciful God, trusting in our own righteousness, but thy manifold great mercies. We are not worthy so much as to gather up the crumbs under thy table. But thou art the same God, whose property is always to have mercy; grant us, therefore, gracious God, so to eat the flesh of thy dear Son, Jesus Christ, to drink his blood, that our sinful bodies may be made clean by his body, our souls washed through his most precious blood. That we may evermore dwell with him, and he with us. Amen."

THE PRAYER OF CONSECRATION.

"Almighty God, our heavenly Father, who of thy tender mercy didst give thine only Son, Jesus Christ, to suffer death upon the cross for our redemption, who made there (by his one oblation of himself once offered) a full, perfect, and sufficient sacrifice, oblation, and satisfaction, for the sins of the whole world, and did institute, and in his holy Gospel command us to continue a perpetual memory of that his precious death to his coming again; bear us, O merciful Father, we most humbly beseech thee, and grant that we receiving these thy creatures of bread and wine, according to thy Son our Saviour Jesus Christ's holy institution, in remembrance of his death and passion, may be partakers of his most holy body and blood: who in the same night that he was betrayed took bread, * and when he had given thanks, he brake it, † and gave it to his disciples, saying, Take eat, ‡ this is my body which is given for you, do this in remembrance of me. Likewise, after supper § he took the cup, and when he had given thanks, he gave it to them, saying, Drink ye all of this, for this ‖ is my blood of the New Testament, which is shed for you and for many for the remission of sins: do this, as oft as ye shall drink it, in remembrance of me. Amen."

When the Archbishop, and Dean of Westminster, with the Bishops' Assistants, namely, the Preacher, and those who read the Litany, and the Epistle and Gospel, had communicated in both kinds, the Archbishop administered the bread, and the Dean of Westminster the cup to the King.

At the delivery of the bread, was said—

" The body of our Lord Jesus Christ, which was given for

---

* Here the Archbishop took the paten into his hands.
† And here broke the bread.
‡ And here laid his hand upon all the bread.
§ Here took the cup into his hand.
‖ And here laid his hand upon every vessel (be it chalice or flagon) in which there was any wine to be consecrated.

thee, preserve thy body and soul unto everlasting life. Take and eat this in remembrance that Christ died for thee, and feed on him in thy heart by faith with thanksgiving."

At the delivery of the cup—

" The blood of our Lord Jesus Christ, which was shed for thee, preserve thy body and soul unto everlasting life. Drink this in remembrance that Christ's blood was shed for thee, and be thankful."

While the King received, the Bishop appointed for that service held a towel of white silk, or fine linen, before him. Then the Archbishop went on to the Post Communion, saying :—

" Our Father which art in heaven ; hallowed be thy name, Thy kingdom come. Thy will be done in earth, as it is in heaven. Give us this day our daily bread ; and forgive us our trespasses as we forgive them who trespass against us. Lead us not into temptation, but deliver us from evil ; for thine is the kingdom, and the power, and the glory, for ever. Amen."

Then this prayer :—

" O Lord and Heavenly Father, we, thy humble servants, entirely desire thy fatherly goodness, mercifully to accept this our sacrifice of praise and thanksgiving ; most humbly beseeching thee to grant, that by the merits and death of thy Son, Jesus Christ, and through faith in his blood, we and all thy whole Church may obtain remission of our sins, and all other benefits of his passion, and here we offer and present unto thee, O Lord, ourselves, our souls and bodies, to be a reasonable, holy, and lively sacrifice unto thee ; humbly beseeching thee, that all we, who are partakers of this holy communion, may be filled with thy grace and heavenly benediction."

Then was said :—

" Glory be to God on high, and on earth peace : good will towards men. We praise thee ; we bless thee ; we worship thee ; we glorify thee ; we give thanks to thee for thy great glory, O Lord God, Heavenly King, God the Father Almighty."

" O Lord, the only begotten Son Jesus Christ.

" O Lord God, Lamb of God, Son of the Father, that takest away the sins of the world, have mercy upon us. Thou that takest away the sins of the world, receive our prayer. Thou that sittest at the right hand of God the Father, have mercy upon us.

"For thou only art holy, thou only art the Lord, thou only, O Christ, with the Holy Ghost, are most high in the glory of God the Father. Amen."

The King returned to his throne upon the Theatre, and afterwards the Archbishop read the final prayers.

THE FINAL PRAYERS.

"Assist us mercifully, O Lord, in these our supplications and prayers, and dispose the way of thy servants towards the attainment of everlasting salvation, that among all the changes and chances of this mortal life, they may ever be defended by thy most gracious and ready help, through Jesus Christ our Lord. Amen.

"O Lord our God, who upholdest and governest all things in heaven and earth, receive our humble prayers with our thanksgivings, for our Sovereign Lord George, set over us by thy good providence to be our King. And so, together with him, bless all the Royal Family, that they, ever trusting in thy goodness, protected by thy power, and crowned with thy favour, may continue before thee in health and peace, in joy and honour, a long and happy life upon earth, and after death may obtain everlasting life and glory in the kingdom of heaven, through the merits and mediation of Jesus Christ our Saviour, who with thee, O Father, and the Holy Spirit, liveth and reigneth, ever one God, world without end. Amen.

"Almighty God, who hast promised to hear the petition of them that ask in thy Son's name, we beseech thee mercifully to incline thine ears to us that have made now our prayers and supplications unto thee, and grant that those things which we have faithfully asked according to thy will, may effectually be obtained to the relief of our necessity, and to the setting forth of thy glory, through Jesus Christ our Lord. Amen.

"The peace of God, which passeth all understanding, keep your hearts and minds in the knowledge and love of God, and of his Son Jesus Christ our Lord. And the blessing of God Almighty, the Father, the Son, and the Holy Ghost, be amongst you, and remain with you always. Amen."

The whole Coronation office being thus performed, the King, attended and accompanied as before, the four swords being carried before him, descended from his throne crowned, and carrying the sceptre and rod in his hands, went up the area eastward of the Theatre, and passed on through the door, on the south side of the altar, into King Edward's Chapel; and as they passed by the altar, the rest of the Regalia lying upon it, were delivered by the Dean of Westminster to the Lords that carried them in the procession, and so they proceeded in state into the chapel; the organ all the while playing.

The King then came into the chapel, and standing before the altar, took off his crown and delivered it, together with his sceptre, to the Archbishop, who laid them upon the altar there; and the rest of the Regalia were given into the hands of the Dean of Westminster, and by him laid there also.

Then the King withdrew himself into his traverse prepared for him upon the western wall of that chapel.

Within his traverse the King was disrobed by the Lord Great Chamberlain of his royal robe of state (which was forthwith delivered to the Dean of Westminster to be laid also upon the altar) and again arrayed with his robe of purple velvet, which was before laid ready in the traverse for that purpose.

When the King, thus habited, came forth of his traverse, he stood before the altar, and the Archbishop being still vested in his cope, set the crown of state, provided for the King to wear during the rest of the ceremony, upon his head. Then he gave the sceptre with the cross into the King's right hand, and the oil with the cross into his left; which being done, both the Archbishop and Dean divested themselves of their copes, and left them there, and proceeded in their usual habits.

Then the King carried his sceptre with the cross in his left hand; the four swords being borne before the King, and the rest of the heralds having again put the rest of the procession in order, he went on from King Edward's Chapel to the Theatre, and thence through the midst of the choir and body of the church, out at the west door, and so returned to Westminster Hall.

The King then proceeded through the door by the side of the communion-table into St. Edward's Chapel, and during his absence, which lasted about ten minutes, the Abbey became literally deserted. As soon as his Majesty disappeared, the throng began to crowd out of the church. The peeresses departed forthwith; the box of the foreign ministers was emptied in a moment; the musicians and principal singers abruptly left the choir; and when the King returned, he had empty benches covered with dirt and litter, on the one hand, and the backs of his courtiers expediting their exits with a *sauve-qui-peut-like* rapidity, presented themselves to his view upon the other. This mode of clearing the Abbey may probably have been found necessary as a measure of convenience, but it certainly was a most unpicturesque arrangement. It had the appearance of a want of due respect to the Sovereign. His Majesty, however, though much encumbered with his splendid attire, moved forward with great seeming good humour, and shook hands with the Princess Mary as she left the Abbey.

The appearance of the Abbey, during the ceremony of the Coronation, was a scene of grandeur of which decription can convey but a faint idea. The King was seated on his throne, dressed in a robe of a most splendid and sumptuous description. It was a silver dress *a la Henri Quatre*, made of silver tissue, trimmed with silver lace. The dress, although called *a la Henri Quatre*, is the old English dress, well known in the time of Queen Elizabeth. Over this dress his Majesty wore a surcoat of crimson velvet reaching to the knee, turned back in front with silver tissue embroidered in gold, representing the crown, surrounded by gloria, laurel trophies, the civic crown, &c. The same embroidery was continued round the skirts and up the back. The sleeves hung loose, and were embroidered in a corresponding style.

Over this surcoat was the sword-belt embroidered in gold. The buckle, scabbard, belt, &c. were completely covered with diamonds.

Gorgeous Appearance of the Nobility.

Over these was worn a crimson velvet robe, nine yards in length, lined throughout with the finest ermine, and most exquisitely embroidered, representing the crown and gloria, trophies, &c. interwoven with laurels, palm, &c. This border was about nine inches wide and of extraordinary workmanship. On the outside run a bullion fringe, and beyond that appeared a narrow edge of ermine, and a part of the robe which hung down in front was also embroidered in every respect as the other part. From the right shoulder of the robe were suspended four massy gold tassels; the body of the mantle was studded all over with the rose, the thistle, and the shamrock, placed alternately.

Around his Majesty stood on one side the bishops with their copes of gold, and robes of black velvet; and close by them the heralds, with their gorgeous and many-coloured vestments. On his right and left were the peers, with their different coronets on their heads, with the robes of state loosely flowing around them, laden with all the pomp of minever and velvet. Before him stood in front, on the extreme right, the Knights of the Bath, distinguished by the taste, lightness, and elegance of their vesture, and the unbounded profusion of their snow-white plumage; and next to them were the Knights of the Garter, not peers, in all the splendid paraphernalia of their order. Their gorgeous appearance contrasted well with the elegant simplicity of the blue dress assigned to the Privy Councillors, who were flanked by heralds and officers at arms. On the King's left there stood in front five officers armed with ponderous golden or gilt maces, and dressed in a most beautiful suit of blue silk and gold. These were mixed up with various officers of arms, who, by the mingled hue of their habiliments, produced a very noble and picturesque effect. In the rear of these gentlemen the grand mass of persons who had marched in the procession was formed in a close and serried phalanx, the Yeomen of the Guard in their splendid liveries being in the centre of it, and forming, as it were, its *point d'appui*. In short, the *coup d'œil,* which was afforded to the spectator by this condensing into one small place of all the proudest ornaments of English chivalry, was one of the grandest and most magnificent scenes which was ever witnessed.

When the procession quitted the Hall, it was followed by the ambassadors and their suites, the peeresses, and all those who had tickets of admission to Westminster Abbey. They proceeded through the passages by the House of Lords, and on from thence through the covered way which led from the House of Lords to Poet's Corner. The Hall, which but a few moments before presented one of the grandest spectacles, became now, for a short time, almost deserted. Those only remained who had not tickets for the Abbey, or whose duties detained them in the Hall. The preparations for the banquet now commenced, and the cloths were soon laid along the tables at which the peers, &c. were to dine. There were three tables on each side of the Hall, each table laid for fifty-six persons. The seats were so constructed, that each could accommodate two, a small space being left between each seat. As soon as the cloths were placed, 336 silver plates (the number of those who were expected to sit down in the Hall) were laid on, each plate having two silver spoons placed near it. This was the first part of preparation. When it was arranged, the officers who had the care of what is termed the Coronation plate, began to place it on two large side-boards placed on the right and left of the throne. The plate thus exposed was entirely of pure gold. It consisted of several large dishes and vases richly embossed. The centre dish on each side presented a fine bas-relief of the Lord's Supper. Below that, on the left, was a large gold tankard, on the side of which was represented, in bas-relief, the story of the Grecian daughter. All the other vessels were richly embossed with various devices. Some of these pieces are of a very ancient date, and have graced the coronation banquets of several of our monarchs. A few of them were marked

A. R. *(Anna Regina)*, and some C. R. *(Carolus Rex)*. Immediately after the arranging of the Coronation plate, the royal table, at which were to dine the King and the several male branches of the Royal Family, was placed opposite the throne, and in part under the canopy. It was nearly of a triangular shape; the throne supplying the place of what would have been one of the angles: at two of the sides were six chairs (three at each) for the reception of their Royal Highnesses the Dukes of York, Cambridge, and Gloucester, who sat at the right of the throne, and the Dukes of Clarence, Sussex, and the Prince Leopold, who were placed on the left. The table was covered with rich damask cloths, on which were wrought the Royal arms and the devices of the several British orders, with their mottoes. On these was placed a large oval mirror, having four square pieces projecting at different sides. In the oval centre were the letters " G. R." In the square compartments were painted the red and white rose, the shamrock, and the thistle. Besides these, there were four small figures and several stands, all in gold, placed on the table. At that end which fronted the Hall was suspended a very rich flowered white satin drapery, with gold fringe and gold bullion tassels: between the festoons were the stars of the several British orders in gold embroidery. At a little before two o'clock, the waiters commenced laying the banquet on the tables at both sides of the Hall. The meats served up were all cold, and consisted of fowls, tongues, pies, and a profusion of sweet meats, conserves, and fruit of every kind. Before the tables were finally arranged (about two o'clock), the candles in the several branches were lit. There were thirteen chandeliers on each side of the Hall, with sixty large wax lights in each. These consisted of very rich cut glass, with a profusion of drops. Besides these, there were twelve table stands, with eighteen candles in each. These, together with candles placed in the choir, amounted to nearly two thousand lights, ex-

2 K

clusive of two branches of Argand suspended at the right and left of the throne. Such a vast display of artificial light would be calculated to add considerably to the splendour of such a scene, if it took place after sun-set; but in the broad glare of an unclouded sun, which beamed through every window, any number of lights could not be found a desirable acquisition. On the contrary, they detracted considerably from its splendour; and certainly from the comfort and convenience of every person in the Hall. To those gentlemen whose seats happened to be placed immediately under the chandeliers, the great increase of temperature—and that was very considerable—was not the only inconvenience; for occasionally large pieces of melted wax fell, without distinction of persons, upon all within reach. The very great heat was no where more visible than in the havoc which it made upon the curls of many of the ladies, several of whose heads had lost all traces of the friseur's skill long before the ceremony of the day was concluded. Before the return of the procession from the Abbey, those ladies and gentlemen who could gain admission from the Hall thither, amused themselves, either by promenading the Hall, or the space outside which was left between the platform and the covered way from the House of Lords to Poet's Corner. In this place many of them were gratified with a sight of the balloon, which ascended from the Green Park, and which, viewed even at that distance, presented a very splendid spectacle.

At about twenty minutes to four the gates of the Hall were thrown open, to admit the procession on its return.

Viewed from the upper end of the Hall through the arched way, the appearance of the white plumes of the Knights of the Bath was most magnificent. On their entrance to the Hall, the Knights took off their hats, but the Peers continued to wear their coronets. The procession then entered in the following order:—

The Procession.

Messenger of the College of Arms.
High Constable of Westminster.
Fife and Drums, as before ⎫ Who on their arrival in
Drum Major ⎪ the Hall, immedi-
Eight Trumpets ⎬ ately went into the
Kettle Drums ⎪ gallery over the tri-
Sergeant Trumpeter ⎭ umphal arch.
Sergeant Porter.
Knight Marshal and his Officers.
Six Clerks in Chancery.
King's Chaplains.
Sheriffs of London.
Alderman and Recorder of London.
Masters in Chancery.
King's Sergeants at Law.
King's Ancient Sergeant.
King's Solicitor General.   King's Attorney General.
Gentlemen of the Privy Chamber.
Barons of the Exchequer, and Justices of both Benches.
Lord Chief Baron of the   Lord Chief Justice of the
Exchequer.   Common Pleas.
Vice-Chancellor.   Master of the Rolls.
Lord Chief Justice of the King's Bench.
Pursuivants of Scotland and Ireland.
Officers attendant on the Knights Commanders of the Bath,
wearing their caps.
Knights Commanders of the Bath, wearing their caps.
Officers of the Order of the Bath, wearing their caps.
Knights Grand Crosses of the Order of the Bath, wearing
their caps.
A Pursuivant of Arms.
Clerks of the Council in ordinary.
Privy Councillors.
Register of the Order of the Garter.
Knight of the Garter, not a Peer, wearing his cap and
feathers.
His Majesty's Vice-Chamberlain.
Comptroller of the Household.   Treasurer of the Household.
A Pursuivant of Arms.
Heralds of Scotland and Ireland.
The Standard of Hanover, borne by the Earl of Mayo.
Barons, wearing their coronets.
A Herald.
The Standard of Ireland,   The Standard of Scotland,
borne by   borne by
Lord Beresford.   the Earl of Lauderdale.

Bishops, wearing their caps.
Two Heralds.
Viscounts, wearing their coronets.
Two Heralds.
The Standard of England, borne by Lord Hill.
Earls, wearing their coronets.
Two Heralds.
The Union Standard, borne by Earl Harcourt.
Marquisses, wearing their coronets.
The Lord Chamberlain of the Household, wearing his coronet.
The Lord Steward of the Household, wearing his coronet.
The Royal Standard, borne by the Earl of Harrington.

| King of Arms of the Ionian order of St. Michael and St. George, wearing his crown. | Gloucester King of Arms, wearing his crown. | Hanover King of Arms, wearing his crown. |

Dukes, wearing their coronets.

| Ulster King of Arms, wearing his crown. | Clarencieux King of Arms, wearing his crown. | Norroy King of Arms, wearing his crown. |

The Lord Privy Seal, wearing his coronet.   The Lord President of the Council, wearing his coronet.
Archbishops of Ireland, wearing their caps.
Archbishop of York, wearing his cap.
Lord High Chancellor, wearing his coronet, and bearing his purse.
Archbishop of Canterbury, wearing his cap.
Four Sergeants at Arms.

| The third sword borne by the Earl of Galloway, wearing his coronet. | Curtana, borne by the Duke of Newcastle, wearing his coronet. | The second sword borne by the Duke of Northumberland, wearing his coronet. |

| Usher of the Green Rod. | | Usher of the White Rod. | |
| The Lord Mayor of London. | The Lord Lyon of Scotland, wearing his crown. | Garter principal King of Arms, wearing his crown. | Black Rod. |

The Deputy Lord Great Chamberlain, wearing his coronet.
His Royal Highness the Prince Leopold, wearing his cap and feathers, and his train borne as before.
His Royal Highness the Duke of Gloucester, wearing his coronet, and his train borne as before.

His Royal Highness the Duke of Cambridge, wearing his
  coronet, and his train borne as before.
His Royal Highness the Duke of Sussex, wearing his
  coronet, and his train borne as before.
His Royal Highness the Duke of Clarence, wearing his
  coronet, and his train borne as before.
His Royal Highness the Duke of York, wearing his coronet,
  and his train borne as before.

The High Constable of Ireland.	The High Constable of Scotland, wearing his coronet.

Four Sergeants at Arms.

The Deputy Earl Marshal, wearing his coronet.	The Sword which had been redeemed, borne naked by the Duke of Dorset, wearing his coronet.	The Lord High Constable, wearing his coronet.

The Lord High Steward, wearing his coronet.
The sceptre with the dove, borne by the Duke of Rutland,
  wearing his coronet.

Twenty Gentlemen Pensioners with standard bearers.	The Bishop of Oxford, wearing his cap.	THE KING, in his robes of purple velvet furred with ermine, and the Crown of State on his head, bearing in his right hand St. Edward's sceptre with the cross, and in his left the orb with the cross, under his canopy, supported as before, and his train borne as before.	The Bishop of Lincoln, wearing his cap.	Twenty Gentlemen Pensioners with the Lieutenant.

Captain of the Yeomen of the Guard, wearing his coronet.	Gold Stick of the Life Guards in waiting, wearing his coronet.	Captain of the Band of Gentlemen Pensioners, wearing his coronet.

Lords of the Bedchamber.
The Keeper of his Majesty's Privy Purse.
Grooms of the Bedchamber.
Equerries and Pages of Honour.
Aides de Camp.
Gentlemen Ushers.

Physicians.	Surgeons.	Apothecaries.

Ensign of the Yeomen of the Guard.	Lieut. of the Yeomen of the Guard.

His Majesty's Pages.

His Majesty's Footmen.

| Exons of the Yeomen of the Guard. | Yeomen of the Guard. | Exons of the Yeomen of the Guard. |

Gentleman Harbinger of the Band of Gentlemen Pensioners.

| Clerk of the Cheque to the Yeomen of the Guard. | Clerk of the Cheque to the Gentlemen Pensioners. |

Yeomen of the Guard closed the Procession.

On entering the Hall, the Barons of the Cinque Ports bearing the canopy proceeded with the canopy as far as the steps of the platform, from whence the King ascended to the throne, and from thence retired to his chamber.

It has been already mentioned, that the several orders of Knighthood returned wearing their hats. This was the case until they got to the entrance of Westminster Hall. There all the Knights of the Bath took off their hats, as did some of the Bishops and several other individuals who took part in the procession. There were only two Knights of the Garter who appeared in the full dress of the order. These were his Royal Highness the Prince Leopold and the Marquis of Londonderry. The noble marquis, as attired in his robes, added very considerably to the splendour of the scene by his graceful and elegant appearance. His lordship's hat was encircled with a band of diamonds, which had a most brilliant effect. On the entrance of his Majesty he was received with loud and continued acclamations—the gentlemen waving their hats, and the ladies their handkerchiefs: his Majesty seemed to feel sensibly the enthusiasm with which he was greeted, and returned the salutations with repeated bows to the assemblage on both sides as he passed up to the platform. His Majesty was evidently fatigued, but he never appeared to be in better spirits. It would be impossible to convey to our readers, who did not witness the procession, an adequate idea of the splendour of the Hall at the moment when the procession had completely passed through the triumphal arch. The rich and gorgeous apparel of the

WESTMINSTER HALL,
as it appeared at the Coronation of George IV.
The Royal Banquet.

Published by J. Robins & Co. Albion Press, London, Aug. 9, 1821.

peers and knights, relieved by the more light though not less elegant dresses of the ladies, gave a magnificence to the scene, which has never been equalled at the coronation of any sovereign of this country, and it may be added of any country in Europe. His Majesty did not ascend the throne on his return, but proceeded immediately to his chamber. The peers took their seats at the tables appointed for them, and began to partake of the banquet.

The guests at the tables on the left hand side of his Majesty, sat in the following order:—

ON THE INSIDE OF THE TABLE, NEXT THE CELLERETS.

The Dukes of Somerset, Grafton, Beaufort, and Bedford.
Earls of Shrewsbury, Winchester, Cardigan, Shaftsbury, Scarborough, Jersey, Cassilis, Morton, Home, Strathmore, Lauderdale, Kinnoull, Elgin, Wemyss, Northesk, Aboyne, Aberdeen, Roseberry, Glasgow, Dartmouth, Aylesford, Cowper, Stanhope, Pomfret, Abergavenny, Grosvenor, Fortescue, Digby, Mansfield, Ormond, Cork, Westmeath, Meath, Athlone, Darnley, Kingston, Roden, Longford, Portarlington, Mayo, Clare, Balmore, O'Neil, Donoughmore, Caledon, Rosslyn, Craven, Romney, Wilton, and Limerick.
Viscounts—Ennismore and Exmouth.
Lords—Audley, Clinton, Zouch, Willoughby de Broke, Howard of Walden, Arundel of Wardour, Clifford of Chudleigh, Saltoun, Colville, Napier, Middleton, King, Montfort, Grantham, Boston, Ducie, Rivers, Foley, Dynevor, Walsingham, Bagot, Ashburton, Rodney, Berwick, Gordon, Montague, Tyrone, Kenyon, Braybroke, and Amherst.

ON THE OUTSIDE OF THE TABLE.

The Lord Chancellor, the Lord President of the Council, the Lord Privy Seal, the Duke of Portland.
Marquisses of Cholmondeley, Hertford, Winchester, Tweedale, Lothian, Buckingham, Londonderry, Salisbury, Bath, Cornwallis, Donnegal, Wellesley, Headfort, Exeter, Nottingham, Camden, Conyngham, Aylesbury.
Earls—Harrington, Portsmouth, Harcourt, Guildford, Ilchester, De Lewarr, Spencer, Bathurst, Clancarty, Gosport, Rosse, Manvers, Oxford, Lonsdale, Harewood, Brownlow,

256   *Arrangement of the Guests.*

St. Germain, Blessington, Glengall, Falmouth, Howe, Somers.

Viscounts—Hereford, Bolingbroke, Torrington, Hampden, Sidney, Killmoray, Bayne, Galway, Powerscourt, Ashbrook, Dungannon, Clermont, Harwarden, Melville, Sidmouth, Norton, Lake, Granville.

Lords—Selby, Calthorpe, Rolle, Carrington, Bayning, Bolton, Northwick, Carberry, Brandon, Massey, Bridport, Longford, Dufferien, St. Helens, Redesdale, Ellenborough, Erskine, Combermere, Hill, Beresford, Prudhoe, Garvagh, Howden, Glenlyon, Maryborough, Stowell, Ravensworth, Delamere, and Forrester.

TABLES ON THE RIGHT OF HIS MAJESTY, INSIDE NEXT THE CELLERETS.

The Archbishop of Canterbury, the Bishops of London, Salisbury, Ely, Gloucester, Peterborough, Bristol, and Raphoe, the Marquis Graham, Lord Charles Somerset, Viscount Morpeth, Lord George Beresford, the Right Hon. John Charles Villiers, the Right Hon. George Canning, the Right Hon. Thomas Wallace, the Right Hon. Charles Arbuthnot, the Right Hon. John Sullivan, the Right Hon. F. G. Robinson, the Right Hon. Wm. Huskisson, Sir H. J. Russell, Sir G. G. Hill, Sir Benj. Bloomfield, Sir Charles Abbot, Chief-Justice of the King's Bench; the Right Hon. Charles Grant, the Right Hon. D. Boyle, Sir James Allan Parke, Sir J. Burrough, Sir Wm. Draper Best, Sir Robert Graham, the Right Hon. the Lord Mayor, Aldermen Sir W. Curtis, Sir R. Carr Glynn, Sir John Eamer, Sir John Perring, Sir Jas. Shaw, Sir Wm. Leighton, J. Ansley, Esq. Sir C. Flower, T. Smith, Esq. J. J. Smith, Esq. the Recorder of London, Eight Barons of the Cinque Ports, Sir John Borlase Warren, Sir A. Clarke, Sir James Saumarez, Sir Richard John Strachan, Sir Alexander Forrester, Sir Brent Spencer, Lord William Bentinck, Sir Galbraith Lowry, Sir Harry Calvert, Sir Thomas Maitland, Sir Henry Johnson, Sir B. Tarlton, Sir G. Hewitt, Sir Hildebrand Oakes.

ON THE OUTSIDE OF THE TABLE.

The Archbishop of York, the Bishop of Bangor, the Bishops of St. David's, St. Asaph, Chester, Orford, Landaff, Ossory, Cloyne, and Limerick.

Viscount Palmerstone, Earl Yarmouth, Lord Charles Bentinck, Lord Binning, the Right Hon. the Speaker, the Right Hon. Henry Pierpoint, the Right Hon. Charles Bathurst, Sir Evan Nepean, the Right Hon. Nicholas

Vansittart, Sir John Nicholl, Sir Thomas Plomer, the Right Hon. Sturges Bourne, Sir Richard Richards, Chief Baron of the Exchequer, the Right Hon. John Becket, Sir John Leach, Sir Robert Dallas, Chief Justice of the Common Pleas; Sir Samuel Shepherd, Sir Geo. Ousley, Sir John Bayley, Sir George Holroyd, Sir George Wood, Sir. Wm. Garrow, Aldermen Sir Claudius S. Hunter, George Scholey, Esq. Sir Wm. Domville, Samuel Birch, Esq. Matthew Wood, Esq. Christopher Smith, Esq. John Atkins, Esq. George Bridges, Esq. Christopher Magnay, Esq. Wm. Heygate, Esq. Rob. Albion Cox, Esq. Richard Rothwell, Esq. —— Williams, Esq. Robert Waithman, Esq. the Sheriffs of London, Eight Barons of the Cinque Ports, Sir Samuel Achmuty, Sir Henry Wellesley, Sir Edw. Paget, Sir George Nugent, Sir William Keppell, Sir John Doyle, Sir Geo. Murray, Sir Richard Browning, Sir George Townsend, Sir C. Morrice Pole, Sir W. H. Clinton, Sir Gordon Drummond, Sir Geo. Cockburn, Sir Thomas Foley.

During this scene the ladies and gentlemen from the galleries promenaded up and down between the tables, and occasionally partook of the refreshments which were so abundantly supplied.

We have been favoured from authentic documents, with an accurate detail of the dishes prepared for the Coronation dinner, from which we have taken the following abstract. We must premise, by stating, that all the cold part of the dinner in the Hall, the dessert, and decorative pastry, &c. were put on the table during the time of his Majesty's absence in the Abbey. The hot dishes were subsequently served through the openings we have described in the back of the cellerets.

HOT DISHES.

160 tureens of soup—80 of turtle—40 of rice—and 40 vermicelli.

160 dishes of fish—comprising 80 of turbot—40 of trout —40 of salmon.

160 hot joints—including 80 of venison—40 of roast beef, with three barons—40 of mutton and veal.

160 dishes of vegetables, including potatoes, peas, and cauliflowers.

480 sauce boats—240 of lobsters—120 butter—120 mint.

COLD DISHES.

80 dishes of braized ham—80 savory pies—80 dishes of daubed geese, two in each—80 dishes of savory cakes—80 pieces of beef braized—80 dishes of capons braized, 2 in each—1,190 side dishes of various sorts—320 dishes of mounted pastry—320 dishes of small pastry—400 dishes of jellies and creams—160 dishes of shell fish, 80 of lobster and 80 of crayfish—161 dishes of cold roast fowls—80 dishes of cold house-lamb.

TOTAL QUANTITIES.

7,442 lbs. of beef—7,133 lbs. of veal—2,474 lbs. of mutton—20 quarters of house-lamb—20 legs of house-lamb—5 saddles of lamb—55 quarters of grass lamb—160 lambs' sweetbreads—380 cow-heels—400 calves' feet—250 lbs. of suet—160 geese—720 pullets and capons—1,610 chickens—520 fowls for stock (hens)—1,730 lbs. of bacon—550 lbs. of lard—912 lbs. of butter—84 hundred of eggs.

All these are independent of the eggs, butter, flour, and necessary articles in the pastry and confectionery departments; such as sugar, isinglass, fruits, &c. Of these, as well as the dessert, we shall be able to give an ample detail hereafter.

Mr. Benois superintended the confectionery department, and Mr. Le Clerc the pastry.

Independent of the dishes prepared for the public banquet, cold dinners were also provided for the following classes:—

The Clerks of the Kitchen, the Master Cooks, the Confectioners, the Silver Pantry, the King's Band, the Yeomen of the Guards, the Footmen, the Pages of the Back Stairs, the Pages of the Presence, the Watermen, and the Attendants.

The following is an accurate list of the covers laid, independent of those in the Hall:—

The Painted Chamber had one cross and two long tables, with 170 covers. The Painted Chamber was set apart for the Ambassadors and foreigners of distinction.

In the old House of Lords there were also three tables, and the accommodations were also on a large scale, for there were 140 covers provided. And in the apartments known by the names of the Members' dining-rooms, there were furnished 48 covers; the Court of Exchequer 200 covers; Common Pleas 36 covers; Judges' room, Exchequer Court, 22 covers; Exchequer Chamber 70 covers; Judges' room, Common Pleas, 35 covers ;- Judges' and Treasurer's room, King's Bench, 50 covers; matted Gallery, 60 covers; Library (common) 20 covers; Committee Room, No. 1, 35 covers; No. 3, 25 covers; No. 5, 36 covers; No. 4, 28 covers: Nos. 10, 11, 12, &c. upwards of 150 covers; in Mr. Ley's house, 50 covers.

All the extra stock of provisions was given, by his Majesty's order, to the poor of St. Margaret's, Westminster.

During the interval between this and the return of his Majesty, the greater part of the ladies and gentlemen who had previously occupied the galleries retired for refreshments, or descended into the Hall, which they promenaded for a considerable time. There were also a great number of persons admitted into the Hall, who it was evident had not been in before. This occasioned some slight inconvenience to those whose duty obliged them to be present. We ought here to remark, that the procession on its return to the Hall was not conducted with any thing like the same regularity which had distinguished its departure. This was probably owing to the great fatigue which all the parties had undergone, and to their consequent anxiety to get to their seats. Some slight derangement was occasioned by the aldermen, who, either from the cause just mentioned, or from a mistake with respect to the regulations of the heralds, had no sooner got within the triumphal arch, than they walked over to one of the tables, leaving several of those behind who ought to have preceded them. This trifling mistake was soon corrected by one of the heralds, who brought the worthy magistrates back to their former station in the procession; but it occasioned some mirth in the Hall, from the well known attachment of the worthy aldermen to the enjoyment of the table.

Precisely at twenty minutes past five the Lord

Great Chamberlain issued his orders that the centre of the Hall should be cleared. This direction occasioned much confusion, not only because many strangers had been allowed to enter the lower doors for the purpose of surveying the general arrangements, but because those who had tickets for the galleries had descended in considerable numbers to the floor. Lord Gwydir was under the necessity of personally exerting his authority with considerable vehemence, in order to compel the attendants of the Earl-Marshal to quit situations intended for persons more immediately connected with the ceremony. A long interval now occurred, during which the various officers, and especially the heralds, made the necessary arrangements for the nobility expected to return with his Majesty. During this pause, silence was generally preserved in expectation of the return of his Majesty from his chamber.

His Majesty's dinner being ready, Garter King at Arms summoned the necessary officers to prepare to serve it up. The requisite arrangements being made, his Majesty came from his retiring room, still wearing the crown; and the moment he again showed himself, he was received with reiterated shouts of applause. His Majesty now seated himself on his throne with infinite grace, his train-bearers throwing the train of his robe over the back, from its immense weight. His Majesty then delivered his orb, to be delivered to the Duke of Devonshire, and the sceptre to the Duke of Norfolk. Every one now looked with the greatest anxiety down the Hall, in the anticipation of seeing the Lord High Constable, the Lord High Steward, and the Earl Marshal, enter on horseback with the first course. Previous to this the Knights Grand Crosses, as well as the Knights of the Bath, had been summoned to the Hall, and at length the procession approached in the following order:—

FIRST COURSE.

The first course was then served as follows:—

Six Attendants on the Clerk Comptroller.
Two Clerks of the Kitchen, in Black Gowns.
The Clerk Comptroller, in a Velvet Gown, trimmed with
silver lace.
Three Clerks of the Board of Green Cloth, in scarlet mantles.
The Secretary of the Board of Green Cloth.
The Master of his Majesty's Household.
The Comptroller of   The Treasurer of
His Majesty's Household.   His Majesty's Household.
Four Sergeants at Arms, with their Maces.
Three Great Officers of State, mounted on horses richly
caparisoned :

| The Deputy Earl-Marshal of England, bearing the Earl Marshal's Staff, and his Coronet on his head, attended by a Page. | The Lord High Steward with his White Staff, his Coronet on his head. | The Lord High Constable, with the Constable's Staff, and his Coronet on his head, attended by two Pages. |

Four Sergeants at Arms, with their Maces.
Gentlemen Pensioners, bearing the Dishes of Meat.

As this procession approached the throne his Majesty seemed to regard it with great satisfaction—and indeed the magnificence of the scene beggars all description. Every person stood up, and every eye was directed to the ceremony. The Duke of Wellington rode a beautiful white charger, richly caparisoned, with a plume of white feathers, surmounted with some heron's feathers on its head. He was himself dressed in his full robes as a peer, with his constable's staff in his hand.

The Marquis of Anglesea, as Lord High Steward, rode in the centre upon his golden dun, likewise richly caparisoned and carrying his wand. He also wore his full robes, with his coronet on his head. The plume on his horse's head was similar to that of the Duke of Wellington's horse.

Lord Howard of Effingham rode on the left, on the little white horse which has so often performed at Covent Garden Theatre.

All the noble lords were attended by their pages and grooms in appropriate dresses.

Then came twenty Gentlemen Pensioners attired in fanciful costume with ruffs, and each bearing a gold covered dish.

On reaching the foot of the platform, the horsemen stopped while the Clerks of the Kitchen advanced to the royal table. The Gentlemen Pensioners then ascended the platform, and delivered their dishes to the Clerks of the Kitchen, by whom they were placed on the table.

After a short pause and all the members of the procession had resumed their places, the whole moved back, the horsemen backing their chargers with great precision.

The most rapturous applause attended this scene, in which his Majesty seemed perfectly to coincide.

The Deputy Lord Great Chamberlain, with his Majesty's Cupbearer the Earl of Abingdon, and his Assistant the Earl of Verulam, being preceded by Black Rod, received then from the Officer of the Jewel House, the gilt basin and ewer for his Majesty to wash, attended by the Lord of the Manor of Heydon with the towel. The King rising, and delivering his Sceptre to the Lord of the Manor of Worksop, and the Orb to the Bishop standing on his left hand, the Cupbearer poured out the water on his Majesty's hand, the Lord of the Manor of Heydon holding the towel. His Majesty having wiped his hands, returned the towel, with infinite grace to the Lord of the Manor.

The King's table being covered, the Earl of Denbigh, as his Majesty's carver, and the Earl of Chichester, as the assistant carver, ascended the royal platform with the customary marks of respect. The dishes were then uncovered, and the King commanded that they should commence their duties. It was now discovered that there were neither soup ladle, spoons, nor carvers on the table. His Majesty smiled; but the omission being observed, it was soon supplied from the sideboard, and the Earl of Denbigh having poured out some soup into a gold soup plate, it was handed to

THE KING'S CHAMPION.

his Majesty; the Royal Dukes were then helped in their turn, the Earl of Chichester assisting.

The soup was then removed, and the carvers again performed their duties on the remaining dishes. It was evident, however, although his Majesty partook of several things which were on the table, that it was a mere ceremony, the forms of which he felt it proper strictly to observe.

On the King's right hand stood the Lord of the Manor of Worksop holding the Sceptre; next to him on the same side, the Lords bearing the Four Swords: on his Majesty's left hand, the Duke of Devonshire with the Orb, and next to him the Deputy Lord Great Chamberlain, and next to him the Duke of Rutland, bearing the Sceptre with the Dove.

On the King's right hand sat the Dukes of Sussex, Cambridge, and Gloucester; and on his left the Dukes of York and Clarence.

The Lord of the Manor of Wymondley, assisted by the King's Cupbearer and his Assistant, then received from the Officer of the Jewel House, and, kneeling, presented to his Majesty, a silver-gilt cup, containing wine; and his Majesty having drank thereof, returned the cup to him for his fee.

The Duke of Argyll, as Great Master of the Household of Scotland, then presented a gold cup of wine; and his Majesty having drank thereof, returned the cup to him for his fee.

THE CHAMPION.

The first course having been removed, the attention of all present was called to the bottom of the Hall by a long and cheerful flourish of trumpets. The great gates were instantly thrown wide open, and the Champion made his appearance under the Gothic archway, mounted on his pie-bald charger; this colour, though perhaps on some accounts objectionable, has a great authority in chivalrous romance in its favour, for Boiardo so describes the horse of Argalia. Having alluded to the *Orlando Innamorata*, we may be excused for quoting the following stanza from the second canto: we have given it a translation only on account of its length, and we feel warranted in inserting it on account of its singular applicability: the poet is describing the entrance of the pagan hero, Sacripante, within the lists, on a noble and generous steed, and comparing the rider with the horse:—

"Like his the pride and courage of the knight,
  Whose vizor up, show'd his bold eyes and keen:
Yclad he was in armour glittering bright,
  Fierce in his look and haughty in his mien.
All hands at once point at the welcome sight,
  For in his frame such well-knit strength was seen,
That every dame and chieftain there might say,
  He, only he, was Champion on that day."

Mr. Dymoke was accompanied on the right by the Duke of Wellington, and on the left by Lord Howard of Effingham; but his polished steel armour, his plumes, and the trappings of his steed, instantly showed the capacity in which he appeared. He was ushered within the limits of the Hall by two trumpeters, with the arms of the Champion on their banners; by the Sergeant Trumpeter, and by two Sergeants at Arms with maces. An Esquire in half armour was on each side, the one bearing his lance, and the other his shield or target: the three horsemen were followed by grooms and pages.

The first challenge was given at the entrance of the Hall, the trumpets having sounded thrice: it was read by the herald attending the Champion in the following terms:—

"If any person, of what degree soever, high or low, shall deny or gainsay our Sovereign Lord King George the Fourth of the United Kingdom of Great Britain and Ireland, Defender of the Faith, son and next heir to our Sovereign Lord King George the Third, the last King deceased, to be right heir to the Imperial Crown of this United Kingdom, or that he ought not to enjoy the same, here is his Champion, who saith that he lieth, and is a false traitor; being ready in person to combat with him, and in this quarrel will adventure his life against him on what day soever he shall be appointed."

After pausing for a few seconds, the Champion drew off his gauntlet, and threw it upon the floor, with a very manly and chivalrous air. As no one appeared to accept the challenge, the herald took up the glove, and returned it to the Champion. The cavalcade then advanced half way up the Hall, when it again halted, and the trumpets having again sounded, the challenge was read as before, the gauntlet thrown down, and restored to the challenger. At the foot of the throne the same ceremony was a third time repeated, the herald reading the challenge at the top of the first flight of steps. We should here remark, that shouts of applause and vociferations of " Long live the King" followed each restoration of the gauntlet to the Champion. His charger was considerably alarmed by the noise, but he seemed to have a complete command over him, and restrained his action within limits suited to the narrow space in which he could be permitted to move, making, in the words of an old English poet,

" A doctrinal and witty hieroglyphic
Of a blest kingdom; to express and teach
Kings to command as they would serve, and subjects
To serve as they had power to command."

The knightly appearance and gallant deportment of the Champion obviously gave considerable pleasure to his Majesty, who taking the goblet that was presented to him by the Cupbearer, drank to the bold challenger with a corresponding air of gaiety. The Champion on his part having received the cup, drank to the King, " Long live his Majesty King George the Fourth." This part of the ceremony passed off with great eclat. After the Champion had drained the cup he gave it to one of his pages, who bore it away as the perquisite of his master.

Immediately after, Garter, attended by Clarencieux, Norroy, Lyon, Ulster, and the rest of the officers of arms, proclaimed his Majesty's styles in Latin, French, and English, three several times, first upon the uppermost step of the elevated platform, next in the middle of the Hall, and lastly at the bottom of the Hall, the officers of arms before each proclamation crying "Largesse" in the usual manner.

Dinner being concluded, the Lord Mayor and twelve principal citizens of London, as assistants to the Chief Butler of England, accompanied by the King's Cupbearer and Assistant, presented to his Majesty wine in a gold cup; and the King having drank thereof, returned the gold cup to the Lord Mayor as his fee.

The Mayor of Oxford, with the eight other burgesses of that city, as assistants to the Lord Mayor and citizens of London, as assistant to the Chief Butler of England in the office of butler, was then conducted to his Majesty, preceded by the King's Cupbearer, and having presented to the King a bowl of wine, received the three maple cups for his fee.

The Lord of the Manor of Lyston, pursuant to his claim, then brought up a charger of wafers to his Majesty's table.

The Duke of Athol, as Lord of the Isle of Man, presented his Majesty with two Falcons.

The Duke of Montrose, as Master of the Horse to the King, performed the office of Sergeant of the Silver Scullery.

The Lord of the Barony of Bedford performed the office of Almoner; and the office of Chief Larderer was performed by the Deputy of the Earl of Abergavenny.

During the performance of these ceremonies, there were repeated bursts of applause, and exclamations of "God bless the King."

The dinner concluded, one of the peers, taking advantage of the pause which followed, rose in his seat, and with his glass in his hand, exclaimed in a loud tone, "Good health and a long and happy reign to King George the Fourth;" with three times three. Every individual at the table rose simultaneously, and filling their glasses, drank the toast, with heartfelt delight. Nine rounds of cheers were then given, which made the building almost shake to its foundation.

The cheers having subsided, the Lord-Chancellor, who had been prominent in this scene, exclaimed in a loud voice, "We drink the health of a subject with three times three; we should have drank that of his Majesty with nine times nine." This was followed by another burst of exultation. "God save the King" was then sung by the whole choir, in the most admirable style. The company seizing several opportunities during the anthem, to express their accordance in the sentiments which it contains.

At the conclusion of this performance, and comparative silence being restored, all eyes were directed to the throne, when his Majesty, who seemed deeply affected, rose, and in a voice heard in every part of the Hall, said, "The King thanks his peers for drinking his health, and does them the honour of drinking their health and that of his good people!!!"

Now again the Hall echoed back the expressions of loyalty from all quarters of the building. His Majesty, turning to all parts of the Hall, bowed most gracefully, with a marked and king-like dignity, which excited general admiration, and then resumed his seat.

The King having dined, "*Non nobis domine*" was sung by all the choir who were present, in a very superior style.

The Lord-Chancellor and several other noblemen, then had the honour of kissing his Majesty's hand; and shortly afterwards (half-past eight) his Majesty quitted the Hall.

Immediately after his Majesty quitted Westminster Hall, he expressed his desire to return to his Palace in Pall Mall, although he had previously intimated his intention to remain for that night at the Speaker's. His Majesty's carriage was ordered, and at eight o'clock his Majesty was conducted to his carriage by the Lord Great Chamberlain, and several of the officers of state. His Majesty was in the highest spirits, and expressed, in the most unqualified manner, the pleasure which he experienced during the ceremonies of the day. Upon the prompt and effective manner in which the Lord Great Chamberlain, the Lord High Constable, the Lord High Steward, the Steward of the Household, the Lord Chamberlain, Sir Thomas Tyrwhitt, and the Members of the Herald's College, performed their respective duties, his Majesty passed the warmest encomiums.

His Majesty was driven off in his private carriage, attended by his usual body guards, amidst loud cheers.

It might appear somewhat singular that so suddenly, on the retirement of the august master of the banquet, and after the praiseworthy order and regularity which had previously subsisted, an opportunity should have been afforded for the active operations of those who seemed to have imbibed a notion that to make spoil of all the decorations and furniture upon the tables, was the indubitable right of those who had the good fortune to be on the spot. The fact is, however, that after the service of the second course, and the subsequent retreat of the Lord High Constable, the Lord Steward, and the Earl Marshal, all those persons who had been extended in double lines, from one end of the Hall to the other, closed, *en masse*, towards the foot of the steps leading to the royal platform. At the same time other branches of the crowd advanced along the passages in front of the cellerets; and as the period for his Majesty's departure approached, these formidable bodies encroached still nearer upon the before sacred presence. Among those thus marshalling as it were for a scramble, we noticed several of the peers' attendants, a great portion of the vocal body who had been introduced to sing "God save the King," and "*Non nobis domine*," together with several ladies and gentlemen, who, having previously quitted their seats in the galleries to promenade in the Hall, instead of retiring to their former places, upon the general order for clearing the space in front of the platform being issued, had only gone behind the dining-tables, and into the passages communicating with the kitchens. At length his Majesty rose, and having passed through the avenue behind the throne, accompanied by the great officers of state and his royal brothers, the gathering crowd of spoilators, by a simultaneous rush, in a moment surrounded the royal table. For a few seconds delicacy, or a disinclination to be the first to commence the scene of plunder, suspended the projected attack; but at last a rude hand having been thrust through the first ranks, and a golden fork having been seized, this operated as a signal to all, and was followed by a general snatch. In a short time all the small portable articles were transferred into the pockets of the multitude. The Lord Great Chamberlain, being alarmed by the confusion, returned to the Hall, and, by the greatest personal exertion, succeeded in preventing the extension of the supposed " licensed plunder" to the more costly parts of the Coronation plate. Thus the spoil which was seized was confined mainly to a few knives and forks, some gold plates, the glasses, a few spoons, and two or three of the gilt figures by which the plateau on the centre of the table had been ornamented. With great difficulty all the remaining part of the plate was removed to Cotton Garden, and all apprehensions on this score having subsided, the marauders were left to the undisturbed exercise of their coronation privileges in the body of the Hall, and hither they forthwith transferred their attentions. The scene which was now presented scarce admits of parallel in modern times. The individuals in the galleries, who had hitherto remained passive spectators to the operations beneath, and many of whom had, from some unfortunate omission in the regulations prescribed by the Lord Great Chamberlain, remained the whole of the day without refreshment, poured down the different stairs and passages to the festive board, which, having been vacated by the peers, and other guests, who had long before satiated their appetites, was attacked with a vigour, only in proportion to the actual exhaustion of the assailants. A raging thirst was the first want to be satisfied, and in a very few moments every bottle on the board was emptied of its contents. A fresh supply was, however, soon obtained from the cellerets; and we believe all reasonable calls of this sort were readily complied with. From liquids the company proceeded to solids, and here the work of destruction was equally fierce; sweet-meats, pastry, and confectionery of all sorts vanished with the rapidity of lightning; the distinctions of sex, and almost the common rules of politeness, seemed to have been forgotten; and it was not till the first cravings of nature were subdued, that something like an anxiety for the accommodation of the ladies found existence. Groups of beautiful women were then scattered at the tables, and every effort made to afford them that refreshment of which they stood so much in need. While some were thus occupied, others still pursued the work of plunder. Arms were every where seen stretched forth breaking and destroying the table ornaments, which were of themselves too cumbrous to remove, for the purpose of obtaining some trophy commemorative of the occasion; thus baskets, flower-pots, vases, and figures, were every where disappearing, and those were followed by glasses, knives and forks, salt spoons, and, finally, the plates and dishes. These last were of pewter, engraved with the royal arms, and the letters "Geo. IV." and were therefore greatly coveted. The dirty state of these articles, however, added to the inconsistency of their appearance with full Court dresses, deterred many from appropriating them to their own use, although some, laying aside all delicacies of this sort, did not fail to take out their handkerchiefs, and, amidst their folds, to conceal the much-prized spoils. As the persons thus engaged satisfied their respective desires, they retreated by the north door to the platform, along which they were seen seeking their respective modes of conveyance, anxious to escape the scene of desolation they had left behind. This, however, was no easy task, and many hours elapsed before they were all enabled to quit the spot.

Several attempts were made to obtain admission into the dining-rooms adjoining the Hall, but these were successfully resisted by Mr. Fellowes, and the persons under his direction. While what may fairly be called the humbler classes of visitants were thus engaged, the peeresses, and those who had been admitted by peers' tickets, and whose wants were not less pressing, were endeavouring to obtain refreshment elsewhere. Many were introduced to the rooms which had been occupied by the different branches of the procession, and here such remnants of the feast as yet remained were greedily seized; but still numbers were so unfortunate as to be unable to obtain any relief, if at all, till a very late hour.

New difficulties now arose from the time which necessarily elapsed before the carriages, which it had been arranged were to come up in turn, and by a particular course, could arrive. All the rooms and passages around the House of Lords were filled with persons of the highest distinction, of both sexes, all manifesting the greatest impatience to escape from a place which had now lost all its attractions, and which presented no object to cheer their drooping spirits. The unusual early hour at which it had become necessary for them to rise in the morning, in order to enable them to be present at the ceremonies, added to the labours and privations through which they had gone during the day, had reduced them to a complete state of exhaustion, and all the ordinary punctilios of society were of necessity forgotten. Peers and peeresses, judges, and privy councillors, knights of all orders, and commoners of all degrees, were alike worn out by fatigue, and lay promiscuously, some on sofas, some on chairs, and a still greater number on the matted floors of the rooms and passages in which they happened to have sought refuge. Many, while in this situation, were overtaken by sleep, and in this happy state of forgetfulness, scenes were presented extremely at variance with the splendid and dignified spectacle which had been but a few hours before exhibited in the presence of the Sovereign, and in which these very individuals had borne so prominent a part. Every polite attention was paid by the Lord Great Chamberlain, Mr. Fellowes, his secretary, and the attendants under their direction; but these persons having been without rest for the two nights preceding, they were ill calculated to relieve distresses in which they were themselves participators. It was three o'clock in the morning before the whole of the company had departed,—and at that hour several of the ladies were so completely worn out, that it became necessary to carry them to their carriages.

No sooner had these difficulties been overcome, than new ones arose. The populace, which during the day had been kept at a distance, as the attention of the guards became relaxed, approached nearer to the Hall, and at length got round to the kitchen gates—where their boisterous demands for admission soon attracted the attention of Mr. Watier, the Clerk Comptroller of the Kitchen. This gentleman, who had taken so active a part in all the arrangements for the banquet, and upon whose responsibility so much depended, now recollected that the whole of the coronation plate was under his charge in Cotton Garden, and that if the crowd which was assembled once obtained entrance, a scene of indiscriminate plunder must follow, hastened to Mr. Fellowes, and represented to him the danger which threatened. Mr. Fellowes, who had just lain down, instantly rose upon this new call, and, first sending for some sentinels, he precipitated himself among the multitude, to whom he addressed himself on the impossibility of their being indulged until the next day. By this means he contrived to keep them at bay till the military guard arrived—when, finding himself thus supported, he made good his retreat, and, by disposing his forces in a judicious manner, prevented the consequences which were so seriously to be apprehended.

We cannot close this part of our history more appropriately than by the insertion of the following letter, supposed to be from the prolific pen of Sir Walter Scott:—

" Sir—I refer you to the daily papers for the details of the great national assembly which we witnessed yesterday, and will hold my promise absolved by sending a few general remarks upon what I saw, with surprise amounting to astonishment, and which I shall never forget. It is, indeed, impossible to conceive a ceremony more august and imposing in all its parts, and more calculated to make the deepest impression both on the eye and on the feelings. The most minute attention must have been bestowed to arrange all the subordinate parts in harmony with the rest; so that amongst so much antiquated ceremonial, imposing singular dresses, duties, and characters, upon persons accustomed to move in the ordinary routine of society, nothing occurred either awkward or ludicrous which could mar the general effect of the solemnity. Considering that it is but one step from the sublime to the ridiculous, I own I consider it as surprising that the whole ceremonial of the day should have passed away without the slightest circumstance which could derange the general tone of solemn feeling which was suited to the occasion.

* * * * * * * *

" The effect of the scene in the Abbey was beyond measure magnificent. Imagine long galleries stretched among the aisles of that venerable and august pile—those which rise above the altar pealing back their echoes to a full and magnificent choir of music—those which occupied the sides filled even to crowding with all that Britain has of beautiful and distinguished; and the cross gallery most appropriately occupied by the Westminster school-boys, in their white surplices, many of whom might, on that day, receive impressions never to be lost during the rest of their lives. Imagine this, I say, and then add the spectacle upon the floor—the altars surrounded by the Fathers of the Church—the King encircled by the nobility of the land and the counsellors of his throne, and by warriors wearing the honoured marks of distinction, bought by many a glorious danger,—add to this the rich spectacle of the aisles, crowded with waving plumage, and coronets, and caps of honour, and the sun, which brightened and gladdened as if on purpose, now beaming in full lustre on the rich and varied assemblage, and now darting a solitary ray, which catched, as it passed, the glittering folds of a banner, or the edge of a group of battle-axes or partizans, and then rested full on some fair form, ' the Cynosure of neighbouring eyes,' whose circlet of diamonds glistened under its influence. Imagine all this, and then tell me if I have made my journey of four hundred miles to little purpose. I do not love your *cui bono* men, and therefore I will not be pleased if you ask me, in the damping tone of sullen philosophy, what good all this has done the spectators? If we restrict life to its real animal wants and necessities, we shall indeed be satisfied with 'food, clothes, and fire;' but Divine Providence, who widened our sources of enjoyment beyond those of the animal creation, never meant that we should bound our wishes within such narrow limits; and I shrewdly suspect that those *non est tanti* gentlefolks only depreciate the natural and unaffected pleasure which men like me receive from sights of splendour and sounds of harmony, either because they would seem wiser than their simple neighbours at the expense of being less happy, or because the mere pleasure of the sight and sound is connected with associations of a deeper kind, to which they are unwilling to yield themselves.

"Leaving these gentlemen to enjoy their own wisdom, I still more pity those, if there be any, who (being unable to detect a peg on which to hang a laugh) sneer coldly at this solemn festival, and are rather disposed to dwell on the expense which attends it, than on the generous feelings which it ought to awaken. The expense, so far as it is national, has gone directly and instantly to the encouragement of the British manufacturer and mechanic; and so far as it is personal to the persons of rank attendant upon the Coronation, it operates as a tax upon wealth and consideration for the benefit of poverty and industry; a tax willingly paid by the one class, and not the less acceptable to the other, because it adds a happy holiday to the monotony of a life of labour.

"But there were better things to reward my pilgrimage than the mere pleasures of the eye and the ear; for it was impossible, without the deepest veneration, to behold the voluntary and solemn interchange of vows betwixt the King and his assembled people, whilst he, on the one hand, called God Almighty to witness his resolution to maintain their laws and privileges, while they called, at the same moment, on the Divine Being, to bear witness that they accepted him for their liege Sovereign, and pledged to him their love and their duty. I cannot describe to you the effect produced by the solemn, yet strange mixture of the words of Scripture, with the shouts and acclamations of the assembled multitude, as they answered to the voice of the prelate who demanded of them whether they acknowledged as their Monarch the Prince who claimed the sovereignty in their presence. It was peculiarly delightful to see the King receive from the Royal Brethren, but in particular from the Duke of York, the fraternal kiss, in which they acknowledged their Sovereign. There was an honest tenderness, an affectionate and sincere reverence in the embrace interchanged between the Duke of York and his Majesty, that approached almost to a caress, and impressed all present with the electrical conviction, that the nearest to the throne in blood was the nearest also in affection. I never heard plaudits given more from the heart than those that were thundered upon the Royal Brethren when they were thus pressed to each other's bosoms—it was the emotion of natural kindness, which, bursting out amidst ceremonial grandeur, found an answer in every British bosom. The King seemed much affected at this and one or two other parts of the ceremonial, even so much as to excite some alarm among those who saw him as nearly as I did. He completely recovered himself, however, and bore, generally speaking, the fatigue of the day very well. I learn, from one near his person, that he roused himself with great energy, even when most oppressed with heat and fatigue, when any of the more interesting parts of the ceremony were to be performed, or when any thing occurred which excited his personal and immediate attention. When presiding at the banquet, amid the long line of his nobles, he looked 'every inch a King;' and nothing could exceed the grace with which he accepted and returned the various acts of homage rendered to him in the course of that long day.

"It was also a very gratifying spectacle to those who think like me, to behold the Duke of Devonshire and most of the distinguished Whig nobility assembled around the throne on this occasion; giving an open testimony that the differences of political opinions are only skin-deep wounds, which assume at times an angry appearance, but have no real effect on the wholesome Constitution of the country.

"If you ask me to distinguish who bore him best, and appeared most to sustain the character we annex to the assistants in such a solemnity, I have no hesitation to name Lord Londonderry, who, in the magnificent robes of the Garter, with the cap and high plume of the Order, walked alone, and, by his fine face and majestic person, formed an adequate representative of the Order of Edward III. the costume of which was worn by his lordship only. The Duke of Wellington, with all his laurels, moved and looked deserving the baton, which was never grasped by so worthy a hand. The Marquis of Anglesea showed the most exquisite grace in managing his horse, notwithstanding the want of his limb, which he left at Waterloo. I never saw so fine a bridle-hand in my life, and I am rather a judge of ' noble horsemanship.' Lord Howard's horse was worse bitted than those of the two former noblemen, but not so much so as to derange the ceremony of retiring back out of the Hall.

"The Champion was performed (as of right) by young Dymoke, a fine looking youth, but bearing, perhaps, a little too much the appearance of a maiden-knight to be the challenger of the world in a King's behalf. He threw down his gauntlet, however, with becoming manhood, and showed as much horsemanship as the crowd of knights and squires around him would permit to be exhibited. His armour was in good taste, but his shield was out of all propriety, being a round rondache, or Highland target, a defensive weapon, which it would have been impossible to use on horseback, instead of being a three-cornered, or heater-shield, which in time of the tilt was suspended round the neck. Pardon this antiquarian scruple, which, you may believe, occurred to few but myself. On the whole, this striking part of the exhibition somewhat disappointed me, for I would have had the Champion less embarrassed by his assistants, and at liberty to put his horse on the *grand pas*. And yet the young Lord of Scrivelsbaye looked and behaved extremely well.

"Returning to the subject of costume, I could not but admire what I had previously been disposed much to criticise—I mean the fancy-dress of the Privy Councillors, which was of white and blue satin, with trunk hose and mantles, after the fashion of Queen Elizabeth's time. Separately, so gay a garb had an odd effect on the persons of elderly or ill-made men: but when the whole was thrown into one general body, all these discrepancies disappeared, and you no more observed the particular manner or appearance of an individual, than you do that of a soldier in the battalion which marches past you. The whole was so completely harmonised in actual colouring, as well as in association with the general mass of gay, and gorgeous, and antique dress, which floated before the eye, that it was next to impossible to attend to the effect of individual figures. Yet a Scotsman will detect a Scotsman amongst the crowded assemblage, and I must say that the Lord Justice Clerk of Scotland showed to as great advantage in his robes of Privy Councillor, as any by whom that splendid dress was worn on this great occasion. The common court-dress, used by the Privy Councillors at the last coronation, must have had a poor effect in comparison of the present, which formed a gradation in the scale of gorgeous ornament, from the unwielded splendour of the heralds, who glowed like huge masses of cloth of gold and silver, to the more chastened robes and ermine of the peers. I must not forget the effect produced by the peers placing their coronets on their heads, which was really august.

" The box assigned to the Foreign Ambassadors presented a most brilliant effect, and was perfectly in a blaze with diamonds. When the sunshine lighted on Prince Esterhazy, in particular, he glimmered like a galaxy. I cannot learn positively if he had on that renowned coat which has visited all the Courts of Europe, save ours, and is said to be worth 100,000*l.* or some such trifle, and which costs the Prince 100*l.* or 200*l.* every time he puts it on, as he is sure to lose pearls to that amount. This was a hussar dress, but splendid in the last degree, perhaps too fine for good taste—at least it would have appeared so anywhere else. Beside the Prince sat a good-humoured lass, who seemed all eyes and ears (his daughter-in-law, I believe), who wore as many diamonds as if they had been Bristol stones. An honest Persian was also a remarkable figure, from the dogged and imperturbable gravity with which he looked on the whole scene, without ever moving a limb or a muscle during the space of four hours. Like Sir Wilful Witwoud, I cannot find that your Persian is orthodox; for if he scorned every thing else, there was a Mahometan paradise extended on his right hand along the seats which were occupied by the peeresses and their daughters, which the Prophet himself might have looked on with emotion. I have seldom seen so many elegant and beautiful girls as sat mingled among the noble matronage of the land ; and the waving plumage of feathers, which made the universal head-dress, had the most appropriate effect in setting off their charms.

" I must not omit that the foreigners, who are apt to consider us as a nation *en franc*, and without the usual ceremonials of dress and distinction, were utterly astonished and delighted to see the revival of feudal dresses and feudal grandeur when the occasion demanded it, and that in a degree of splendour which, they averred, they had never seen paralleled in Europe.

" The duties of service at the banquet, and of attendance in general, was performed by pages dressed very elegantly in *Henri Quatre* coats of scarlet, with gold lace, blue sashes, white silk hose, and white rosettes. There were also Marshal's-men for keeping order, who wore a similar dress, but of blue, and having white sashes. Both departments were filled up almost entirely by young gentlemen, many of them of the very first condition, who took these menial characters to gain admission to the show. When I saw many of my young acquaintance thus attending upon their fathers and kinsmen, the Peers, Knights, and so forth, I could not help thinking of Crabbe's lines, with a little alteration—

'Twas schooling pride to see the menial wait,
Smile on his father, and receive his plate.'

It must be owned, however, that they proved but indifferent valets, and were very apt, like the clown in the pantomime, to eat the cheer they should have handed to their masters, and to play other *tours de page*, which reminded me of the caution of our proverb, ' not to man yourself with your kin.' The Peers, for example, had only a cold collation, while the Aldermen of London feasted on venison and turtle; and such similar errors necessarily befel others in the confusion of the evening. But these slight mistakes, which indeed were not known till afterwards, had not the slightest effect on the general grandeur of the scene.

* * * * * * * * * *

"You will have from others full accounts of the variety of entertainments provided for John Bull in the Parks, the River, in the Theatres, and elsewhere. Nothing was to be seen or heard but sounds of pleasure and festivity; and whoever saw the scene at any one spot was convinced that the whole population was assembled there, while others found similar concourse of revellers in every different point. It is computed that about five hundred thousand people shared in the festival one way or another; and you may imagine the excellent disposition by which the people were animated, when I tell you that, excepting a few windows broken, not the slightest political violence occurred to disturb the general harmony; and that the assembled populace seemed to be universally actuated by the spirit of the day, namely, loyalty and good humour. Nothing occurred to damp those happy dispositions; the weather was most propitious, and the arrangements so perfect, that no accident of any kind is reported as having taken place. And so concluded the Coronation of George IV. whom God long preserve. Those who witnessed it have seen a scene calculated to raise the country in their opinion, and to throw into the shade all scenes of similar magnificence, from the Field of the Cloth of Gold down to the present day.

"AN EYE WITNESS."

We shall now advert to some of the minor circumstances connected with the august ceremony which we have just described; and in the first place great praise is due to the government for the plan which they adopted in dividing the population of the metropolis, by various exhibitions in different parts of the town, and which ultimately tended to preserve the peace and harmony of this celebrated day. Thus, after the procession had entered the Abbey, the greater part of the populace moved off to the Green-Park, to witness the ascent of Mr. Green in a magnificent air balloon. At about a quarter past one the gentleman took his seat in the car, and the ropes which held it to the earth being removed, he ascended steadily and almost perpendicularly for a few moments. It then obliqued in a north-easterly direction, which it held until it was lost sight of, which was not for a considerable time, in consequence of the extreme clearness of the atmosphere. When at the height of several hundred yards, it was observed stationary for a few moments, until three or four bags of sand were seen descending from the car, when it immediately rose with rapidity to a distance from which it appeared no larger than a peer's coronet, and soon after it dwindled to the size of one of the balls with which such coronet is decorated, (and which, by the bye, it much resembled from the reflection of the noon-day sun upon one of its glossy silken sides,) until it finally disappeared, as if it melted into ether. The place from which it ascended was an enclosed piece of ground, between the Basin and Piccadilly. The aerial voyager continued waving a flag to the people below, so long as he was visible. He descended at South Mimms, in Essex.

The crowd then moved forward to Hyde Park, to witness a boat race which took place a little before two o'clock on the Serpentine river. Upon this occasion four boats started, and were obliged to double a standard, erected at either extremity of the river, twice. The race was won by about two lengths of the winner's boat. The river was covered with boats filled with ladies and gentlemen regaling themselves upon the water; and its banks lined by carriages and well-dressed persons, who appeared to derive much enjoyment from the scene before them. But what excited the greatest share of attention from the spectators, was a splendid triumphal car drawn by two elephants, one before the other, as large as life, and caparisoned after the Eastern manner, with a young woman, dressed as a slave, seated on the back of each, and affecting to guide the animals with an iron rod. The machine was constructed on a large raft, which was towed by three or four boats, manned with watermen in blue uniform. Upon the whole, the appearance of the river, with its animated banks and bosom, combined with the beautiful surrounding scenery, and a perfect cloudless blue sky, presented to the view a *coup d'œil* production of no ordinary effect.

By his Majesty's command all the theatres were thrown open on the evening of the Coronation; and we are enabled to state it as a fact, that his Majesty offered 2,000*l.* to the proprietor of Vauxhall Gardens to throw them open to the populace, but the offer was rejected, unless an indemnity was given for the injury which the Gardens might sustain.

At Covent Garden Theatre every part of it was as closely crowded as it was possible to pack human beings. Of the respectability of the company it may be unnecessary to say any thing. The bundles of hats and bonnets and shawls suspended from the front of the dress boxes, formed a very grotesque exhibition, and was as much contrasted with the usual elegance of that circle as imagination could have contrived it. The play was Henry IV., and every incident or expression of broad humour or forced conceit was sufficiently applauded. When the company on the stage sang "God save the King," the shouts of "The Queen" were quite deafening, and the popularity of the amendment was testified by every species of applause.

DRURY LANE.—The crowd in this theatre was both numerous and well dressed. The play, "The Spectre Bridegroom," seemed to give them unbounded delight. The preference of a "Sovereign to a Guinea" was cheered without interruption. Here, too, "the Queen" was shouted with great applause.

HAYMARKET THEATRE.—This new building was thrown open to the public, and was filled in every part by a decent and respectable assemblage of persons. The comedy of "The Heir at Law" was followed by the farce of "The Agreeable Surprise;" and between the play and afterpiece the appropriate anthems of "Rule Britannia," and "God save the King," were sung in full chorus.

LYCEUM.—The performances at this place of summer amusement, were conducted on the same principle, and without interruption before a crowded audience.

FIRE-WORKS IN HYDE PARK.

An immense concourse of persons flocked to Hyde Park in the evening to witness the expected exhibition of fire-works. The entrance at Hyde Park Corner was rendered extremely dangerous to pedestrians, by the throng of carriages and horsemen which blocked up the way. Upon entering the Park, the appearance of the trees illuminated by variegated and Chinese lamps; a long line of tents lighted up in different fanciful modes; swings in full motion; the appearance of an illuminated stage peeping over a clump of trees near the cascade; together with incessant discharges of very splendid rockets flashing a glaring light upon the solid mass of spectators as far as the eye could reach; but above all, the glimpses caught through the foliage of the trees, of the tastefully illuminated waters of the Serpentine, formed a scene the most picturesque and delightful that can well be conceived. This beautiful piece of water was adorned at one extremity by an illuminated transparency which was erected nearly over the cascade, representing, amongst other things, his Majesty in a triumphant car drawn by milk white horses; nearly opposite to which, on the right bank, was a handsome lighted temple, surmounted by a crown. It was also illuminated at the other sides; in addition to which, the car and elephants before mentioned were brilliantly lighted up with lamps, which, together with those of the towing boats, which were blue, had a very singular and pleasing effect, moving along the surface of the water; and this was considerably heightened by the fantastic appearance of occasional splendid water rockets, resembling the gambols of some fiery monster of the deep. The river was, as in the morning, covered with boats filled with company. The fire-works, which were displayed at a short distance to the right of the river, were extremely magnificent, some showers of very beautiful rockets in particular. They were prepared under the management of Sir W. Congreve.

The fire-works were of the most magnificent description, consisting of rockets, catherine wheels, turbillions, parachute rockets, and every other ingenious device that distinguishes the Pyrotechnic art. The display of these did not commence until half-past nine o'clock, when even Hyde Park was crowded in almost every part of it to inconvenience. At this moment we do not consider it any exaggeration to state, that there must have been more than half a million of persons present. The fire-works commenced with a discharge similar to small arms of infantry firing a salute. It was answered by a discharge of the same nature from Kensington Gardens, this was followed by a profusion of stars, catherine wheels, &c. and concluded by a discharge of rockets the most brilliant that could be formed. On the western extremity of the river a fire-work was exhibited, which from its magnitude, and the multitude of sparks that it emitted, gave the spectator no bad idea of a volcano. The dark gloom of the trees of Kensington Gardens behind this magnificent fire-work added greatly to the beauty of the effect. From the Park the frequent discharge of rockets from Primrose-hill could be perceived. The occasional brilliancy of the fire balloons drew forth the admiration of the multitude.

If, however, the Coronation was a source of profit to particular individuals, it was, on the other hand, a ruinous speculation to many, and especially to those who, at a great expense, had erected the booths for the accommodation of the public. As success has ever been popularly considered the criterion by which judgment is to be pronounced upon the merit of any speculation, no doubt the proprietors of these booths will be generally blamed for a want of foresight in their respective undertakings. It has been said in their justification that equal prices were demanded and paid with avidity for seats at the old coronation, and that therefore speculators were entitled to calculate upon a similar result again. Upon this we need only to observe, that the space to be filled at the former coronation was not more than one-third of the extent covered in for spectators at the late Coronation. The great improvements of late years in the vicinity of Westminster Abbey, have entirely altered the locality of that neighbourhood, and thrown open an area two-thirds larger than the previous line between Westminster Hall and Abbey, independent of the great difference in the size of the houses on the spot. So that the calculations founded upon what was done at the coronation of George III. did not at all apply to the arrangements for that of George IV.

We are sorry to have to add, that some mischief was done by the mob which followed the Queen. After her Majesty had arrived at South Audley-street, the mob separated into two bodies, the one proceeding up to Grosvenor-square, and the other down Hill-street, where they broke the windows of Lord de Grouchy and of Mr. Williamson, at whose houses preparations were making for illuminations. They then proceeded to the house of Earl Powis in Berkeley-square, and demolished many of the windows at the houses of noblemen and gentlemen in Dover-street and Albemarle-street, where preparations had been made on a scale of splendour adequate to the occasion. They also attacked Grillon's Hotel, from whence they proceeded down Piccadilly, and broke the windows at almost every house where preparations were made, and in some instances they did not leave until they had demolished the devices entirely. They took a circuit from Piccadilly down Jermyn-street, where many windows were broken, to St. James's-square, and set themselves down before the house of the Marquis of Londonderry, whose windows they proceeded to demolish with the utmost fury. They were somewhat disturbed by one of the Horse Guards, whom, however, they assailed with missiles, and he was obliged to retreat. He galloped to the head-quarters and returned with a reinforcement, at the appearance of which this detachment of the first mob dispersed. They had, however, made the best of their time, and had done most serious mischief to the premises of the noble marquis. The majority of the other detachment of the mob, which had proceeded to Grosvenor-square, set to work in the same manner upon the house of the Duke of Montrose, and after having demolished a number of the windows, and done other injury, they set themselves before the house of Lord Whitworth, where they made similar havoc, not only with the glass, but the frame of the windows. Whilst they were proceeding in this manner, a sergeant's guard of foot soldiers took a circuit round the square. At the appearance of the soldiers, the rioters desisted for a few minutes, but recommenced as soon as they had passed. The mob was chiefly composed of boys and men of the humblest sort. Nothing could exceed the deliberation with which they proceeded about their work, whilst groups of persons stood aloof to watch them. There was a great scarcity of stones, or the mischief that would have been done, with the opportunity the rioters had in the absence of the civil force, would have been incalculable. When they could not find stones, they amused themselves by pelting the servants and carriages who were conspicuous for splendid liveries with mud, when their order to pull off hats for the Queen was not instantly obeyed. A report having been spread that a body of military were coming, the mob dispersed.

We shall now take a cursory view of the rejoicings which pervaded the more distant part of the country, and which will sufficiently testify that a spirit of loyalty and attachment to our glorious constitution still exist in the country, and that George IV. is, of all the monarchs who have dignified the English throne, not the least worthy of the love and veneration of his people.

At BRIGHTON, as early as four o'clock in the morning, persons were seen moving from all parts of the town towards the spot selected for the day's amusements, (the beautiful field known by the name of the Prince's Cricketing-ground,) where two fine oxen, placed before capacious fires the preceding night, were still in rotatory motion. From near sunrise to noonday, vehicles of all descriptions, filled with country people, and crowds of equestrians and pedestrians, came pouring into the town from East, West, and North, adding many thousands to the local population. The shops were closed, business was suspended, care forgotten, and nothing but ideas of pastime, merriment, and festivity, seemed to engross the public mind. On the Level, all sorts of manly exercises were resorted to by the stout and agile; and to promote their wishes, in this respect, foot-balls were distributed. At twelve o'clock, sixty-three guns, or, as it is termed, a Coronation salute, was fired from some small ordnance, planted in a wagon, belonging to Messrs. Vallance. About one o'clock, a presentation of medals took place on the Steyne, by the Rev. Mr. Everard, to all the children belonging to the various charity-schools of the town: on one side was the head of George IV., and on the other the following inscription:—" *Crowned July* 19, 1821. *May his reign be long and happy !"* The children afterwards, two and two, walked out to the field. The oxen being well roasted, one of them was taken from the fire, and placed on a platform, when Mr. Palmer, of London, his Majesty's cutler, (who had brought on the ground a large wagon, decorated with colours, bearing loyal inscriptions, and laden with stingo, for gratuitous distribution,) presented to John Vallance, Esq. an immense carving knife and fork, requesting that he would use them in cutting the first slice, and then present them, as a token of his respect, to the town of Brighton, for its use on public occasions. The gift was accepted; and Mr. Vallance made the first cut with this sabre-like instrument under a salute of sixty-three guns. The laborious office of carving now commenced, and provisions, sufficient to give substantial dinners to 8000 persons, were, in one hour, distributed and demolished.

At POOLE, the Mayor and Admiral, accompanied by the Corporation, Jury, and many respectable persons, formed a procession from the Guildhall to the Quay, preceded by a band of music, colours, &c. The ships in the harbour were decorated with colours, numberless boats were on the water; added to which, the firing of cannon, the ringing of bells, and the acclamations of the populace, formed a grand and interesting scene. A party of 300 gentlemen, sat down to a sumptuous entertainment, provided for them in a spacious booth erected on the shore. The Mayor presided on the occasion. In the evening there was a grand display of fire-works.

TAUNTON.—The morning was ushered in by the ringing of bells, and the town bore the appearance of a holiday. The Taunton Troop of Yeomanry, assembled for a field-day, and on their return to the parade, fired three vollies, as did also the staff of the First Somerset Militia. In the afternoon, the poor inhabitants were regaled with several hogsheads of strong beer and cider, to drink the health of his Majesty. At half-past four o'clock, a party of nearly seventy sat down to an excellent dinner, in the great dining-room at the Castle Tavern. The ladies entertained the children of the several charity schools, with a liberal feast of roast beef and plum-pudding, in the Crescent Field, and good humour regulated the amusements of the day.

BRIDGEWATER.—The bells rung through the day, and cannon were fired during the intervals. The poor inhabitants of the town were regaled under an awning on the Quay, with beef, mutton, and pork, and several hogsheads of cider were distributed at different parts of the town.

WEEDON.—An excellent dinner was provided by the officers and men employed under the civil branch of his Majesty's ordnance, three tents were pitched and decorated with laurel and flowers in the arsenal; at half-past one, thirty-three sat down to partake of roast beef and plum-pudding, and strong ale, &c. A royal salute was fired with twelve-pounder carronades planted on the batteries, and salutes of four guns each were fired at intervals.

MONMOUTH.—Some of the members of the True Blue Club made a collection for the purpose of gladdening the hearts of the poor, and gathered sufficient to give to upwards of 600 persons, a plentiful dinner of beef, bread, cider, ale, &c. About seventy gentlemen dined on the Kymin Hill, the guns of which were fired at intervals during the day, and rockets, &c. let off at night.

NORTHAMPTON.—At an early hour, the bells of the respective churches commenced their merry peals, and bands of music paraded the streets, performing several favourite national airs, which were continued at intervals throughout the day. At twelve o'clock, part of the 19th regiment, the troop of Volunteer Cavalry (dismounted), and the staff of the Regular Militia, assembled in the Market-square, and fired some excellent vollies, &c.; afterwards, the staff of the Militia dined in a booth on the Market-hill, and great numbers of the population, together with the boys and girls of the Corporation and Blue Schools, sat down at nineteen tables, arranged in the Market-square, to partake of plum-pudding and beef, and drank the health of his Majesty in good ale, provided by public subscription; towards which the Corporation contributed 100*l*. and two Representatives in Parliament 50*l*. each.

WARMINSTER.—Two roasted oxen, and two sheep, with ten hogsheads of beer, and 4000 loaves were distributed indiscriminately to all the poor, men, women, and children. An excellent dinner was served up at the Bath Arms, to the gentlemen of the town, and a fat buck (a present from the Marquis of Bath) was among the dishes. In the evening, there was a display of fire-works.

At COGGESHALL, 1622 persons were supplied with roast-beef and plum-pudding, and several hogsheads of ale.

SUNDERLAND.—The morning was ushered in by ringing of bells, the ships in harbour were decorated with colours. A subscription was raised, which afforded a comfortable dinner to about 2000 poor people, each having a ticket, for which they got two pounds of beef, a threepenny loaf, and threepence in money.

At FROME, a procession of the principal friendly societies with their splendid flags took place from Spring Gardens, attended by three excellent bands of music, each individual was decorated with purple ribbons. On their return to the Market-place, " God save the King" and other loyal tunes were performed. An excellent dinner was provided at the George Inn, (for which the Marquis of Bath provided a buck,) at which the principal inhabitants were present.

EXMOUTH.—About 700 poor families sat down to a plentiful supply of roast-beef and plum-pudding, and ale. After dinner the " health of our patriotic King" was drank with enthusiasm by the happy dinner party, with nine times nine, when a royal salute was fired. The vessels lying in the Port were decorated with flags. The whole of the arrangements were under the direction of John Sweetland, Esq. An excellent dinner was given at the Globe Tavern, Sir Digory Forrest in the chair. In the evening there was a most brilliant display of fireworks.

At WITHAM, with the aid of a liberal subscription, upwards of 1400 individuals in the parish received one pound and a half each of the best mutton, a half-quarter loaf, and a pint of strong beer. After the distribution, the children of the National School, amounting to nearly 200, were regaled (through the liberality of Mrs. Sarah Ducane, the Lady of the Manor) with a bountiful dinner of roast beef and plum-pudding, under the beautiful avenue of trees in the Walk Field, belonging to that lady, adjoining the Grove. The children of the Protestant Dissenting School, amounting to about the same number, partook of a similar bountiful repast in the same place, through the liberality of W. H. Pattison, Esq.

BOGNOR.—Nearly 200 of the children belonging to the schools in this neighbourhood were regaled with roast beef, veal, mutton, plum-pudding, &c. and ale, by the Earl of Arran, in the Lawn before his house.

DONCASTER.—The morning was ushered in by the ringing of bells, and an extensive procession paraded the streets. On arriving at the Mansion-house, " God save the King" was sung with the greatest effect. The Corporation joined the procession in their robes, and the whole proceeded to the south entrance, when a *feu de joie* was fired by the West York Militia. Upwards of 2000 persons were regaled with roast beef and plum-pudding in the Parsonage-yard, and a plentiful supply of ale, to drink the health of our beloved Sovereign. In the evening a ball and supper was given by the Mayor and Corporation at the Mansion-house, which was beautifully illuminated in various devices. Upwards of 500 tickets were issued.

CHELMSFORD.—A subscription of 300*l.* having been collected, a committee was formed, and the money was devoted to the purpose of making every humble heart rejoice in the observance of the Coronation. On the preceding evening a fat ox was put down to roast, and tables were erected in the High-street, reaching from the Black Boy to the Saracen's Head. In the morning of Thursday, the discharge of cannon and the ringing of bells announced the commencement of the glorious ceremony; at one o'clock the bugles summoned the guests to the hospitable board; as soon as they were seated, the Rev. J. G. Ward, Rector, assisted by the Rev. Mr. Hutchinson, the Curate, pronounced a blessing from two chairs elevated for the occasion. About four o'clock, nearly 100 gentlemen sat down to an excellent dinner at the Shire Hall, John Crabb, Esq. in the chair. In the evening the town exhibited some excellent fireworks and was brilliantly illuminated.

TROWBRIDGE.—A procession to church, consisting of the Benefit Societies (about 1200 persons), and the Charity Schools (about 1000 children), took place. The sermon was preached by the Rev. G. Crabbe. Dinners were provided for the poor, and a party of gentlemen dined at the George, where many loyal toasts were drank.

CHIPPENHAM.—Upwards of 200 of the inhabitants, with the children of the Sunday Schools, were regaled in the open streets, with an excellent dinner. A number of gentlemen and the principal inhabitants afterwards dined together at the White Hart Inn.

WISBEACH.—About 4000 persons dined together in the Market-place, and at six o'clock the rustic sports commenced. The Coronation ball, at the Rose and Crown Inn, was numerously and respectably attended.

HUNTINGDON.—A liberal subscription was entered into, to provide a dinner for the poor, and every family who chose to accept it.

PETERBOROUGH.—The clergy, magistrates, and

principal tradesmen, dined together at the Talbot Inn; and in order that the poor might participate in the rejoicings, a subscription was made amounting to 160*l*. of which sum Earl Fitzwilliam gave 20*l*. Lord Milton 10*l*. and the Bishop of Peterborough 10*l*. and a good dinner was provided for them, and afterwards, such as chose, were supplied with tea.

ABINGDON.—Upwards of 1800 persons were supplied by subscription with a dinner, and plenty of excellent beer. The women and children dined in the County Hall, and the men in the Market-place. The Corporation and principal inhabitants acting as carvers at the various tables, and others supplying the beer. The Corporation and a large party afterwards dined in the Council Chamber. At seven o'clock, according to ancient custom, 1000 cakes were thrown from the Market House, and several barrels of beer given to the populace by the Corporation.

ROMSEY.—The day was observed with the ringing of bells, the shops were all shut. At four o'clock, a party of gentlemen sat down to an excellent dinner at the Swan Inn, at which the Mayor presided, supported by the Recorder and Archdeacon of Gloucester. His Majesty's health was drank with enthusiasm. Broadland's Park, the seat of the Right Hon. Viscount Palmerston, also presented a scene of great festivity; two fine sheep were roasted whole in the Park, and cut up in the presence of several thousand spectators; after which, about 100 of his lordship's labourers with their wives and families, sat down to excellent fare provided for them.

SHERBORNE.—The houses in this town were decked with oak and laurel. Five oxen and three sheep were roasted, and given away, together with a liberal supply of strong beer. An excellent dinner was provided in the Town Hall, where the health of the King was drank, and after circulating the glass freely, the gentlemen adjourned to a field in Cold Harbour, where tea and coffee were provided, which was served up by all the beauty in the town. In the evening, brilliant fire-works were exhibited.

COLCHESTER.—A public dinner was given at the Three Cups Inn, at which Sir G. H. Smyth presided. The Mayor and Corporation attended divine service, at St. Peter's Church. A subscription had been collected, amounting nearly to 300*l.* which was expended among the poorer inhabitants, to provide a comfortable dinner at their own houses, and bread and meat, and money for beer, were supplied to 6000 persons for this purpose. The town was decorated with flags and boughs, and the shops were shut. The bells rang during the day, and a display of fire-works took place in the evening.

CARLISLE.—At sun-rise, the flag was hoisted at the castle; they have, unfortunately, no bells to ring on such occasions, though they can boast of a cathedral and two parish churches. At one o'clock, the artillery of the castle fired a royal salute; the infantry on the castle walls, and the cavalry in the New-road, near the castle, firing a *feu de joie* every seventh gun. As soon as this ceremony was over, 36 barrels of ale, and 3500 two-penny loaves were distributed to the people.

BURTON-UPON-TRENT.—The morning was ushered in by the musical peal of bells, which continued at intervals until midnight. At ten o'clock, a procession was formed, consisting of the ladies and gentlemen, the bailiff, Sir J. D. Fowler; the Burton troop of Yeomanry Cavalry, the clergymen, the children of the Sunday Schools, (about 600) &c. &c. after parading the streets, they proceeded to church, where an excellent sermon was preached by the Rev. H. Jones: 1000 men were afterwards regaled at the different public houses, with roast beef and plum-pudding, and two quarts of strong ale each.

At OXFORD, the illuminations were never more brilliant. The poor had meat and beer distributed amongst them, and an excellent dinner was given to the children of the City and University charity schools. The prisoners and debtors in the goal were not forgotten by Sir Edward Hichings, the Mayor.

EXETER.—The morning was ushered in by the ringing of bells, and the firing of cannon. The Mayor, Recorder, and Corporation, attended by the corps of constables, and the incorporated trades, with their banners, were met at St. John's Hospital by the Forty Guardians of the Poor, and a highly respectable and numerous body of gentlemen of the county of Devon and city of Exeter, and officers of the army and navy, accompanied by the children of the Blue School, went in procession to the Cathedral, when on entering, " God save the King" was played by the organ. The Anthem—" The King shall rejoice," was sung by the choir, and Mr. Archdeacon Jones preached an excellent sermon. At twelve o'clock, the East Devon Militia fired four vollies, in the Barrack-square. About half-past five, 230 gentlemen sat down to dinner. The new ball-room was thrown open at nine o'clock, and it soon filled with a brilliant assemblage of the rank, fashion, and beauty of Exeter and its neighbourhood.

SAFFRON WALDEN.—A noble ox was roasted whole, in honour of the day. At twelve o'clock, it was deposited upon a table in the centre of a ring-fence, 800 feet in circumference, and there distributed in the most quiet and orderly manner, amongst the crowd without the ring. A plentiful supply of good old beer was apportioned to their poorer neighbours, superintended by several gentlemen of the town.

PORTSMOUTH.—The morning was ushered in with merry peals of bells, colours displayed on the churches, the shipping, and at all the public, and many of the private buildings; the interests of which was increased at noon by the assembling of the military around the lines of the garrison, who fired, in succession with the salutes from the batteries, a *feu de joie*, as did the ships of war a royal salute of twenty-one guns each; and they being dressed with their colours,

presented a most lively and picturesque sight.—
Amongst the numerous festivities on the joyful occasion was a meeting of the Captains of the Navy afloat
and on half-pay, to dine at the George Inn in this
town, Commodore the Honourable Sir Charles Paget
in the chair, and J. R. Glover, Esq. Vice: 500 of
the children of the National School, were regaled
with a dinner of roast beef and plum-pudding, the
children sang " God save the King."

BIRMINGHAM.—The morning was ushered in with
the ringing of bells, and joy and good humour appeared in the countenance of every one. The churches
and chapels of the Establishment were opened, and
sermons suitable to the great occasion were preached
to. the different congregations, which were numerous.
At one o'clock, upon the firing of a royal salute by
some six-pounders, upon Bennet's-hill, the dinners
commenced. The aged and infirm, full 1600, male
and female, were regaled with roast and boiled beef,
and plum pudding, and ale, the old folks heartily
singing, after dinner, " God save the King."

DURHAM.—The bells of the churches rang many a
merry peal. A subscription was entered into for the
purpose of presenting meat, bread, and ale, to such
persons as might apply for it; and an immense number of families received the gift. An ox was roasted
at the head of Old Elvet, and was, together with a
quantity of ale and bread, attempted to be distributed,
but owing to the pressure of the crowd, the greater
part of it was wasted.

BEVERLEY.—There was a procession; and a subscription was opened for the poor; to which G. L.
Fox, Esq. M. P. for the borough, contributed 50
guineas.

PONTEFRACT.—The mayor, corporation, gentlemen of the town, and military, formed a procession,
which passed through the principal streets in the
town. The poor, to the number of 900 or more, had
an excellent dinner given to them in the Marketplace.

SCARBOROUGH.—A public dinner was provided by the corporation, who also gave 50*l.* to the poor, in tickets of 1*s.* each.

SHEFFIELD.—The day was celebrated by a grand procession, by laying the foundation stone of St. George's Church, and by public dinners.

LEEDS.—The morning was ushered in by the ringing of bells, and the display of flags from the steeples of the churches and from private houses. The shops and warehouses, with a very few exceptions, were shut up, and it was, in every sense of the word, a holiday. The Leeds volunteers, under the command of Lieutenant-Colonel Hardy, joined by the 15th Royal Hussars, and the Leeds squadron of the Yorkshire Hussars, proceeded to Woodhouse-moor. Soon after five o'clock, the Mayor went to the Music Hall to receive his brother magistrates, the members of the common council, the clergy, the hussar staff, yeomanry, and volunteer officers, and the gentlemen who had been invited to the corporation dinner, about 115 in number.

NEWPORT, ESSEX.—In this village, the day was announced by the ringing of bells, which continued until the evening, when all the poor were plentifully regaled with an excellent entertainment, and plenty of strong ale ; and money was given with the greatest liberality to those who preferred it from choice.

ETON.—The young gentlemen of Eton College had a whole holiday, in honour of the Coronation. A very liberal subscription was made by the Provost and Fellows, and the inhabitants of the town. The poor were regaled at their own houses with meat, bread, and ale. In the evening the town and college were splendidly illuminated.

In the two neighbouring parishes of Ingatestone and Fryering, in Essex, a dinner was provided for the poor, to which about 300 sat down, and were plentifully supplied with good English fare.

The rural village of East Hanningfield, Essex, presented a most jovial and loyal appearance. The poor were regaled with beer and provisions ; and the choral band of the parish, joined by the inhabitants, during a display of fire-works, sang and played the national anthem of " God save the King."

CHESTER.—As early as four o'clock flags were hoisted, and at half-past five o'clock the bells commenced their merry peals. Royal salutes were fired. There were various triumphal arches, and numerous transparencies. A grand procession consisting of the members of the Corporation, the clergy, and most of the companies and societies in the city, attended divine service in the Cathedral.— The procession consisted of about 5000 individuals, and extended nearly a mile. As it passed along from the Abbey-square to the Castle-yard, different military bands played " God save the King." Several gentlemen of fortune, and eminent tradesmen gave treats to the people in their employ, and other poor inhabitants.

SHREWSBURY.—About half-past ten o'clock the various incorporated companies, bands, &c. assembled in the Quarry Walk, and thence proceeded to St. Mary's Church. There were numerous public dinners at different inns : and 27 sheep were roasted and distributed with ale, &c. An ox, the gift of the Right Hon. the Earl of Powis, was roasted in the Market-square, and distributed to 300 poor persons. The poor in the Alms-houses were generously supplied with meat, tea, &c. by J. St. Anbin, Esq. and Mrs. Meredith. The sum of 10l. was allotted to the poor in the House of Industry, who fared luxuriously on beef and plum-pudding ; and each prisoner in the County Goal received 2lbs. of beef, &c. Similar festivities took place in most other parts of the country.

The inhabitants of West Cowes celebrated the day of the Coronation, not by wasting an immense quantity of candles ; but by giving a comfortable dinner to about 2000 poor persons belonging to the town and parish ; including men, women and children.

A dinner in honour of the Coronation was given to

the poor of Croydon, on Duppas-hill, for which a large subscription had been collected. So great anxiety was shown to render the arrangements complete, that the gentlemen by whom it was planned were on the hill by four o'clock in the morning. The company, consisting of about 1000 persons, sat down by two o'clock.

KIMBOLTON.—Ten fat sheep were distributed to the parishioners. In the evening, the men were provided with ale, and their wives and families with tea, and in the evening the town was illuminated.

BIGGLESWADE.—Upwards of 200l. was collected to provide a public dinner for the poor. Three bullocks were roasted, and 2000 persons were entertained on the Market-hill. The chair was taken by Charles Barnett, Esq. at a dinner, under a booth, which was partaken of by the gentlemen of the town, and a variety of rustic sports concluded the day.

CHICHESTER.—The standard of England was hoisted on the Saxon tower, in the Cathedral yard. The Duke of Richmond's troop of Horse Artillery, the staff of the Sussex Militia, and the recruits of the 73d regiment, marched to the Broyle, where a *feu de joie* was fired. The Duke of Richmond was at the head of his regiment; the different inns were occupied with dinner parties, all emulous to testify their loyalty. The Bishop of Chichester held his annual visitation, and afterwards entered the dining-room, where, after addressing a few emphatic words to the President (William Ridge, Esq. Mayor), the venerable prelate drank " health and prosperity to the reigning Monarch." The town was illuminated in the evening.

NEWARK.—The subscriptions were liberal beyond all precedent. A plentiful entertainment of plum-pudding, roast beef, and strong ale, with every vegetable in season, was served up to the number of 7000 persons and upwards, of the immediate neighbourhood. At the Town Hall there was an elegant dinner provided, of which the Mayor and Corporation, together with the Newark troop of Yeomanry Cavalry, partook.

CHATHAM.—The whole of the troops in garrison, consisting of the Royal Sappers and Miners, Royal Marines, 71st and 86th regiments, assembled at 12 o'clock, under the command of Lieutenant-General Desborough, Commandant of the Garrison, and fired a *feu de joie*, in honour of the day; the Artillery at the same time firing a royal salute from the batteries, after which all the troops gave voluntarily three hearty cheers.

HARWICH.—At an early hour the houses and vessels in the harbour were decorated with flags. At twelve o'clock, royal salutes were fired from the batteries, at the Landguard Fort, from the vessels, and by the military at the barracks. About 1400 poor persons were regaled with an excellent dinner in the West-street.

STAMFORD.—The bells rang throughout the day. At six in the evening a most numerous and splendid procession took place from the Town Hall through all the principal streets. Many hogsheads of ale were given away to the populace; and the evening concluded with a brilliant and general illumination of the town.

WARWICK.—Two oxen were roasted in the Market-place, and distributed to the populace. A band of music paraded the streets playing "God save the King," and other loyal airs, and in the evening an illumination took place in every principal street; the front of the House of Correction, the Gaol, and the County Hall were illuminated. At Leamington Spa, the Regent, Bedford, and Royal Hotels, several boarding houses, and the front of the Theatre, were illuminated with lamps, &c.

HEMEL-HEMPSTEAD church was decorated with flags and boughs, the bells rung, and about 2500 persons were regaled with beef, bread, and beer. The children of the National School and School of

Industry, had roast beef and plum-pudding. The town was brilliantly illuminated.

KNUTSFORD, NORTHWICH, MIDDLEWICH, NANTWICH.—The Coronation of his Majesty was celebrated in these towns in the most marked and joyous manner: the day was observed as a day of rejoicing: the Yeomanry and Volunteers were assembled, bands of music paraded the streets, and the most lively demonstrations of duty and attachment to the Throne were exhibited by all classes.

Having now concluded our account of the festivities which took place in different parts of the country on this memorable occasion, we shall proceed to notice some further particulars, which may be considered as precedents for future coronations, and which, in some instances, have received the sanction of antiquity for their use.

The proceedings of the Court of Claims have already appeared in a former part of this work, and the following is an account of the quantity of plate which was given at the time of the Coronation, according to the claims delivered in to the Lord High Chamberlain of England for that day:—

1. The Lord High Almoner for the day, according to claim, two edge-gilt basons - - - 305 oz.
2. To the Duke of Norfolk, as Earl Arundel, claiming as Chief Butler of England, a gold cup of a wine quart - 32 oz.
3. To the Lord Mayor of London, as assistant to the Chief Butler, and to serve the King with after dinner, a gold cup - - - - - 30 oz.
4. To the Mayor of Oxford, as assistant to the Lord Mayor of London, a gilt cup or potole, weighing about 110 oz.
5. To the Lord of the Manor of Great Wimondley, in Hertfordshire, as Chief Cupbearer, a silver gilt cup, weighing about - - - - - 32 oz.
6. To the Champion of England,* as Lord of the Manor

---

* There is one circumstance attending the challenge of the Champion, which appears to have been overlooked by Taylor, Thomson, and others, who have written on the subject, which is, that the challenge to any person to deny the King's right *to be* crowned is not made until the ceremony of the Coronation has *actually* been performed; thus, how can any person come forward to gainsay or deny of Scrivelsby, in Lincolnshire, now in the Dymocke family, a gold cup of Winchester pint - - - 30 oz.

7. To the Barons of the Cinque Ports, for their claim of supporting the King and Queen's canopies, each by twelve silver staffs of eight feet in height, with bells to each staff, weighing 40 oz.—The twenty-four staffs and bells weigh in all - - - - - 960 oz.

8. The staff of the Lord High Constable of England is of silver, the ends are gold enamelled with the King's arms and his own, weighing about - - - 12 oz.

9. The staff of the Earl Marshal of England is of gold, enamelled black at each end, and engraved with the King's arms and his own, in length twenty-eight inches, and weighs about - - - - - 15 oz.

10. The gold coronet for Garter King at Arms, weighing about - - - - - 24 oz.

11. The sceptre or rod for Garter, part silver and part gold - - - - 8 oz. 19 dwts.

12. The gold chain and badge for Garter - 8 oz.

13. The gilt collar of SS. with badges for Garter 30 oz.

14. The same for Lord Lyon, King of Arms of Scotland, in all - - - - - 70 oz. 19 dwts.

15. The same for Bath King of Arms, in all 70 oz. 19 dwts.

16. The silver coronet for Clarencieux King of Arms, about - - - - - 18 oz.

17. The silver-gilt collar of SS. for the badges of Portcullis, only - - - - - 20 oz.

18. The gold chain and badge - 7 oz. 19 dwts. 17 gr.

19. The same for Norroy King of Arms, in all about 18 oz.

20. The collar of SS. partly gilt and partly white, for the six Heralds - - - - 120 oz.

21. The collar of SS. all plain silver for the four Pursuivants - - - - - 80 oz.

22. The Usher of the Black Rod of England, whose garniture is of gold lace, upon a fine black ebony stick or rod, about - - - - - 5 oz. 6 dwts.

---

a right which has been actually put in execution. The challenge is always made at dinner between the first and second course, and consequently the whole ceremony of the challenge sinks into an act of mere state and pageantry. The ceremony of the Championship was introduced into this country in the reign of William the Conqueror, when that Monarch rewarded Robert de Marmion, the hereditary Champion of the Dukes of Normandy, with the Castles of Tamworth and Scrivelsby, in Lincolnshire. He also gave him the office of hereditary Champion of England, to be held by the tenure of either of those two grants—it is not known which.

23. The Usher of the Green Rod of Scotland, whose garniture is of silver, part gilt, upon green, about 20 oz. 15 dwts.
24. The wedges of gold which the King and Queen offer at the altar, each two wedges at 20 oz. each—in all 40 oz.

To those of our readers who were not so fortunate as to see any part of the splendid ceremonial, the following information respecting the dresses of the peers may be of some service.

The Barons of England, who constitute the lowest part of the peerage, had formerly neither coronets nor velvet robes, but only a cap of scarlet lined with fur, and a habit of cloth of the same colour. In the thirteenth year of the reign of Charles II. he issued a grant, permitting them to use the coronet which they now wear, and which consists of a plain circle of gold, having six pearls set upon the upper rim, the lower part of the circle edged with ermine, and the whole surmounted by a cap of crimson velvet, with a tuft and tassel of gold. At the coronation of King James II. in 1684, the barons petitioned for robes conformable to their coronets, and accordingly a grant was issued, stating, that for the future their robes should be of crimson velvet, with capes and edgings of white miniver, and two rows of ermine as a distinction.

A Viscount, which is the next degree upwards, has for his coronet a circle of gold, richly chased, edged with ermine, and sixteen pearls placed on the rim, with a cap and tassel similar to a baron's. His robes are also of crimson velvet, lined with white sarsenet, and white fur capes, and two doublings and a half of spotted ermine.

The coronet of an Earl is a circle as before, richly chased, having eight pearls raised upon high points of gold, which spring out of the upper rim, with an equal number of strawberry leaves, formed of the same metal, standing upon lower points between them. It has also a doubling of ermine, cap and tassel as already described. An earl's mantle is similar to the former, except that it has three guards of ermine.

A Marquis's coronet differs from an earl's in the

number of pearls and strawberry leaves, and in the manner of placing them. It consists of four of each ornament, placed alternately on short equal points, with the same doubling, cap and tassel; the robes have three guards and a half of ermine.

A Duke's coronet is formed of eight golden strawberry leaves only, raised on short points of the same height above the rim. The fur, cap and tassel are the same as before. The robes belonging to this degree have four rows of ermine.

It is necessary, however, to observe that robes, as well as coronets, are regulated by the Earl Marshal's order at every coronation. Thus on the present occasion, an order was issued that the pearls on the coronets should be dispensed with, and that silver balls gilt should be their substitute.

There was one department connected with the ceremony of the Coronation to which his Majesty paid particular attention, which was the selection of the music to be performed in the Abbey. On this subject, his Majesty, whose judgment and taste in these matters are universally recognised, suggested many alterations and improvements. At his Majesty's command the Hallelujah Chorus from the Messiah was added to the selection already made, and was performed on the entrance into the Abbey. By his Majesty's desire too, "God save the King," and "Non Nobis Domine," were rehearsed, preparatory to the banquet in Westminster Hall. During the rehearsal, his Majesty found that the instrumental part of the band was too powerful for the vocal—he therefore commanded that the voices should be increased, and this took place as far as the extent of the orchestra would permit.

His Majesty, at the end of the rehearsal, was pleased to express his gracious approbation of the persons engaged on this important occasion. He particularly complimented Messrs. Attwood and Knyvett, the composers of the two new anthems, on the talent which they had displayed.

Mr. Kramer, the master of the King's Band of wind instruments, also signalized himself on this occasion. He was the composer of the music to Kent's celebrated anthem of "Blessed be thou, Lord God of Israel," the last piece performed in the Abbey on the day of Coronation. This anthem is a peculiar favourite with the King.

The Solos and Verse parts in the anthems were sung by Mr. Gore, Mr. W. Knyvett, Mr. Evans, Mr. Salmon, jun., Mr. Nield, Mr. Vaughan, Mr. Hawes, Mr. J. B. Sale, Mr. T. Welsh, Mr. R. Clark, and the young gentlemen of the Chapel Royal and Westminster Abbey. Among the others who assisted in the full pieces, were the Rev. Dr. Holmes, Sub Dean of the Chapel Royal; the Rev. Dr. Dakin, Precentor of Westminster Abbey; the Rev. Messrs. Beckwith, R. Webb, Dr. Fly, J. Pridden, E. Cannon, W. Hayes, J. W. Vivan, Beckwith, jun. Shelton, Champness, Beck, Rodburgh, Moore, Knapp, of the Chapel Royal, Westminster Abbey, and others; also Messrs. Sale, sen. Sir G. Smart, Messrs. Leete, C. Knyvett, Mitchelmoor, Kellner, G. Sale, Greatorex, Goulden, Cooper, Marguet, Roberts, Braham, Blackburn, Turle, sen., Turle, jun., George Clarke (of Worcester), Henshaw, J. Elliott, Harris, Watts, Neate, Doane, Cooper, Windus, Wilson, Broadhurst, Greatorex, jun., Taylor, Collyer, Neate, Horn, Gwilt, Harris, Gore, jun., &c. &c.

Mr. Shield, the master of the King's State Band, appeared as conductor, and led off the whole of the band. Mr. Kramer, the master of the King's wind instrument band, appeared at the head of twenty-nine wind instrument performers.

Mr. Knyvett, as senior organist to the King, presided at the organ. Mr. Kramer was appointed to lead the band upon this memorable occasion, and had the honour of having eight other leaders of bands to play under him.

The first violins were—Messrs. Keitzweiter, H.

Smart, Reeve, Loder (of Bath), W. Griesbach, and Anderson.

The second violins were—Mr. Dance, principal; Spagnoletti, Mori, W. Ware, Calkin, Cole, and Schram.

Violins—Mr. Mountain, principal; Messrs. Blake, Ware and Schram.

Violincellos—Mr. Crossdill, principal, who only performs upon great public occasions before the King, being violist to his Majesty, having retired from the profession; Mr. Lindley, principal second, who only plays second to Mr. Crossdill; Mr. Schram, a third violincello.

Double Basses—Mr. Dragonetti, principal; Mr. Boyce, principal second; Mr. Hill, another double bass.

Mr. Hedgly, distributor of the music; Mr. Field, music porter. The organ was built for the occasion by Elliot, of Tottenham-court-road.

It was not only previous to, but subsequent to the Coronation, that several base attempts were made by some disaffected and revolutionary spirits to inflame the public mind, by decrying the whole ceremony as a useless gorgeous pageant, and entailing an expense upon the country, which its impoverished finances could not support. Their jaundiced vision beheld in the preparations for it, nothing but an unbounded extravagance, and a wasteful expenditure of the public money. They discovered on the part of ministers an extraordinary degree of culpability, in advising the performance of the ceremony, when the public mind was in the highest state of irritation at the indignities which had been offered to the Queen, and when it was generally known that she would not be allowed to participate in the ceremony, and finally they beheld in the illustrious individual, who was to perform the principal part, nothing but a disregard to the public voice, and a puerile attachment to show and ostentation. But on the other hand they could not behold the benefits which the trading community received from the enormous sum of money, which was put in circulation, nor the advantages which accrued to thousands by the employment which it afforded them. There was scarcely a single branch of trade which was not benefitted by it, and in several departments, an impetus was given to the manufactory of the respective articles, from which the most important benefits resulted. If we look to the article of porcelain, which was extremely splendid, we there find that on this occasion only were provided 6794 dinner plates, 1406 soup plates, 1400 dessert plates, 288 large ale and beer pitchers. China services for 122 covers were laid in the Painted Chamber; for 108 in the Court of Exchequer; for 138 in the old House of Lords; for 66 in the Exchequer Chamber; for 38 in the Long Galleries; for 44 in the Princes' Chamber; for 38 in the Judges' Room; for 34 in the Common Pleas; for 42 in the Serjeants' and Treasurers' rooms; for 46 in the House of Commons' Coffee-room; for 26 in the Lords' committee room; for 106 in the members' waiting-room (inner and outer); for 17 in the Library.; for 40 in Mr. Ley's room, and for upwards of 200 covers in the several committee rooms.

In the article of table linen alone, 240 yards of elegant damask table-cloths were provided for the Hall: 1000 yards more were laid on the tables: 150 dozen of damask napkins were used at the different tables, besides nearly half the quantity for waiters, knife-cloths, &c.

When we consider the quantity of timber which was required for the various erections—the cloth that was used for the covering the different articles which were used for the embellishment, and beautifying of the Hall and Abbey, we cannot but compassionate those wayward and disaffected individuals, who could only see in the splendid pageant a desire to increase the oppressive burthens of the people.

Besides, there is another very material point to be

considered, from which the snarlers at the expense of the Coronation appear wholly to have withdrawn their attention, and perhaps with that wilfulness which generally distinguishes them on all subjects which bear upon the expenditure of the country. We make no allusion to those expensive speculations which were entered into by private individuals, the failure of which is to be attributed to a total want of calculation, and to the extortionate demands which were made upon the pockets of the public, by the grasping disposition of the speculators. We shall confine ourselves to the erections and the embellishments, the expense of which was defrayed by government, and in this we shall be able to show, that barring the claims which were made by certain individuals and clerical bodies to a portion of the erections, the expense fell far short of that which has been so industriously and insidiously reported to the public, and which was circulated with a design disgraceful to those in whose distempered minds it originated. If we look to the article of timber, the cost to the public must have been enormous, and on the first view it appears to carry with it a most extravagant aspect; but it should be taken into consideration, that the timber being the property of the public, was again sold, and the proceeds transmitted to the Treasury. Thus, a Mr. Page purchased the whole of the timber-work erected by government, with the exception of the erections in Westminster Abbey, which were claimed by the Dean and Chapter as their perquisite, but which was rightly resisted by the Board of Works.*

---

* Had the same custom been prevalent here as in Germany at the Coronation of the Emperor, the expense to the public would have been much greater. I was present during the whole of the Coronation of Leopold II., and the people of Frankfort, in claiming their perquisites, are by no means inferior to the English in violence and outrage. The platform, which extended from the Rathshaus to the Domkirch at Frankfort, the cloth which covered it, the house in which the ox was roasted, the whole of the scaffolding from which the wine was distributed to the populace; in fact, every thing which had been erected at the public expense, became the perquisite of the people.

In the same manner we may speak of the splendid chandeliers which decorated the Hall, they were afterwards purchased by Mr. Perry of Bond-street; and thus it may be said that Government merely paid for the loan of the necessary articles, and the accusation of an unbounded and careless expenditure falls immediately to the ground.

It is, however, in a political point of view, that the importance of the Coronation ought to be duly appreciated, but no doubt can exist that there are many who, from religious motives, most ardently wished that it had never taken place. Few of our readers can be ignorant of the gigantic strides which have been lately made, not only in the former but in the present reign, towards the emancipation of the Catholics, and still fewer of our readers can be ignorant of the firm and unshaken manner in which his late Majesty adhered to his Coronation oath. But for that unshaken and inflexible adherence, the reign of George III. would have been marked by an act at once dangerous and ruinous to the welfare and constitution of the country. It was the tone and temper of the mind of George III. on the important question of Catholic emancipation— it was the knowledge possessed by his ministers of the certain failure of every attempt which had been made to induce him to violate his oath, that saved the country from the direful consequences which would have resulted to it, had the emancipation of the Catholics been carried into effect. It was an obstacle the ministers knew they could never surmount—they might like a tub thrown to the whale, amuse the Irish

---

The Emperor and the procession had no sooner passed the platform, which extended nearly as far as that at the Coronation of George IV. than it disappeared as if by magic; it appeared to be riven up with a single crash by an earthquake, and no fanatic coming from the Holy Land with a newly-discovered thumb of St. Peter, (although to my certain knowledge there are no less than twelve of St. Peter's thumbs already to be seen amongst the invaluable reliques of the Catholic churches,) could possibly place a higher value upon his treasure, than an inhabitant of Frankfort placed on a bit of the board on which the Emperor had trodden. *Fiat Lux.*

Catholics by declaring to them that they were the strenuous advocates for their emancipation—that it should not be considered a government question, and they might carry their duplicity so far, and court the popularity of the Irish Catholics, by introducing the question to the consideration of the legislature, and even vote for its adoption. They, however, well knew that, although the question might be carried in both Houses of Parliament, not one of them dare to propose the ratification of it to the Sovereign.

If, therefore, it be considered that the existence and purity of the Protestant religion be essential to the well-being and the prosperity of the country, (and who that has experienced its benign influence can doubt it?) it becomes a matter of state necessity that the reigning monarch should enter into that solemn compact with his people by which he swears " to the utmost of his power to maintain the laws of God— the true profession of the gospel, and the Protestant reformed religion established by law—to *maintain and preserve inviolably the settlement of the united church of England and Ireland, and the doctrine, worship, discipline and government thereof as by law established within England and Ireland, and the territories thereunto belonging.*"*

---

* It is rather singular that in the Supplement to the Gazette which was published on the 3d of August, 1821, giving an official account of the Coronation, the oath which his Majesty took is not given. It differs in a very essential manner from the oath which was taken by his Illustrious Predecessor, it being as far as regards the Protestant religion, much more forcibly and distinctly stated. In the oath as taken by George III. it is merely said, "Will you grant and keep and by your oath confirm to the people of England the true profession of the Gospel established in this kingdom?" It is true, that at the Coronation of George III. the Union of Ireland had not then taken place, but still it was an integral part of the kingdom, and the Sovereign was as indisputably as much at the head of the church in Ireland at that time, as he was after the Union. The hydra of Catholic Emancipation had not then, indeed, reared its head so high; but there is something more in the wording of the oath as taken by George IV. than is at first apparent, and the omission of it in the Gazette, may have perhaps been wilful.

If, therefore, we take into our consideration the importance of the Coronation Oath, as administered to a sovereign of this country, in the face of the nobles, the clergy, and the representatives of the people, by which he enters into a solemn compact with them to preserve their laws inviolable, and particularly to maintain and uphold the Protestant religion, without which there is no real safeguard to the lives, property, nor liberty of the people, our surprise almost kindles into indignation, that any individual, possessing the real character and virtues of an Englishman, could have risen up in opposition to the celebration of a ceremony, with which the best interests of the country are identified; and without which an inroad is established to the introduction of a religion as an integral part of the state, which in former times diffused anarchy and rebellion, rapine and murder, over the country, and the scenes of which would be renewed, were the persecuting and intolerant spirit of the church of Rome ever again to have an undisputed sway in this country. It is well known that it was the conscientious fidelity of George III. to his Coronation Oath, which at one time saved the country from the afflicting ills which would have resulted to it from Catholic Emancipation; and in this very circumstance we find the solution of the enigma, which presented itself to the contemplation of the country during the Coronation of Geo. IV.

PATRIOTISM is certainly a high and sounding word; it carries in its implication all that is great and grand —all that ennobles the human character; for a real and substantive patriot, not taken in the jargon of the present day, but in its true and legitimate sense, must be, consequentially, a great and good man. The virtues which adorn the real patriot are well known, and

---

The declaration against transubstantiation and the authority of the church of Rome, was signed by George III. in the Abbey immediately after the Coronation Oath. It was signed by George IV. before the Houses of Parliament. The latter, we believe, to be without a precedent.

they are such which ought to be the aim and scope of every individual to attain. But in the same manner that many persons wrap themselves up tightly in the cloak of religion, in order to practise fraud, deception, and every species of uncharitableness, as the possession of that eminent virtue presupposes the absence of every degenerate vice, and also an utter incapability of wilfully adhering to an immoral course of life; so the *pseudo* patriot disclaims with stentorian lungs against any of those acts of government, by which the constitution of the country is preserved in its native integrity, or by which his own treasonable or rebellious designs are frustrated.

Thus, in the case of the Coronation, a number of individuals, pretending that an almost vesuvian fire of patriotism was glowing within them, crept from their hiding holes, and sounded an alarm through the country, that ruin must necessarily ensue to it, from the tremendous and overwhelming expense with which that ceremony was attended. The radical, who having nothing to lose, might, perhaps, gain something in the general scramble of a revolution, put on the cloak of patriotism, and mounting his rostrum in the ale-house, bellowed forth his frothy tirade against those improvident, impolitic, and evil-designing ministers, who dared in times like these to propose the celebration of such a ceremony; and the discourse was, as usual, wound up with a tremendous phillippic against the Illustrious Individual who, according to the expression of one of the most notorious of the radicals, could so far degrade himself as to become the principal puppet in the performance of a state pantomime. The leaders of the revolutionary tribe, who if they do not like the country had better leave it, knew well that they had only to disseminate the poison of such discourses amongst a certain few, in order to establish its free and uncontrouled circulation amongst those classes of the people whose minds are easily warped and biased to receive an unfavourable impression of the Illustrious Individual who now fills the throne of this country, and of the ministers who manage the intricate machinery of its vast concerns.

But if we could disrobe these pretended patriots of the garb which they have assumed, and view them in their true and ludicrous light, we should discover that it is not their nice and tender feeling for the interests of the country—it is not the thrilling alarm which they testify for the integrity of the glorious constitution, sealed with the blood of our forefathers—it is not the righteous horror which they feel for the political sins of the rulers of the nation: no, it is that these very rulers, by their vigorous measures, circumvent them in their designs—that they are able to penetrate through the flimsy texture of treason and rebellion which they have woven in secret, and, lastly, that by advising the celebration of the Coronation, these very incapable and unconstitutional ministers deprived them of one of their chief sources, on which they had fondly calculated, of revolution and ruin to the country. It was in vain that the clamor was raised that the functions of government could be carried on equally as well without the ceremony of the Coronation as with it; and this clamor was grounded on the principle, that the simple act of coronation does not invest the King with any power or authority which he did not previously possess, or which was indispensable to the administration of his government. Another curious argument was adduced in support of this principle, which was the singular and certainly unprecedented spectacle which Europe presented at this time, of not a single reigning monarch having put his nation (as the expression ran) to the expense of a coronation, ergo—as all the reigning monarchs of Europe could do without a coronation, it was only befitting in the King of this country to follow so laudable an example, and do without one also. This argument might certainly hold good in the climate of Petersburgh, Berlin, and Vienna. There, the monarchs are possessed, *de jure*, of a power above the people; and the compact which they enter into with the people at their coronation, is to uphold that power by every possible means. It is not, therefore, surprising that the people should not be very anxious respecting the performance of a ceremony the sole intent and purpose of which is to rivet those chains closer, which at present they feel, in many instances, too galling to support. But it is very differently constituted with the King of this country. The laws are enacted as much for the restraint of the monarchial power, as for the establishment of its administration, according to the limits laid down by the constitution; and it becomes a vital part of the duty of an English monarch to swear obedience to those laws, which have been confirmed by his predecessors, and in the confirmation of which he was no party whatever, but descends to their administration by heritage. On the other hand, he exacts homage and fealty from his subjects; and if the Coronation Oath be on one part binding on the monarch, the Oath of Allegiance is on the other part binding on the subject; and thus a mutual compact is entered into, by which the constitution of the country is preserved inviolable—the due administration of the laws established beyond the power of either party to infringe it—and that regular balance is preserved between the monarch and the subject, by which (to use the phraseology of the statesman) the machinery of the state works well, and its general and individual interests promoted.

But of all the benefits which flow from the solemn compact entered into by the sovereign with his subject, that which secures to them the maintenance and preservation of the Protestant religion, is certainly the most important. When we consider the torrents of blood which deluged this country, before such an invaluable blessing as the Protestant religion was confirmed to us, we ought to look with a most jealous and watchful eye, upon every act which could tend to disorganize the country, by the introduction of, or more properly speaking, by a legislative acknowledgment of that very mode of faith, which has caused almost all the rivers of Europe to run with blood, and has occasioned the fairest portion of the world to shudder at the dreadful scenes which its bigoted and fanatical votaries have enacted.

From a renewal of these scenes, the Coronation Oath of his Majesty has decidedly guarded us; and, therefore, the ceremony, which confirmed that pleasing prospect to the people of this country, cannot have been viewed with feelings of satisfaction neither by those who profess the Catholic religion, nor by those deluded and misguided men, who thought to find in the ruin of their country the establishment of their own power and prosperity.

We cannot close these remarks on the importance and necessity of the Coronation of the Kings of England, more appropriately than with the following reflections.

The best and dearest interests of the country are identified with the ceremonies of the Coronation;—the constitution of the land becomes confirmed, and when the love of that constitution is known to be implanted in the bosom of the sovereign, the same spirit will diffuse itself through all orders of his subjects; his example will secure it—his influence will improve it—his countenance will create emulation in every heart to perpetuate it, and the fruit of his conduct will be mutual confidence, strength, and glory. When great and good kings reign, they are the means by which God blesses a people. It is not said, because the Lord loved Solomon, but because He loved Israel, therefore made He, Solomon King; and may the holy spirit of that God, in whose presence the King and people have declared their mutual engagements, pour into their hearts a sincere zeal for each other's happiness, and unite them in the strictest bonds of affection. May the sacred oath which George IV. took at the Altar of the King of kings, ever recur to his mind, as the genuine intentions of his own heart. May justice and judgement be the habitation of his throne. May mercy and truth go before his face. May the Almighty mark every year with fresh instances of his goodness, to him and to his people. May every blessing of public prosperity, and abundance of peace, be in his day; late may he be called to a heavenly crown of eternal glory! And here on earth, through the mercy of the Most High to this kingdom, may his crown flourish long with unsullied lustre, under the guidance of that wisdom, in whose right hand are length of days and honor.

FINIS.

J. Robins and Co. Albion Press, London.

LIST OF PLATES.

	Page
Westminster Hall, with the ceremony of the Champion's Challenge } to face the Title	
The Crown of State, &c.	47
The Coronation Procession of King George the Fourth	207
King George the Fourth in his Coronation Robes	232
Westminster Hall—the Royal Banquet	255
The King's Champion	262

www.ingramcontent.com/pod-product-compliance
Ingram Content Group UK Ltd.
Pitfield, Milton Keynes, MK11 3LW, UK
UKHW020644250925
8075UKWH00047B/1030